The Bucks $tart Here

How Great Digital Companies Create Lasting Business Value

Ian McDonald Wood

CAPSTONE

Copyright © Ian McDonald Wood 2000

The right of Ian McDonald Wood to be identified as the author of this work has been asserted in accordance with the Copyright, Designs and Patents Act 1988

First published 2000 by

Capstone Publishing Ltd
Oxford Centre for Innovation
Mill Street
Oxford OX2 0JX
United Kingdom
http://www.capstone.co.uk

All rights reserved. Except for the quotation of short passages for the purposes of criticism and review, no part of this publication may be reproduced, stored in a retrieval system, or transmitted, in any form or by any means, electronic, mechanical, photocopying, recording or otherwise, without the prior permission of the publisher.

British Library Cataloguing in Publication Data
A CIP catalogue record for this book is available from the British Library

ISBN 1-84112-1037

Typeset by
Forewords, Oxford
Printed and bound by
T.J. International Ltd, Padstow, Cornwall

This book is printed on acid-free paper

Substantial discounts on bulk quantities of Capstone books are available to corporations, professional associations and other organizations. If you are in the USA or Canada, contact the LPC Group for details (tel: 1-800-626-4330; fax 1-800-243-0138); everywhere else, contact Capstone Publishing (tel: +44-1865-811113; fax: +44-1865-240941).

Contents

Foreword	vii
Introduction Fortune favours ... well, anyone who tries!	1
Success for the taking	1
It could be you!	2
A guide to shaping your fortunes	3
Introducing the e-champions	4
Just regular guys	8
A sixth sense for technology	9
More than a passing interest in customers	10
Vision emerges	12
A matter of teamwork	15
Turning dreams into reality	18
Part One Technology shapes the landscape	**21**
1 New society, new economy, new rules	**23**
Beyond the third wave	26
The first wave revisited	28
A revolutionary economy	30
The age of opportunity	31
Creating not destroying value	33
Summary	34
2 Powerful forces at work	**37**
The drivers of technology	39
The drivers of business performance	45
Summary	51
3 Network dynamics	**53**
Convergence	56
Network returns	59
Information over estimation	62
Immediacy	64

	Buyer ascendancy	66
	Provider equalization	69
	Buyer–seller re-engagement	71
	Interconsumer collaboration	73
	Summary	75

Part Two Customers to the fore — 77

4 The rise of customer power — 79
Marketing and the customer — 82
Managing the transfer of power — 84
Changing behaviours — 85
Collective power of individuals — 87
Summary — 88

5 Society calls the tune — 91
24/7 society — 93
Flexible working — 96
Social fragmentation — 100
Self-determination — 105
Beliefs erosion — 108
Metamedia consumption — 112
Summary — 116

6 New customer dynamics — 117
Experience richness — 119
Attention scarcity — 123
Individualism — 126
Now mentality — 128
Active participation — 130
Trust deficit — 133
Access freedom — 136
Affinity gap — 139
Summary — 143

Part Three Doing business digitally — 145

7 A fresh approach required — 147
New mindsets needed — 149
Understanding the difference — 151
Getting first-mover advantage — 152
The quest for digital business tools — 153
Summary — 156

8 In search of value — 157
Competition, customers and value — 160

	The Value Levers	162
	Summary	187
9	**Digital value profiles**	**191**
	How Value Lever pairings can make the net work for you	193
	Digital Value Profiles	195
	Summary	226

Part Four Building for success   229

10	**Creating virtual value**	**231**
	A Value Lever checklist	235
	Turning connections into dollars	240
	From business plan to action	242
	Summary	243
11	**Creating the network-sensitive organization**	**245**
	Ideas intensive	248
	Action oriented	250
	Partner biased	251
	People centred	252
	IT integrated	253
	Customer centric	255
	Risk conversant	256
	Channel fluent	257
	Lean focus	259
	Summary	260
12	**Transformational options**	**263**
	But change is not easy	267
	Transition to digital business	269
	Transform, disaggregate or perish	272
	Summary	276

Reflections The bucks start here   277

13	**A personal agenda**	**279**
	Time for departure	283
	Rush!	285

References   286

Index   293

Foreword

Success in the unfamiliar landscape of digital business is about creating and applying new knowledge. A book contains information – it is you, the reader, who then turns that information into the knowledge you need. The utility and value of your new knowledge will depend upon the quality of the information and how it has been presented. With this reality uppermost in my mind I have written *The Bucks Start Here* to be a source of knowledge that will make this new landscape more familiar and accessible. Moreover, I have aimed to present the content in a format that should engage as well as inform you.

Exploring this virtual prairie, and making sense of the opportunities it offers, has been a long and testing journey. I could not have got this far without the contribution of colleagues and fellow explorers, notably Dr Melvyn Reader, my Research Manager, and Christopher Barnatt, academic, author and expert on future developments in a technology-driven world.

Yet there is a also a wider band of pioneers and would-be settlers, each of whom has in some small way contributed to the quest. These are the managers of so many client organizations who have participated in our Research & Development programmes over the last five years, or with whom I have had the privilege to work in client workshops and consulting projects. They have helped to evaluate and test new concepts, co-creating new knowledge about digital business and the emerging network economy.

Knowledge, as Peter Drucker noted long ago, is the only meaningful economic resource. Use *The Bucks Start Here* to increase your own capital.

Ian McDonald Wood
Millennium Group
Winchester, UK
http://www.millenn.co.uk

Introduction

Fortune favours . . . well, anyone who tries!

■ Success for the taking

Vast fortunes are being made overnight by merely launching Internet-based businesses, so it seems. One could quite easily believe that the world has taken leave of its senses. On an almost daily basis we learn of the latest multi-millionaire to amass a fortune within days if not hours of his or her company making its first public offering of shares. Billionaires, too, are no longer the rarity of the recent past.

Sceptics believe we are witnessing yet another of the periodic episodes in human history when new technology promises discontinuous change and, with it, huge rewards to the early-mover entrepreneurs. They hark back to the railroad mania of the nineteenth century and, in Britain, to the canal mania of the late eighteenth century that set in motion the industrial revolution. Investors piled into just about every project going in the hope of making a rapid capital gain. The prospects of profit were remote and in most cases proved wholly absent. In the end only a few ever made any significant gains and all too many lost their investments.

There are similarities today as human nature repeats the experience, stampeding in search of elusive investment profits, bestowing astronomical stock prices indiscriminately on the good as well as the not so good long before the true potential of each new Internet business can be fairly assessed. Yet, what we are experiencing now is very different and more extreme than those earlier moments of change driven by advancements in transportation technology. We are presently undergoing a radical and rapid transition to a much-modified world in which how we live, how we think, how we behave and how we do business is altering fundamentally and for ever. As if that is not enough, it is occurring now, around us and at an alarming rate of acceleration.

To the businessperson this challenges every shred of hard-won experience and undermines many of the basic tenets of late twentieth-century management practice that they have learned to apply. Moreover, the speed of this occurrence leads to confusion and uncertainty – and for some gives away to fear, denial and even rejection. It needn't be so.

It could be you!

So runs the advertising slogan encouraging Britons twice weekly to buy tickets in the UK's national lottery with a 14 million-to-one chance of winning the jackpot. When it comes to the chances of Internet-based business success in this new network economy the odds are high but far less daunting than any lottery. Yet they can be reduced further to quite acceptable and even attractive levels of risk. All that is required is the confidence that comes from understanding what is driving this rapidly evolving business environment and the provision of a simple set of tools to make Internet-based business success a less risky and more certain proposition.

Appreciating also how some of the most successful Internet entrepreneurs have built their successes using an implicit understanding of the key dynamics and critical success factors of this new competitive landscape can only help in reducing further the perceived odds against digital business success. In addition the varied nature of these well-known successes – from almost accidental start-ups to the transforming of institutions – will be relevant to you whether your challenge is to 'Internet-enable' an established business in which you are an employee, or to undertake a wholly new venture.

A guide to shaping your fortunes

This, then, is the intended purpose of this book, to be a guide to shape your fortunes. Explore the nature of major digital success stories using the thinking, tools and framework presented and explained in the following chapters. With this knowledge you can define the shape and assess the potential for your own digital venture, and gain the confidence to galvanize yourself into action, and success. To achieve its purpose the book pursues a logical process.

Part One will help you to take the first step, to discover how technology is reshaping society and business. In Chapter 1, appreciate the nature and extent of the revolution that is transforming the world around you. Identify, in Chapter 2, the new forces at play in this changing business environment, and observe how, at a macro level, technology plays a pivotal role in shaping the new competitive landscape. Then, in Chapter 3, explore at a micro level the distinctive nature of these new competitive realities – the dynamics of the network economy – and begin to learn how they redefine successful business behaviour.

Part Two is the second step in the process, providing you with insights into how customer power is now the unrivalled driving force in digital business. Perceive, in Chapter 4, the nature and extent of customer influence in the new economy and how it is the source of power. In Chapter 5, evaluate key social and cultural trends, many of these long running and with a trans-national dimension, which conspire with one another and interact to impel the network economy. Then, in Chapter 6, comprehend how particular customer dynamics emerge from a nexus of social trends to create the context for successful business in the digital age.

Part Three unfolds a distinctive method for doing digital business successfully, building on this fresh perspective of new competitive forces and emergent customer dynamics. Appreciate, in Chapter 7, why a changed mindset, new tools and an original approach are required for effective business performance in the digital age. Understand, in Chapter 8, why a value-based approach to digital business is critical and acquaint yourself with the 'Value Lever' framework. Then, in Chapter 9, grasp the power of Value Levers by comprehending how the framework confirms and explains the success of seven celebrated Internet entrepreneurs.

Part Four, the fourth step in the process, is about applying Value Levers to your own new digital intiative – whether your exploits will be as employee or as entrepreneur. In Chapter 10 get to grips with a practical process to turn your own dream into a digital business. Success demands more than just a smart business plan, and in Chapter 11 evaluate the new imperatives for how you need to organize your prospective digital venture to sustain future success. If your task is to transform an existing real-world organization, whose achievements are rooted in the physical economy, then Chapter 12 will help you to put your intiative into context, laying out the transformational options that present themselves.

Finally, in Reflections, the spotlight falls upon you, the reader, the principal factor in determining the extent of your own personal digitally based success. In Chapter 13, match your own capabilities and character traits to those of the seven celebrated Internet entrepreneurs whose experiences are a thread that runs throughout this book.

Introducing the e-champions

What makes the experiences of Internet entrepreneurs, or e-champions as we have called them, so important to this book? It is simply because, for all seven of those whom we have selected, their success stories are still in the making. Being a celebrated Internet business success is all well and good but it's not, it seems, reason enough to rest on your laurels. 'There's no rest for the weary', reflects Jeff Bezos of Amazon, 'But, hey, we're trying to invent the future of e-commerce – it's not supposed to be easy' (Preston, 31/3/99). Each of these e-champions believes they have much yet to do, so we can learn from the experiences of already successful people who are continuing to shape their own fortunes. Throughout the book we will draw on and refer to their successes and experiences to support and explain the various steps outlined above

The sense of a task only half-completed extends to all of our e-champions. This is irrespective of whether they have been start-up pioneers, such as Jeff Bezos, Jay Walker and Pierre Omidyar; Internet business developers in their own real-world pre-Internet companies, such as Charles Schwab and Michael Dell; or, Internet innovators in long-established and conservative companies, such as Mike Harris of UK's Prudential Corporation and John Pluthero of Dixons, the UK electrical goods retailer. So who are these guys?

Jeff Bezos is the youthful founder and Chief Executive of Amazon, the company that billed itself as 'Earth's Biggest Bookstore' (although it now sells more than just books), and one of the world's best-known Internet companies. Because Bezos owns 41 percent of Amazon's shares, he holds a fortune in stock and – on paper at least – he was worth more than $7 billion in May 2000. Jeff calls himself a 'nerd', having studied computer science and electrical engineering at Princeton, but he is a highly sociable individual, who enjoys having fun as well as working hard. Even though, in its fifth year, Amazon has yet to turn a profit, most of Bezos's investors keep faith with him and with his vision of creating the world's most customer-centric company.

Jay Walker is the founder and Vice-Chairman of Priceline, the name-your-own–price, customer-driven auction system. He is a multi-billionaire through his 47 percent stake in Priceline, but he is much more than that. Jay is also Chairman and Chief Executive of Walker Digital, an 'intellectual-property laboratory' where a couple of dozen people – mainly inventors, marketers and lawyers – work at developing patentable business models that can be licensed or spun off into new companies. The first patent established by Walker Digital research and development centre cost more than $2.5 million to develop and was subsequently used by Priceline. Just like Bezos, Walker sees much still to achieve. 'You can't let the paper wealth distract you', says Jay. 'Like the song says, don't count your money while you're still at the table' (Halper, 1/10/99). He still has big plans for Priceline, and eventually wants to see the company's name-your-own-price service extended to include almost anything people can buy. When Priceline added groceries to its service in late 1999, Walker simply commented that 'This is just the start' (Brady, 22/9/99).

Charles R. Schwab – known to his friends and family as 'Chuck' – is the founder, Chairman and co-Chief Executive of the Charles Schwab Corporation, one of the USA's largest financial firms as well as one of the largest and most profitable electronic commerce businesses in the world. Born in 1937, Schwab is the oldest of our group of e-champions, but his pioneering spirit appears undaunted by his success. He founded his brokerage firm, Charles Schwab & Company, in 1971 with a total customer focus and the intention to create change and initiate progress. Over nearly thirty years he continued to do this, with his greatest achievement being the Internet development of eSchwab. His co-Chief Executive David Pottruck captures this sense of boundless energy. 'Our advantage is in our ability to innovate faster – to make the discontinuous leap' (Lappen, 29/4/96).

Pierre Omidyar is Founder and Chairman of eBay – the Internet's most popular person-to-person auction house. He holds around one third of eBay's common stock and is a multi-billionaire. A software developer, Pierre has focused on making computing accessible to ordinary people, who do not share his technological abilities. 'He was always one to apply the technology in a way that was useful to ordinary people', comments Steve Schramm, Omidyar's former boss at General Magic. People who know Omidyar best say that he has always been very serious, very deliberate and very good at finding the cutting edge, but they are surprised at the extent of his success. Conscious of his limitations, it seems, and keen to maintain a balance between work and leisure, Pierre has appointed a Chief Executive for eBay so that he could focus on the company's long-term strategy.

John Pluthero is Chief Executive of Freeserve, the UK-based Internet business launched by Dixons Group – the UK's largest electronics retailer – on the back of a pioneering free Internet access service. As Head of Corporate Development John had long felt that there was an opportunity for Dixons to develop a genuine Internet business. Together with colleagues he hatched the concept of free

Internet access, persuaded Dixons' senior executives of its merit and then drove through the rapid launch of Freeserve in September 1998, as well as its subsequent flotation in July 1999. Flotation was only the start to an even greater task and Pluthero now faces the challenge of turning prospective value attributed by investors to Freeserve into serious returns. His reward for his endeavours in creating a business valued at $3.5 billion on flotation was a million shares valued then at around $3 million, which made him a multi-millionaire, but not yet in the league of some in this gaggle of e-champions. At only thirty-five Pluthero is one of the youngest ever chief executives of a UK publicly quoted company. If anyone can make it happen and realize Freeserve's potential, one suspects that John Pluthero may well be the person – articulate, creative, ambitious and a driven man for whom twelve-hour days are the norm.

Michael Dell is founder, Chairperson and Chief Executive Officer of the Dell Computer Corporation, currently the second largest PC maker in the world. Annual sales at Dell have grown at a startling rate during the course of the last decade, with revenues rising from $389 million in 1990 to over $23.6 billion in 1999. As well as being the youngest ever CEO of a company to earn a ranking on the Fortune 500 listing, Michael Dell is the computer industry's longest-tenured CEO. He is also the fourth-richest businessperson in North America, holding a fortune in stock valued at more than $25 billion in May 2000. *Fortune Magazine* recently commented that 'the closest person we have to Henry Ford is Michael Dell'. Michael qualifies as an e-champion, because his migration of Dell Computer to the Internet is arguably his most outstanding achievement to date. By late 1999, the company's sales over the Internet exceeded $35 million a day, representing annual gross revenues of $13 billion!

Mike Harris is Chief Executive of Prudential Banking and of Egg, the recently launched online banking and financial services arm of the UK-based Prudential Group. A career banker, Mike had been the launch Chief Executive of First Direct, the Midland Bank's ground-breaking and highly successful telephone banking venture inaugurated in 1988. Mike has been rated by the *Sunday Times* (26/9/99) as one of the most influential figures in UK personal finance. So far, Egg – launched at the cost of £150 million by Prudential – has proven to be an immense success, having hit its five-year target of $5 billion new savings in just six months. Mike is a charismatic and valued leader. He is also highly creative, willing to experiment and prepared to take a risk. These seem to provide the perfect combination of attributes for someone at the cutting edge of transforming the UK's personal finance sector. Mike has yet to receive financial rewards on a scale to match our other e-champions. Once Prudential has successfully floated Egg, realizing the multi-billion dollar valuation that analysts forecast, then Mike will surely be rewarded handsomely. Like John Pluthero, Mike has much yet to prove.

Just regular guys

Perhaps the most reassuring factor that should encourage every would-be Internet entrepreneur to leap into action is that all of these e-champions are quite human and in many respects no different to anyone else. Chuck Schwab attributes much of his business success to his dyslexia, and to the particular learning style he developed that enabled him to graduate from Stanford Business School, though not without a struggle. This alternative approach to learning clearly helps him to see things differently, a great advantage to the serial innovator. Jeff Bezos read a report on the astronomical growth of the Internet that acted as 'a huge wake-up call' to the former computing graduate. Jay Walker is a self-confessed admirer of Thomas Edison and seems to strive constantly to emulate his hero, inventing the digital equivalents of the electric light bulb or the phonograph. John Pluthero is an economics graduate and chartered accountant turned Head of Corporate Development who for four years had thought his company, Dixons Group, should have an Internet strategy. Then there is Pierre Omidyar, the soft spoken and unassuming individual, whose eBay fortune seemed to his former colleagues to be almost accidental. Even Mike Harris fits the 'regular guy' label. He may first have achieved corporate success with the launch of First Direct, but Mike only joined Prudential after he quit his telecoms employer because a cost-cutting regime was not enough for him – he needed to develop business too.

▪ A sixth sense for technology

Technological drivers play a key role in shaping and enabling the emerging network economy, laying the foundations for a new social and commercial environment. This brings with it a very different set of dynamics that challenges the prevailing view of competition between businesses. It is clear from the successes of our e-champions that they are highly sensitive to this and recognize the fundamental role that technology plays in every aspect of their businesses. Yet it is clear that you don't need to be a technologist to become an e-champion – just to have a healthy interest in IT is sufficient.

Chuck Schwab was always looking to use technology as a way of adding value to the service he provided to customers and as a means of getting closer to them – applying a 'high tech, high touch' approach. Indeed, the success of Schwab is based upon a whole series of technological innovations. Jay Walker's ideas factory, Walker Digital, has a strong technological focus in its quest to find new ways of doing business via the Internet. Similarly, banker Mike Harris and accountant John Pluthero each have a technological awareness that has enabled them to perceive potential advantage from Internet-based business at an early stage.

For those e-champions who have been technologists first and foremost, their perspectives are much broader than the narrow application of information technology to meet business needs. Jeff Bezos, a systems developer originally, recalls that he had always been interested in anything that could revolutionize computing, hence his immediate interest when he first read about the remarkable growth of the Internet. Pierre Omidyar developed a passion for computing at an early age and became a software developer at Apple and then General Magic. Yet throughout his various career moves, Omidyar remained focused on making computing accessible to ordinary people, who did not share his technological abilities. Similarly, Michael Dell has always had a strong interest in computers. 'As a child he was interested in two things – computers and money' (Lynn, 26/4/99). Michael was quick to see the potential of the Internet for both his customers and his business.

■ More than a passing interest in customers

Perhaps even more striking than their attitude to technology is the apparent total preoccupation of these e-champions with their customers. Clearly, just as you don't need to be a technologist to succeed, you don't need to be a marketer. For these e-champions, delivering outstanding value to customers seems to come before everything else. It is almost as though creating shareholder value is the last thing on their minds. This may seem odd, yet it does typify the true entrepreneur for whom personal wealth and value creation are more a scorecard than a primary personal objective.

Perhaps the most extreme e-champion on the customer issue is Jeff Bezos. Ask Bezos what particular vision has provided the inspiration for the creation and development of Amazon, and his reply is almost certain to include the phrase 'customer-centric'. 'Our vision is to be the world's most customer-centric company', says Bezos, 'where customers can come to find anything they want to buy online' (Hunter 21/6/99). He explains some of Amazon's more recent departures in the same way, 'We are not trying to be a book company – we're trying to be a customer company'(Bezos, 16/9/99). As the Schwab website proudly proclaims, Chuck Schwab set out to 'provide customers with the most useful and ethical financial services in the world'. This is no marketing puff – it comes from the heart. Jay Walker may be less explicit about customer value, but the patented name-your-own-price, customer-defined business model betrays his focus on value to customers as the driver of value creation for Priceline and its shareholders. Mike Harris is just as intense on this issue. Rupert Howell of HHCL & Partners, the advertising agency used by Harris to help launch First Direct and then Egg, links Harris's desire to be creative to his concern to deliver something that is truly of value to customers: 'What is really remarkable about him is his passion for customer service. That's something everybody talks about, but he really believes in it and makes it happen' (Cozens, 6/11/98). Michael Dell is no less excessive. He knew that the Internet could make a major difference to his customers. 'The World Wide Web provided a way to link our customers with all the information they needed to buy and manage their computers and do it in real time. . . . We knew that our customers – and potential customers – would be there first'(Dell, 1998).

Yet it is John Pluthero's experience that illustrates the extreme nature of this customer obsession. Pluthero had been working for several months on the development of a stand-alone, free Internet access service for Dixons. Two key individuals had helped him, Mark Danby, until recently the Chief Operating Officer at Freeserve, and, Peter Wilkinson, the multi-millionaire Managing Director and co-founder of Planet Online, the Energis-owned Internet service provider that Pluthero had earlier signed up as a business partner. In July 1998 a major breakthrough occurred. Wilkinson was on a train journey from Leeds to London, when he decided to make some calculations on the back of a napkin. These roughly written calculations turned out to be of great significance, since they showed that – by winning advertising revenues and obtaining a share of the telephone charges collected from the users of the service – a free Internet access service would indeed be a financially viable prospect for Dixons. On his arrival in London, Wilkinson showed his calculations to Pluthero, who – after repeatedly checking the figures for errors – became sufficiently convinced of their veracity to put the concept of a free Internet access service to Dixons' Chief Executive. 'I phoned John Clare that evening . . . and explained it to him, remembers Pluthero. He gave me that instinctive retailer's reaction, which is "Giving it away – just run that by me again". But he rapidly understood what it might mean' (Waples, 13/6/99). Clare is CEO of a very streetwise customer-focused retailer, yet even he had to think twice even to accept the principle of free Internet access, let alone the underlying business model.

This almost fanatical addiction to providing customer value does appear to be a critical factor in e-champion success. As John Clare discovered it goes far beyond even a retailer's concern for customer focus. Yet this obsession has another side to it that translates into a deep sensitivity for society that can be found in many if not all of the e-champions. With eBay Pierre Omidyar has created a socially aware and community-minded organization. Both Omidyar and his co-founder, Jeff Skoll, are enthusiastic supporters of the eBay Foundation, a charitable organization run by company employees to issue grants to community-oriented projects. This social conscience spills over into eBay's commercial operations, and even Omidyar's rivals acknowledge the fair-mindedness and modesty that characterizes his organization. A number of Jeff Bezos's associates predict that he will take his extreme generosity and philanthropy to higher levels over time, whatever those may be. Having conquered his own learning disability, Schwab has invested significant amounts of money in the Schwab Foundation for Learning, which aims to help children with dyslexia appreciate that 'They're not stupid. They just learn differently'. This deep awareness beyond any customer-based obsession does reflect one of the most distinctive characteristics of the world of the Internet – a sense of mutuality and shared experience. Mike Harris captures the spirit precisely: 'The Internet is above all a medium which connects human beings together, allowing individuals to communicate, groups to collaborate and people to gather together in like-minded communities' (Harris, 16/1/99).

Vision emerges

A sixth sense about the broad role of technology in shaping society, and a profound commitment to customers provide ideal conditions to encourage an active imagination and lateral thinking. For our e-champions it seems that their visions have emerged from this fertile ground. Michael Dell captures the sentiment in a manner almost too modest for someone whose achievements speak for themselves, 'Dell is proof that people can learn to recognize and take advantage of opportunities that others are convinced don't exist. You don't have to be a genius or a visionary, or even a college graduate to think unconventionally. You just need a framework and a dream' (Dell, 1998).

Long before the emergence of the Internet and the network economy, Chuck Schwab envisioned his brokerage company becoming the custodian of his clients' dreams. Add to that his early appreciation of how the Internet changes the rules for society and for business, and you have a potent mixture. Who could challenge the milestone achievements of his firm towards a vision 'to provide customers with the most useful and ethical financial services in the world'? (Charles Schwab website).

Jeff Bezos is customer obsessed. Having received 'the wake-up call' he wanted to see if there was a business opportunity in the Internet. The scale of his ambition is evident, as he himself points out. 'Amazon isn't for the faint of heart. We're trying to build something important and lasting' (Hunter 21/6/99). His investors clearly agree and they stick with him. They continue to believe that Bezos's vision – to be the world's most customer-centric company – will deliver significant long-term profitability. But for Bezos vision is more than just the dream, it plays an important role as a management tool in prioritizing action. 'Once you have the big vision, you'll see that within it there are hundreds of smaller ones, and you need the ability to do brutal triage, to be able to say: 'No, we don't do this, that, and that; we're going to focus exclusively on these three things." For Jeff communication of that vision is a close second to prioritization. 'Also key', says Bezos, 'is consistently articulating the vision of what is to be achieved. You can have the best people, but if they're not all moving toward the same vision, it's not going to work' (Hazleton, 7/98).

John Pluthero had evidently been shaping a vision for an Internet business for some years. In fact, John says that he had been mulling about an Internet strategy since 1994, when Dixons had started to package AOL's subscription-based service with PCs sold by the company. It was then that the thought first crossed his mind that Dixons could offer a cheaper Internet access service than AOL with content that would appeal more to UK users. It required that fateful train journey from Leeds to London by Peter Wilkinson to hatch the free Internet access concept, and that was all Pluthero needed to let his vision take shape and fly. The scope of this vision and the scale of his ambition are clear to see in the argument he couched to John Clare for floating Freeserve. 'If this is as big as we think it could be, then we are going to have to play on a level playing field with other Internet businesses. This means we will need to float and generate our own currency and resources because that is the way this market is going' (Waples, 13/6/99).

Mike Harris's creativity and preparedness to be a heretic and to challenge conventional thinking suggest a person who has a vision suited to this new world. Mike's conviction that the Internet will rapidly revolutionize businesses, and his passion for customer service and delivering customer value, have enabled him to see the possibilities in UK personal financial services. 'I believe that two-thirds of all financial services purchases or transactions will be done via electronic means in fifteen years' time' (Harris, 16/01/99), says Mike. This has led to a clear and unambiguous vision. 'Our primary objective when we launched Egg was to create an e-commerce led business', comments Harris, 'We will be introducing a stream of innovations which will encourage a large, permanent switch in personal finance habits' (Darby, 25/3/99). Important to Mike Harris, the intrapreneur – a word coined in the 1980s for an internal, corporate entrepreneur (Pinchot, 1985) – is the support from a top-level sponsor who can act as mentor and smooth the way. Mike could do no better on this count than to have Sir Peter Davis, then Group Chief Executive of Prudential Corporation, fulfil this role for him. Sir Peter's commitment to Egg and its future role within the Prudential Group of companies indicated that he undoubtedly shared Mike's vision.

Yet, when it comes to vision, Jay Walker is perhaps the most interesting. Priceline is a brilliant concept that is being well executed, a fact readily acknowledged by leading analysts. 'In our view, Priceline.com's business model lends itself to being one of the most successful we've ever seen' says Keith Benjamin at BancBoston Robertson Stephens. Mary Meeker of Morgan Stanley Dean Witter is equally admiring, crediting Priceline with having a 'strong brand name, first-mover advantage, and a unique business model' (Stone, 29/4/99). Walker's vision for Priceline is to extend the name-your-own-price service to include almost anything people can buy. As testimony to this, Priceline has moved into groceries – in addition to the airline tickets, hotel rooms, cars and mortgages already available in the USA. However, Jay has appointed Richard Braddock, a former President of Citicorp, as CEO and Chairman of Priceline, placing his trust and the aspirations of his investors in a man who shared this vision. Why relinquish his position at the helm of Priceline? Because Jay Walker has a much broader vision that is being pursued by Walker Digital, his intellectual property laboratory, of which Priceline is but one product. 'Computing is becoming universal. Mips [millions of instructions per minute] will be free and ubiquitous. Mips trend to zero [cost] and bandwidth trends to infinite. What we do at Walker [Digital]', says Jay, 'is ask, how will business be reinvented given that reality? It's a question most businesses are not working on' (Machan, 17/5/99). Walker argues that Internet has the potential to radically alter what he refers to as the 'DNA' – that is, the building blocks – of business. He believes that the Internet's rapidly evolving ability to support fast, personalized communication will change the normal rules of brand strategy, so that products and services will no longer need to have a particular brand attached to them before customers will decide to make a purchase. 'The base pairs of the DNA of business are, for the first time, accessible and recombinable', claims Walker, 'We have the opportunity to assemble a business method that looks unlike any business method before, because we now have tools to reassemble the information layer of society' (Walker, 16/9/99). With Priceline as evidence of his thinking, one should pay very careful attention to these radical perspectives, before dismissing them!

A matter of teamwork

The typical perception of the successful entrepreneur is of an individual slaving away in solitude to generate success. This may be the case when the ideas are first hatched, but execution of the idea on a scale that will generate real success is a matter of teamwork and an enlightened approach to organizational design. This is a reality of which our e-champions are all aware, irrespective of whether their successful e-venture has been a start up or an initiative started within an established company.

When it comes to making start ups work, Jeff Bezos readily acknowledges it's a major challenge. 'I think ideas are easy. It's execution that's hard. If you and I were to sit here for an hour and scribble on this chalkboard on the wall, we could come up with a hundred good ideas. The hard part is making them work' (Hazleton, 7/98). To Bezos, teamwork is second nature. He is a highly sociable individual, who enjoys having fun as well as working hard – the company motto is 'work hard, have fun and make history'. In fact, Bezos is a decidedly merry fellow, whose loud and infectious laugh constantly sends echoes round the Amazon office in Seattle. That sense of fun is important. You would probably also find it if you were to join the two dozen or so people – inventors, marketers and lawyers – working in the Walker Digital intellectual property laboratory developing patentable digital business models. Working at eBay is likely to be an equally rewarding experience. eBay is that socially aware organization with a charitable organization run by company employees issuing grants to community-oriented projects. This is a company with a social conscience and, like Amazon and Walker Digital, it reflects the values of its founder in the way it works and in the way its employees behave.

For the Internet business initiative started within an established company the issues are more complex. How do you nurture and grow the new digital business free from the pressures and interventions of the existing business? Mike Harris's achievements at Egg have been dependent upon assembling the right group of people and motivating them in the right way. Mike has that innate ability to inspire others. 'I like to create things. I like creating an environment of creativity and I believe in inherent human creativity. But there is a deal you have to do to get people to bring their creativity to work. You have to treat them like human beings' (Hall, 11/10/98). Again, teamwork is fundamental. Mike also walks the talk. Shortly after Egg's launch, when the company was literally swamped with a flood of applications, Harris himself pitched in with the mundane task of sorting these out. In fact, he dealt with over five hundred applications personally, and even went so far as to ring customers when their recorded messages were unclear. Mike's achievement within Prudential is all the more notable considering the restraining cultural influences that a UK financial institution is likely to exert upon any new initiative of this nature.

Freeserve would probably never have achieved its success had John Pluthero, Mark Danby and Peter Wilkinson not worked together for several months to establish the business, create the business model and then sell the concept to Dixons' Chief Executive and Chairman. Pluthero also had to wrestle to establish a separate identity for Freeserve and its small team of only thirty people prior to its launch. In July 1998 Dixons did not expect the management of Freeserve to be a full-time job, making Pluthero responsible also for Dixons' distribution and after-sales arm. This span of responsibility was quickly refocused after the ensuing meteoric success of Freeserve. In April 1999 Pluthero was appointed Chief Executive of Freeserve and put in charge of its flotation.

The development of Dell Corporation's Internet business has required a strong commitment to teamwork. Michael Dell recognizes the importance of acquiring talent and then cultivating it. His style is collaborative, and he is willing to delegate and share responsibilities. It will therefore come as no surprise to learn that the founder of Dell frequently asserts that his company is allergic to hierarchy. A strong sense of team underpins his success.

It is the launch of eSchwab in 1996 that really puts the teamwork issue into perspective. In late 1995 a software demonstration was set up for Chuck Schwab by the company's 'tech guru', Dawn Lepore, now Vice Chairperson as well as Chief Information Officer at Charles Schwab Corporation. Lepore's computer engineers decided to carry out a simple Internet-based stock trade in order to show one possible advantage of an experimental piece of communications software. This involved a Schwab server taking an order from a web browser on a PC, routing it through all of Schwab's sophisticated back-end systems, executing the trade, and then sending a confirmation of the trade back to the original PC. When the patched-together demonstration worked successfully, both Schwab and Lepore (unlike their less business-aware engineers) felt stunned as they quickly grasped the implications of what they had just witnessed – the birth of Internet-based stock trading. Within a couple of weeks, Schwab had got Lepore to put together an independent – and initially secret – project team, which was assigned the task of getting Internet-based trading up and running at Schwab. The project team quickly grew to involve a couple of dozen people and was then formed into a separate brokerage unit, called eSchwab, which reported directly to Chuck's right-hand man – David Pottruck, President and Co-CEO of Schwab. The decision to set up a separate electronic commerce unit was in part done to enable Schwab to compete with deep-discount brokerages, such as E*Trade and Ameritrade, which were also working hard to offer an Internet-based service. 'We had to figure out how to compete with these small brokerages' comments Pottruck, 'So we needed a group that felt like they did: nimble, unshackled from the larger bureaucracy.' However, an element of caution was also involved in the decision to develop eSchwab in isolation from the rest of the company, and as Dan Leemon, Schwab's Head of Strategy points out: 'We created eSchwab because we wanted to learn. But we did not want to risk the whole company' (Gunn, 7/12/98).

History then speaks for itself, for the launch of eSchwab proved to be enormously successful and the separate story of eSchwab's subsequent reintegration into the main business of Charles Schwab Corporation is explored in a later chapter. Customer focus and technology-based innovation were critical to eSchwab's success but so to was absolutely first class teamwork. 'Teamwork is the only way we can accomplish anything', asserts Chuck. 'We are not built like a traditional brokerage house. We are not about outselling everyone else but about growing the company, which will create jobs and allow people to grow their careers.' The company's very low staff turnover rates demonstrate that this is more than mere lip service on the part of Schwab, as does the strong sense of genuine loyalty expressed by everyone at the company, ranging from office clerks to those in senior management. 'This is the best company I have ever worked for', comments Joan Joyner, Assistant Manager of the Schwab branch on San Francisco's Montgomery Street, whose past employers included two traditional brokerage houses.

■ Turning dreams into reality

When it comes to success in digital business and creating value in the network economy, it is clear that you don't need to be a technologist, a marketer or a strategist, judging by the experiences of our e-champions. What does seem important is:

- a basic literacy in information technology and an awareness of its role in shaping society;
- a profound commitment to customers and to providing value to them above almost everything else;
- a willingness to let your imagination loose; and
- the preparedness to build a team around you that can help you to achieve the success you seek.

Michael Dell maintains that to take advantage of the opportunities all you need is a framework and a dream. In *The Buck Starts Here* you will find the framework. You will be able to develop an appreciation of the way technology is reshaping society and business, from which you can begin to develop that sixth sense. You can explore key societal trends and their influence in shaping customer power. You can evaluate a set of tools and a framework of Value Levers to help you in building your own digital business. You can also address key organizational issues to ensure your business not only becomes a reality, but also achieves a level of success to match your aspirations. *The Buck Starts Here* will even provide some of the material for your dream – all you need to do is shape the dream itself.

Part One
Technology shapes the landscape

1

New society, new economy, new rules

▶ The inescapable nature of the new business environment and the need for the Value Lever framework
▶ The three waves of human society and what we need to learn from them
▶ How the information society metamorphosed into a network society
▶ The distinctive features of the network economy and the opportunities they create
▶ Misconceptions and conventional beliefs of e-business and the role that value plays in overcoming them

Filling the business vacuum

As the business world is turned upside down by the tumultuous events that are unfolding around us, so a sense of unease and uncertainty creeps into boardrooms and management meetings. The last vestiges of a stable predictable competitive landscape cling on, as flourishing Western economies disguise the underlying sea change that is taking place. Most senior managers have long managed to deny or ignore the social and technological changes taking place around them. They have pursued the easy path of business as usual, sticking to time-honoured sales-driven business models. Throughout the 1980s and 1990s major companies the world over tried to renew, reinvent or revitalize themselves. The results portray a dismal catalogue of failure and shortcoming, with only a handful able to boast success of any magnitude. For most, such radical evolution was important but deemed not absolutely essential to survival. So, when the going got tough, risk-averse boards and management teams reverted to business as usual, discarding troublesome partially completed initiatives, jettisoning them like so much useless flotsam.

What was optional over those last two decades has now become inescapable as the new economy rapidly reveals itself with all its ramifications. In Europe at least, more than three-quarters of companies report that their senior managers do not understand the implications of the new landscape. Only a small proportion of managers have truly understood the social changes taking place around them and the implications for consumer, and customer, behaviour. Even fewer have really grasped the enormity of information technology developments and their radical effects, preferring to delegate the thinking to IT functions held fast in the time warp of legacy systems.

But there is now a realization that what is going on is more akin to revolution than evolution in business thinking and practice. An orderly progression in the direction of both e-business and new economy thinking shows signs of panic. It is turning into headlong stampede, as managers discover that they need new tools and new ways if their businesses are to sustain pre-network offline economy successes. The challenge they now face is that, while there is much commentary on the Internet, the network economy and all matters digital, there is only limited output of truly practical help that managers can seize upon actively to help them transform their businesses or introduce entrepreneurial traits. No longer can you contract in all the thinking from major consulting firms – they too are struggling to find their feet in the knowledge that their relevance and *raison d'être* are much more restricted in this fast-moving, ideas-driven world.

There is a need to fill that vacuum and provide a lifeline for budding entrepreneur and seasoned business manager alike. To this end the Value Lever framework developed in this book is pivotal. Through evaluation of the new competitive forces and dynamics generated by technological developments and social trends, and their interaction, the author and his research colleagues have distilled an understanding of this new business landscape. This has produced a rigorously developed approach to digital business that offers a tangible means of overcoming the negative influences driving network economy competition. To comprehend fully the power of the Value Lever framework and its application, it will pay to understand not only the drivers of new competition, but also the origins of the network economy. As you will shortly discover, there is nothing new under the sun.

Beyond the third wave

There is a sense of real excitement about living in present times. Something fundamental is taking place around us – the emergence of a new society driven by information technologies. The last decades of the twentieth century have been fertile times for social commentators and analysts who have noted this growing influence of computer power. Japanese scholars first wrote of the 'Information Society' in the late 1960s as they observed the insidious role that computer-based technologies were playing in the growth of the Japanese economy. Western observers and writers quickly picked up this theme and began to analyse the nature and future of this Information Society. What emerged was a consensus about the past, present and future development of human civilization. Alvin Toffler explained this as the three waves of human evolution (Toffler 1970, 1981):

- The first wave involved the development of an *agrarian society*. This centred on man's transition from the hunting of animals and the gathering of wild plants for food to the growing of grain-crops and domestication of livestock. This agrarian revolution is believed to have commenced around 8000 B.C.
- The second wave involved the emergence of an *industrial society*. Mankind learned how to use inanimate sources of energy, such as steam and electricity, to power machinery. The industrial revolution began in Europe at around the end of the seventeenth century and then spread to many other parts of the world
- The third wave, observed Toffler, leads us to the development of an *information society*, in which mankind is learning to leverage the power of computer technology to store and process information. The origins of this information revolution lie in the technological advances made after the Second World War, but it was only in the 1970s that the revolution started to have an impact upon society as a whole.

During the 1990s the third wave revolution took on almost tsunami proportions. It is now driving us beyond an Information Society, to a '*Network Society*' in which the information-transmitting power of telecommunications is hugely enhancing the information-processing power of computers. 'We are witnessing the unleashing of a technological revolution of historic proportions, which will transform the fundamental dimensions of human life', observes Manuel Castells, eminent sociologist and Professor at University of California. 'This revolution is opening up unlimited horizons of creativity and communication', he reflects, 'and it is challenging our societies to engage in a process of structural change' (Castells, 1996).

As time moves on and the rate of change around us accelerates, Castell's foresight appears increasingly valid. There is a growing sense that we are living through an extraordinary period in human history, in which we are reorganizing our entire civilization around the digital power of telecommunications-enabled information technology. Yet we are only at the start, and our vision of how this may unfold is limited only by our imaginations.

The first wave revisited

The first wave of Toffler's evolution of human civilization was an agrarian society. It represents the longest phase of human experience and prevailed until the early part of the eighteenth century. In this agrarian society people lived out their lives mostly in villages and towns, aware only of their immediate surroundings. Few travelled – there was neither reason nor affordable means – and few were educated or could read. The written word was for the few, the privileged and the learned. It was used principally for law and religion. Survival depended upon knowledge exchanged within each local community. Communication was by spoken word, and the economy was local and largely self-sufficient. This was a primitive form of network economy. One-to-one communication predominated in face-to-face encounters. One-to-many and many-to-one communication occurred at meetings. Market days and marketplaces provided the context for many-to-many communication. Affiliations were strong, personal and static.

Over the ensuing 250 years much changed in the wake of the industrial revolution. Migration and widespread travel became more commonplace. Education meant the written word was no longer the preserve of the few and was now used for widespread communication. Letters and newspapers gradually proliferated as a means of keeping in touch with distant family and friends or familiar surroundings. The bounded and self-contained world of the local network economy-based community started to break down. As the industrial revolution continued into the twentieth century, new forms of communication were invented. Radio and then television made their impact but, though they have the effect of generating a more global perspective on life, they did little to restore the strong sense of community engendered by the more personal forms of intercommunication that existed in the agrarian era. Each contributed to developing a society where mass awareness created mass markets waiting to be served. Marshall McLuhan spoke of the 'global village' but most of the communication in this embryonic worldwide community was broadcast, one-way and impersonal in nature. Intercommunication still depended upon the spoken word exchanged on a face-to-face basis – only the telephone provided remote communication and this was limited to a one-to-one basis.

While society developed a global perspective through broadcast media, the telephone, with its one-to-one communication limitations, did little to arrest the decline of that basic sense of community in society. 'Face-to-face' remained the predominant means of buyer–seller interaction, for the consumer at least, even though economies had moved from local to national, and ultimately on to an international scale. Unlike the agrarian society that preceded it, affiliation had become weaker, relatively impersonal and more fluid in this industrial society.

During the latter part of the twentieth century industrial society increasingly gave way to an information society where civilization developed and proliferated computer technology, learning to store information and to process it in a far more effective manner than was ever previously thought possible. Advances in computing power led to the creation of repositories of data. Significant benefits accrued but this new computing capability was largely applied, without question, to automate existing processes and practices developed in the society and markets of the earlier industrial era. It took the convergence of the information-processing power of computers with the information-transmitting power of telecommunications in the last decade of the twentieth century to indicate just how radically society and business might begin to change. The global emergence of the Internet enabled once more the instant interactive communication of that earlier agrarian society. This time instead of face-to-face communication, technology enabled remote connections – one-to-one, one-to-many, many-to-many and many-to-one – independent of location and temporal constraints. With an end to the tyranny of distance and time, society now had the means of unlimited global, multimedia interactive communication to complement the increasingly cosmopolitan nature and status of its communities and economies. Thanks to this we now have at least the capacity, if not yet the collective will, to create an economy that is truly global in nature.

A revolutionary economy

Technology-based connectivity and intercommunication create the potential for an explosive network revolution. Scope, scale and pace of occurrence defy our experience and our ability to imagine them. 'We are at the beginning of a 'network revolution' – an economic and social transition comparable to the Industrial Revolution', proclaims the European Commission in a recent report.

> This revolution reflects the migration of significant amounts of commercial and social activity from the physical world to interactive, digital networks built upon open standards. This revolution is creating a new economy and presents momentous challenges and opportunities for businesses. . . . Such familiar indicators as usage growth rates, changing end-user attitudes, and business investment decisions suggest that the network economy is already spreading rapidly throughout the developed world, significantly altering the way that firms and individuals conduct business. (Condrinet, 1998)

Network revolution leads to network economy. 'We now live in a new economy created by shrinking computers and expanding communications', says Kevin Kelly, former Executive Editor of *Wired* magazine.

> This new economy has three distinguishing characteristics: It is global. It favors intangible things – ideas, information, and relationships. And it is intensely interlinked. These three attributes produce a new type of marketplace and society, one that is rooted in ubiquitous electronic networks. . . . Networks have existed in every economy. What's different now is that networks, enhanced and multiplied by technology, penetrate our lives so deeply that 'network' has become the central metaphor around which our thinking and our economy are organized. (Kelly, 1998)

So what precisely is a network economy? It is an economy that creates significant value from and via digitally based technological, human and organizational connections. It can only flourish when many involved parties have the potential to connect. Such are the benefits of Internet technology – deployed inside organizations, as well as externally for communication with customers – that businesses cannot afford to underestimate the importance of the 'network' metaphor.

The age of opportunity

But what is different about the network economy? It is, after all, subject to the same fundamental economic laws and principles as the conventional and familiar economy. Yet there are some subtle and important differences that influence the way consumers and businesses behave, creating significant new opportunities and challenges. These differences also translate into new and different competitive dynamics, such as:

- A major shift in market alignment from seller or provider bias towards buyer bias – in effect putting power and control much more in the hands of the customer.
- The remarkable effect of 'increasing returns' – where the more customers for a product or service that there are, the more value accrues to *all* customers with each additional customer added
- The opportunity to create all sorts of new interfaces between buyer and seller – auctions, quote services, aggregators and many more.
- The role that inter-connection may play in helping to re-establish community in a sense no longer bounded by physical location.

In the conventional economy businesses create value by focusing their strategies on entities, such as the firm, its suppliers, its channels to market and its customers. But in the network economy businesses create value by focusing on the relationships that exist or can be created between these various entities (Figure 1.1).

The proliferation of 'connections' is pivotal. Each connection is

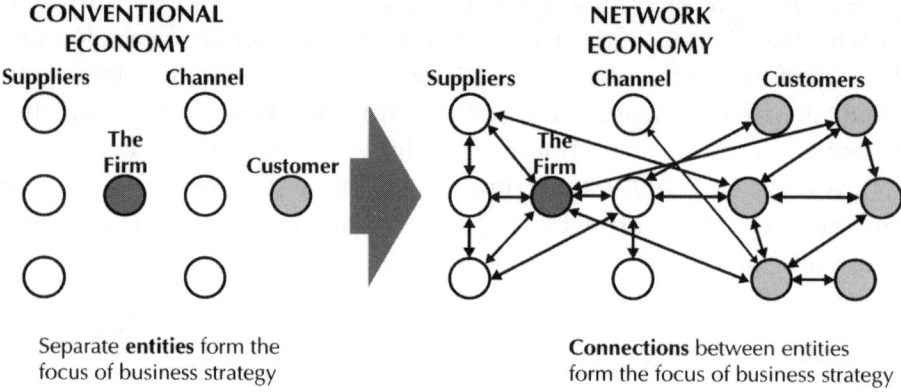

Figure 1.1 Creating value from connection

also a real or possible relationship and, from a business perspective, every relationship is a potential financially based exchange – in other words, a latent source of value and profit. Our e-champions have an implicit awareness of this, and they have used this knowledge as a key source of their successes. For example, Freeserve depends upon an understanding of the various connections between its customers, its portal website and the suppliers of content and services to that website. Each connection has been evaluated as a potential relationship and for how that relationship can be converted into a financially based exchange. For Schwab's online customers the full service they access and enjoy is determined by the host of connections that Schwab has with suppliers of investment management-related information and services. These suppliers are external to the Charles Schwab Corporation.

Even in these early stages of its development these subtle but powerful differences of the new network economy will have a widespread impact upon the competitive landscape of every business sector. We shall explore these differences in detail later in this section.

Creating not destroying value

While these new dynamics offer enormous opportunity to the creative, imaginative and bold, they present a source of enormous concern for those business folk less comfortable with information technology and the inherent rapid pace of change. Informed that the Internet is likely to change most aspects of the way they do business, the first reaction of the less adaptive businessperson is one of denial and rejection. This inevitable and natural reaction to something new and alien to their experience has spawned a number of widely held misconceptions:

- that digital business is really just another channel to market, and nothing more;
- that it is a matter of choosing between either digital business or familiar physical real-world business and that they require discrete treatment;
- that in the network economy relationships with customers will inevitably become more remote;
- that the primary impact of digital business is to drive down prices – to commoditize, and remove any chance of differentiation (and profit);
- that digital business destroys value through disintermediation – that is to say, removing the need for intermediaries because consumers can access comprehensive information about available suppliers quickly and more easily.

There is some truth in all of these, but they are likely to hold true only if managers persist in ignoring the nature of digital business and the emergence of the network economy. The experience of the physical, bricks-and-mortar world naturally positions digital business as just another channel, but it is much more than that. It influences every aspect of the way we organize our firms to create and deliver value to customers and shareholders. Nor is it a binary choice. Real business advantage may well be obtained by evolving existing and successful real-world business models to a form that is part physical and part virtual. In other words, migrate some business process events online and maintain others as before still using existing physical assets. This has become known as the 'clicks-and mortar' approach to the network economy. Among our e-champions who started with purely virtual businesses, some have already recognized that they may need to develop a physical presence in order to achieve fully their potential. For example, Amazon has recognized that its future success depends upon some physical assets. Jeff Bezos and is now opening distribution centres across the USA and there has been a suggestion of flagship bookstores. In moving to auctions Jeff was quick to establish an alliance with Sotheby's. Being wholly virtual is unlikely to be a guarantee of large-scale success.

As for the perceptions that the network economy may make customer relationships more remote, may commoditize and could possibly destroy value through disintermediation, these too may hold true. Apply existing physical-world business thinking and models without appreciation of the unique competitive dynamics of the network economy and these concerns may well prove correct. Try to understand the new competitive dynamics in order to grasp how to create value rather than let it be destroyed by others, and these perceptions will most definitely turn out to be false. Following in the tracks of our e-champions, creating value is what this book is about. Understand the unique properties of the network economy and you can emulate their successes. The opportunities are far greater and more abundant than the challenges.

Summary

A technological revolution of historic proportions is transforming our world and challenging the very structure of our societies. It is clear we are living through an extraordinary period in human history, when we are reorganising our entire civilization around the digital power of telecommunications-enabled information technology. Yet we are only at the start, and our vision of how this may unfold is limited only by our imaginations.

Technology-based connectivity and intercommunication create the potential for this explosive network revolution, where connections are key. Each connection is a real or possible relationship and, from a business perspective, every relationship is a potential financially based exchange – in other words, a latent source of value and, in turn, profit.

Our e-champions have an implicit awareness of what is going on and have used this knowledge as a key source of their successes. You can develop a similar understanding of network society and network economy to match theirs, and then apply this new knowledge yourself to build a truly effective digital business.

In the next chapter we will consider:

- How major technological forces drive commercial conduct and business performance
- How information processing and transmission create the bedrock for the new economy
- The four technological forces that impel society and business
- The four macro-realities of business performance that shape competitive behaviour

2

Powerful forces at work

- ▶ The largely unseen influential forces shaping business in the third millennium
- ▶ The interacting powers of information processing and information transmission and the technological drivers they spawn
- ▶ The critical role interconnectivity and the twin concepts of 'critical mass' and 'more value to all users of a network'
- ▶ The shaping of competitive behaviour by the powers of information technology and the macro-realities of business performance
- ▶ The distinctive nature of the virtual world and its impact on the economics of information.

There are major forces afoot that are shaping the business world around us. These are taking place at a high level, almost unseen and so far only partially interpreted. If we are to buy into any evaluation of these forces at a micro-level where business success is determined by specific and definable response, then we need at least to have an appreciation of what is going on at the macro-level. At this high level, there are two distinct sets of forces at work, the one shaping the other. There are the technological drivers that fundamentally enable and mould the network economy. What technology enables, society and business will adopt, and the macro-realities of business performance are the principal forces shaping the new business landscape and the competitive environment for all businesses.

In this chapter we will explore first the drivers of technology, and then how these technological powers actuate the drivers of business performance.

The drivers of technology

There are two primary aspects of technology that have enabled the network economy. One was critical to the emergence of the information society: the processing of information; the other fuelled the ensuing transition to the network society: the transmission of information. To grasp how to create value when doing business in this new landscape we need to appreciate what is driving these two facets, and how they are likely to influence the nature and scope of this network world. Note that we will overlook the storage of information in this particular context. It is an important and developing aspect of information technology. However, it is passive and is unlikely directly to influence the competitive dynamics.

In understanding the two aspects – information processing and information transmission – there are four key technological drivers with which we need to concern ourselves: digitization, processing power, interconnectivity, and transmission speed.

Digitization
Digitization is 'the encoding of previously physical products and information media into an electronic format which may be stored

and processed within computers' (Barnatt, 1997). This encoding of information not only enables information to be stored and processed by computers, but also allows it to be transmitted via electronic networks over long distances without any loss in quality.

Nicholas Negroponte, the Director of the Media Laboratory at MIT, has no doubt about the critical role of digitization. He argues that business is now shifting away from the production and transportation of *'atoms'* – physical things – to the production and transportation of *'bits'* – that is digital data. As a result of this shift, Negroponte believes that bits – the binary digits represented by either a '1' or a '0' – are eventually destined to become the primary unit of world trade. In his book *Being Digital* Negroponte acknowledges that the shift from atoms to bits will not be able to transform every industry in its entirety. While industries such as manufacturing, food produce, clothing and construction will always have to include a significant role for atoms, he argues that the global economy will in time come to be dominated by 'digital business' (Negroponte, 1995).

Just as Negroponte speaks of 'digital business', so Don Tapscott, author and futurist, talks of a 'digital economy':

> In the new economy, information in all its forms becomes digital – reduced to bits stored in computers and racing at the speed of light across networks. Using this binary code of computers, information and communications become digital ones and zeros. The new world of possibilities thereby created is as significant as the invention of language itself, the old paradigm in which all the physically based interactions occurred. (Tapscott, 1995)

Processing power

The rise in computer processing power that has occurred in the last three decades has followed the prediction of Moore's Law, a forecast made in 1965 by a computer engineer, Gordon Moore, while working at Fairfield Semiconductor. Moore forecaste that the processing power (or speed) of computers would continue for the foreseeable future to double every 18–24 months, while the price to the end-user would remain roughly the same. Moore's conviction as to the sound-

Powerful forces at work

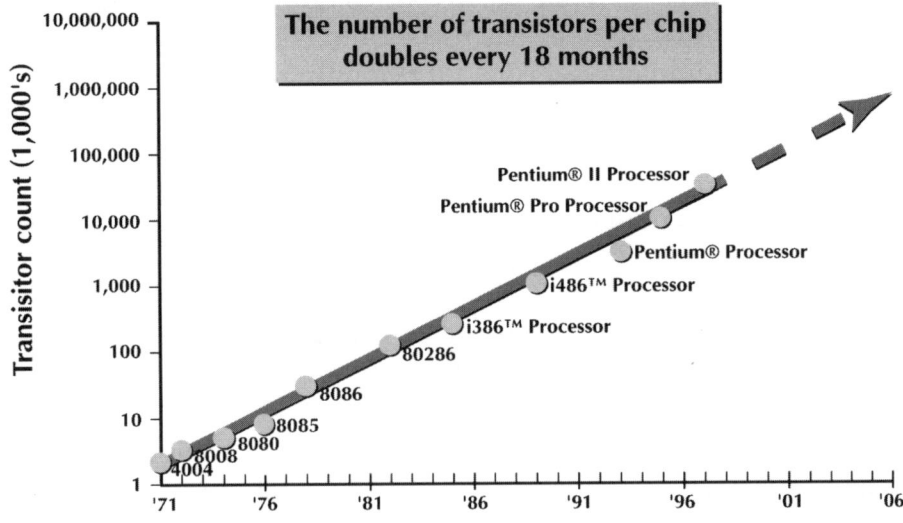

Source: Intel Corporation

Figure 2.1 Moore's Law

ness of his prediction was one of the reasons that led him in 1969 to become one of the co-founders of the Intel Corporation (an organization in which Moore now holds the office of Chairperson Emeritus).

Subsequent history, which Intel's successful evolution into the world's largest microelectronics company has helped to write, has proved the accuracy of Moore's prediction. In the thirty years since Intel engineer Ted Hoff developed the world's first mass-produced microprocessor (the Intel 4004) in 1971, there has indeed been, as Moore predicted, an exponential rise in computer processing power (see Figure 2.1). Observers have maintained for many years that the exponential gains made in the performance of microprocessors would slow down. Yet, it appears likely that Moore's Law will continue to operate well into the next decade (one study predicts that finite physical limitations will begin to have an increasingly significant impact by 2017).

At the beginning of the 1970s computing power cost about 280 times as much as it did in 1997; in 1989 it cost three times as much as in 1997. The steadily reducing cost of computer processing power over the last three decades has fuelled the phenomenal increase in numbers of computers and computer chips in use around the world. In 1997 it was estimated that there were around 200 million computers and 6 billion computer chips in use, and it was predicted that these figures would rise to at least 500 million computers by 2002 and 10 billion computer chips by 2005 (Hutchings, 2/10/97). Virtually every manufactured item now contains a microprocessor computer chip. As Nicholas Negroponte observed: 'you can expect to have on your wrist tomorrow what you have on your desk today, and what filled a room yesterday' (Negroponte, 1995).

Interconnectivity

Interconnectivity refers to the increasing number of communications links between everything and anything that contains a computer chip. Presently we think of those links as relating to devices such as mainframes, PCs, interactive televisions and maybe mobile phones linked through the Internet. With virtually every manufactured good soon likely to have communications as well as microprocessing capability built into it, most of the interconnectivity on the Internet will be from thing to thing, rather than person to person or business to business. So, your washing machine will negotiate with the power utility as to when it will turn itself on to get the most economic rate for power; or, your mobile phone might let each network, to which you are a subscriber, bid for every call you make. Dr Stephen Emmott of NCR's Knowledge Lab maintains that by 2008 thing-to-thing connectivity and automated commerce will result in everyone, willing or unwilling, participating in the Internet by proxy, if not directly.

Just as Moore's Law concerns processing power, so Metcalfe's Law addresses networks and interconnectivity. Robert Metcalfe developed the Ethernet protocol for localized computer networks, and in 1981 he founded 3Com Corporation, the US computer network company. Metcalfe had noticed that linked computer networks needed to achieve a certain critical mass before their users would regard them as worthwhile. This led Metcalfe in 1980 to formulate a rule of thumb that later became known as Metcalfe's Law. The law states that the usefulness, or utility, of a network rises with the square of the number of people using it: that is, utility of a network = (number of users)^2. It implies that the more people that join a given network, the more valuable the network will become to each and every user – not just the new joiners.

A telephone network illustrates the application of Metcalfe's Law. If only two people are connected to a telephone network, then only one conversation can take place; however, if a further person is connected to the network, then it is possible to have three different conversations. If ten people are connected to the same network, then it is possible to have forty-five different conversations. It applies equally to the Internet; as the number of Internet users expands, each and every user enjoys increasing utility. This increasing utility has already reached a critical mass and is now snowballing, so that financial investments in the Internet's infrastructure and in the commercial services on offer are being made at an ever-increasing rate. As if this astronomic rate of growth is not sufficiently alarming, some argue that the value of the Internet may actually increase faster than Metcalfe's Law predicts. Unlike the standard telephone, the Internet allows individuals to interact with more than one other person at the same time – many-to-many connections. Certainly, the exponential growth rate of the Internet shows how highly it is valued by its users, and demonstrates the importance of interconnectivity as a driver of the network economy.

As we will discover when evaluating the unique competitive dynamics of the network economy, Metcalfe's Law has great significance. The twin concepts of critical mass for a given network, and more value to every user from more connections leads to the *Law of Increasing Returns*. This is fundamental to our understanding of why investors are so keen to invest in Internet-based businesses. They believe their investments will enjoy significant long-term value even though short- to medium-term profitability is as yet uncertain. Our e-champions have all demonstrated how they have leveraged this law to the benefit of their businesses and their investors. Jeff Bezo's investors still believe that Amazon has a long way to go before it exhausts the potential of increasing returns to customers, so they continue to accept the absence of profitability. Freeserve's remarkable growth from nothing to 1.4 million users occurred in five months before competitors arrived to slow down progress. Prudential's Egg achieved its five-year target of users and fund under management in five months. All of these businesses are leveraging the remarkable properties that interconnectivity enables.

The scale of what is going on almost defies our imaginations. As Craig Barrett, Intel's Chief Executive, observed: 'We are moving rapidly towards one billion connected computers. This does not represent an online community: it represents the formation of a "virtual continent"' (quoted in Taylor, 7/4/99).

Transmission speed

The rate at which data can be passed across any particular point within a system or network is known as bandwidth. Bandwidth is the principal constraint on the growth of traffic over the Internet. The bandwidth provided by global communications systems has increased rapidly in recent years through better infrastructure in the form of fibre optic cables and enhanced switching, as well as through improved data compression technologies. This has the effect of speeding up data transmission. Yet bandwidth is continually insufficient and manages only just to keep pace with the rapid increase in volume of users and the increased volume of traffic per user. Bandwidth has given rise to a third 'law' – Gilder's Law – formulated by George Gilder, a 'radical technotheorist' as one analyst described him. Gilder forecast that, for the foreseeable future, or at least until the end of the first decade of the new millennium, the total bandwidth of communication systems will triple every twelve months.

The prevalent view is that Gilder is right and that bandwidth will continually increase ahead of demand, ceasing even to be an issue as technological advances produce step changes in bandwidth availability. If Gilder's Law does prove true we will shortly be able to transmit enormous amounts of data over the Internet and other computer networks without creating major bottlenecks, and without incurring the delays with which Internet users are all too familiar. This will allow the development of real-time, multimedia services such as video-conferencing, and full-screen, broadcast-quality video.

Based on his forecast, Gilder also predicts that the price per bit of computer data transmitted over a network will increasingly tend towards zero over time. This will make these real-time multimedia services affordable to both businesses and consumers alike.

Many believe ubiquitous broadband, when unlimited bandwidth is enjoyed by all, will be the point at which the network economy will truly come into its own. John Pluthero has no doubt of its importance to Freeserve's future success. He is certain that broadband will extend the functionality and utility of his portal business to his customers. The next generation of mobile phones due for launch in 2003, if not earlier, is forecast to have full interactive multimedia networking capability. When instantaneous full multimedia capability is the basic standard for all access devices, the utility of the Internet will increase markedly. At that point the technology of the network economy will begin to seem transparent as it delivers a level of usefulness that matches or even begins to exceed society's expectations.

The drivers of business performance

Technological factors are undoubtedly the primary drivers of the network economy. They determine its growing impact upon our lives and portend its dominating influence on society and commerce globally. They fulfil the same role as those earlier technological developments that led to new sources of power and to new forms of machinery, paving the way for the industrial revolution.

The specific commercial impact of these technological drivers is to induce powers that challenge prevailing commercial conduct and business performance. Research confirms there is a clear progression from the technological factors described above to macro-realities of network-based business. These macro-realities then shape the Network Dynamics that, at the micro-level, drive business competition, as Figure 2.2 illustrates. Four distinct forces make up the macro-realities: global interactivity, hypermedia environment, friction-free transactionality and physical asset independence. We will now consider each of these four in turn before exploring the individual network dynamics in Chapter 3.

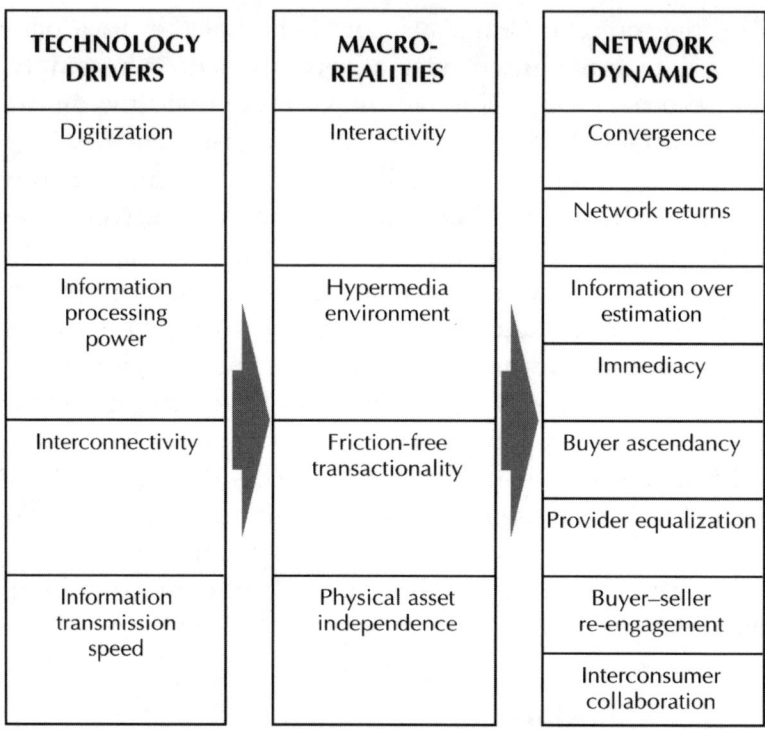

Figure 2.2 Competitive forces in the network economy

Global interactivity

The deployment of networking technologies creates an environment characterized by global interactivity. This is an environment in which it becomes possible to link together people, organizations, systems and processes by means of relationships that are interactive or essentially reciprocal in nature. Investors in Amazon are banking on truly global interactivity to justify its high stock price. Anlaysts estimate that, if Amazon can retain its share of the online global book market as the network economy expands, then its inflated stock price may be quite reasonable.

Global interactivity is a major feature of the network economy as consultants, McKinsey & Co., eloquently explain:

> A convergence of technologies is set to increase our capacity to interact by a factor of between two and five in the near future. This

enhanced interactive capacity will create new ways to configure businesses, organize companies, serve customers, and have profound effects on the structure, strategy, and competitive dynamics of industries. . . . Until now, our ability to manipulate and process data has far outstripped our ability to communicate and interact. However . . . [new] networking capabilities, technologies that enhance connectivity and bandwidth, and standards that drive new applications are coming together in an environment of spiralling processing power and deepening technological penetration. This potent combination heralds a new age of abundant interactive capability. (Butler *et al.*, 1997)

The concept of a 'new age of abundant interactive capability' truly captures the imagination. 'The Internet can be thought of as a two-way broadcast system. . . . It combines the characteristics of two-way communications, such as telephone and fax (one-to-one communications), with those of broadcast media, such as radio and television (one-to-many communications)', observe Yong Choi and colleagues at the Center for Research in Electronic Commerce, University of Texas. 'It is not an exaggerated prediction that the Internet, spurred on by the World Wide Web . . . will some day supersede all these communication mediums' (Choi, Stahl and Whinston, 1997). Even their perspective falls short of conveying the full power of interactivity that extends beyond the interface of customers and suppliers to the whole value chain of a supplier's organization. It will touch every aspect of business systems and processes.

Hypermedia environment

Hypermedia refers to the interaction of abundant content with diversity in available forms of media. A hypermedia environment is one where this abundance of material can be quickly and easily accessed through a diverse range of media – textual, audio, graphical, visual and video. Christopher Barnatt refers to this richness of forms of media as 'metamedia' (Barnatt, 1997). Content adds another dimension, hence hypermedia. The amount of material available in electronic form is enormous and growing. More information has been published in the last three decades than during the whole of the previous five millennia, while an average copy of the *Times* contains more information than the average person would have experienced in their lives in the seventeenth century (Pritchett, 1994). Hypermedia depends upon networking technologies that process, store and enable networked transmission of information in numerous different formats.

We have been able to observe this hypermedia environment evolve as new forms of media have been deployed. RealAudio's audio-streaming technology enables the transmission of real-time audio signals over the Web. Real.com's video-streaming technology enables the transmission of real-time video and audio signals via the Web, although its truly effective use is still limited by bandwidth constraints. We have also seen the deployment of imaging technologies that enable the generation of three-dimensional images of objects, people and locations that can also be manipulated.

Hypermedia remains for the time being the least significant of the four macro-realities. It will truly come into its own as bandwidth increases to enable the instant transmission of any media, including full-broadcast video. In time it will play a critical role in extending the human interface with the network and will contribute strongly to the creation of a personalized bubble of content and experience around each user.

Friction-free transactionality

Bill Gates first used the phrase 'friction-free capitalism' in his book, *The Road Ahead*, to capture the idea that the Internet facilitates the creation of Adam Smith's vision of an ideal marketplace, in which buyers and sellers could quickly locate one another without spending time or money (Gates, 1995). Friction-free transactionality builds on Gates's concept to convey the idea that the network economy brings about significant reductions in the time and cost required for carrying out of all kinds of transactions. 'Transactions' in this context has a much broader meaning than merely the interaction of buyers and sellers. It refers to all communications, interactions and exchanges between people and businesses in a network environment.

These reductions in time and cost have very important consequences for the business world, since many companies are still largely reliant upon the existence of friction in the flow and control of information between buyers and sellers to sustain their profit margins. This is one principal reason that the role of intermediaries will transform significantly as the network economy evolves. Intermediaries who fail to grasp what this friction-free world entails run the risk of dis-intermediation, while other organizations that understand the implications will take advantage of the changes, spot opportunities and succeed through new forms of intermediation. This is precisely what Jay Walker has done with Priceline. Contrast Jay's name-your-own-price airline ticket service with the conventional travel agency that still depends upon friction for a major part of its business.

The impact of changing transaction costs upon the business world was highlighted in the twentieth century by economist Ronald Coase. He discovered that businesses could be expected to undergo major structural adjustments when significant shifts occurred in the cost to a firm of performing transactions internally or via the open market. Since information provides the substance of most transactions and can be exchanged for almost no cost via digital networks, it follows that transactions costs in a network economy will also tend to drop toward zero. This means that the cost of carrying out transactions within a firm, as well as via the open market, will be significantly reduced in a network environment. Consequently we can expect major changes to occur in the business world as it embraces the network economy. Costs of doing business will decline with consequent gains in productivity and efficiency, producing transient benefits offsetting inflationary tendencies in economies.

The actual reductions in transaction costs that occur due to the effects of the network economy are quite remarkable. According to data collected by the American Banking Association, the average costs of a typical retail transaction were $1.07 via a branch, $0.68 via the telephone, $0.27 via an ATM, and $0.10 via the Internet. The US Department of Commerce reports that a typical airline reservation costs $8 via a travel agent or $1 via the Web. Parcels and freight company UPS cite the cost of answering a customer query to be around $2 over the phone compared with only $0.07 via the Web. Perhaps we should not therefore be surprised that research company

Forrester estimates retail prices for goods sold via electronic channels to decline by at least 30 per cent over the next 10–15 years.

The effect of friction-free transactionality will be to influence the whole process of creating and delivering value. Its outcome will lead to the deconstruction and reconstruction of the value systems and chains of the business world. It will change the shape and nature of organizations, as well as helping to redefine the interfaces between buyers and sellers.

Physical asset independence

Physical asset independence is created by the capacity of networking technologies to transcend the limitations of the physical world of bricks and mortar. This is all about the virtualization of business. Physical location becomes gradually less important to the daily activities of people and businesses. Businesses discover that the Internet can enable them to expand the scope or scale of their activities through alliances or outsourcing; many are also finding that they can tap previously inaccessible regional and global markets. Consumers too are making similar discoveries. They are finding that they no longer need to visit their local supermarket, music store or bank, and that they can access these quite effectively using their PCs. Some are already discovering that they can do this using their mobile phones as well, with the additional benefit of securing virtually any commercial service wherever they themselves happen to be.

We are now witnessing what Frances Cairncross, the Senior Editor of the *Economist*, refers to as the 'death of distance', where location becomes an irrelevance to the conduct of business (Cairncross, 1997). Yet, it is not just the death of distance. We are also seeing the death of time, as networking technology enables real-time communications and instant awareness of happenings in remote and distant locations. This demise of both time and distance has important implications for established real-world businesses, enabling them to embrace the 'Martini Principle', and provide customers with access to their products and services 'any time, any place, any where'. A key outcome is that many businesses, big and small, will in the very near future become truly global as they find themselves able to provide a local, around-the-clock service globally. As these global businesses unfold, human beings will come to view the current divide between the virtual and the physical worlds as an irrelevant anachronism – the two worlds will have effectively merged into one. For Michael Dell's customers this is already the case, as they order their PCs online and take delivery of their personalized computer within a few days, just as many of Jeff Bezos's customers no longer visit a bookstore to purchase books.

Summary

The powers shaping the business world around us are awesome and unstoppable. In a matter of decades the humble computer has evolved from clumsy number cruncher of limited scope to the pervasive tool that runs like a thread through every aspect of our lives. The four powers of digitization, processing power, interconnectivity and transmission speed illustrate the enormous influence that information technology exerts, and some would say that this is only the beginning. As transmission speed, and bandwidth in particular, expands to offer the potential of ever richer communications, so the nature of human interaction looks set to transform.

The powers of technology shape the network world, both society and economy. From the business perspective they unleash forces that in turn define the future business landscape and the basis of competition. Global interactivity, hypermedia environment, friction-free transactionality and physical asset independence are four powers of business performance. All are important and interact to fashion network dynamics that at the micro-level inform businesses' response and competition. None is more critical than interconnectivity and its underlying network effect.

In the next chapter we will explore:

▶ The impact of these powers at the micro-level
▶ The evident intuitive understanding of these by our e-champions
▶ The distinctive character and influence of each of the eight network dynamics
▶ What this actually means in respect of business competition

3
Network dynamics

▶ The specific forces that determine business conduct and competitive behaviour in the new economy
▶ Definition of the eight distinct network dynamics: convergence, network returns, information over estimation, immediacy, buyer ascendancy, provider equalization, buyer–seller re-engagement, and interconsumer collaboration
▶ Detailed explanation and evaluation of each dynamic and its digital business context
▶ Examples of dynamics in action and related e-champion application
▶ Underlying business imperatives that the each of these competitive forces commands

Network dynamics

The competitive forces of the network economy are in many respects new and different from those in the familiar physical business world. Fail to understand them and you will find it difficult, if not impossible, to shape an effective business response to them. Price is the blunt instrument of competition, and its usual effect is to erode profits. This was one of the tenets underlying Michael Porter's seminal work *Competitive Strategy* (Porter, 1980). There is a widely held belief that the network economy will lead to perfectly efficient markets, and that the resulting transparency can lead only to price-based competition and to inevitable commoditization. Take this to its logical conclusion and the inescapable outcome for your business is likely to be indiscriminate price-driven competition and a failure to build value, let alone discover profitability in embracing digital business. The positive alternative is to understand the dynamics of the new competitive environment and then begin to shape an effective business response that will lead to digital business success.

In the previous chapter we explored the two principal groups of macro-level powers – technology and business performance drivers. In this chapter we will explore the dynamics that these macro-level powers bring into play, and that is the purpose of this chapter, to provide you with a detailed appreciation of these micro-level network dynamics as an essential input to the evolution of the Value Lever framework.

Our e-champions have built their successes on an intuitive and experience-driven approach to the new business environment. Charles Schwab Corporation continues to charge a stock trade fee almost 100 per cent higher than its nearest online competitor and is still the market leader, enjoying the remarkable benefits of increasing returns. Jeff Bezos uses low pricing deliberately to build value-based, long-term relationships with ever-growing numbers of customers. He understands the full range of competitive forces and can with confidence use price deliberately but not bluntly. Mike Harris is building Egg on similar principles. UK financial services have long been based on high costs and high prices. Mike believes he too can build value-based relationships with his customers where low price helps to seal the loyalty and trust between supplier and customer. Companies such as Priceline and eBay are fee-based intermediaries and are consciously using price as a key factor in their highly innovative business models. To emulate our e-champions' success we therefore need first to understand the competitive landscape.

There are eight network dynamics: convergence, network returns, information over estimation, immediacy, buyer ascendancy, provider equalization, buyer–seller re-engagement, and interconsumer collaboration.

■ Convergence

Network dynamic definition
Influenced by the growing integration of computing, communications and content, the boundaries between companies, industries, economies and even cultures begin to blur.

In the old familiar world of physical business, companies were distinct entities competing in bounded industry sectors. They were like armies manoeuvring for strategic and tactical advantage upon a defined battlefield. This was the world that Michael Porter saw and of which he made sense for the world of business in the early 1980s. Many business people still think and even behave as though that was still the commercial world we now inhabit. Many of us have known for some years that this is no longer the case, aided by the insights of observers and commentators such as Gary Hamel and C. K. Prahalad (Hamel and Prahalad, 1994). Technology and the information society had begun to blur the boundaries of company and sector alike throughout the last decade of the recent millennium. This, however, was only a prelude to the emergence of the network economy.

The World Wide Web, that remarkable invention of Tim Berners-Lee in 1990, indicated just how the information transmitting and processing capabilities of information would come together in full graphical and visual splendour. The realization dawned among the most forward thinking that this would have a marked influence on media and content as well. Nicholas Negroponte was among the first to observe this convergence. He commented that a new industry sector was emerging through the convergence of three, previously separate, industry sectors: computing (computers, software, services), communications (telephony, cable, satellite and wireless) and content (entertainment, publishing and information providers) sectors (Negroponte, 1995). Picking up on this theme, Don Tapscott described the new sector that resulted from the merger of these three 'C's' as the 'Interactive Multimedia' sector, and forecast that it would grow to be worth at least $1.47 trillion by the year 2005 (Tapscott, 1996).

The concept of an interactive multimedia sector was only a start. In old-world thinking it inferred that this was to be something clear-cut and separate from other sectors. The wide application of networking technologies that underpin this interactive multimedia sector is already helping to blur the boundaries between many other business sectors. This is a development that has contributed to the benefit of many of our e-champions. Amazon has moved from bookseller, to music and on to a range of additional categories, including home improvement products and toys, and this is only the start for this customer-obsessed company. As Freeserve builds its relationships with its users, it too is expanding the number of services from previously distinct sectors.

Possibly one of the most marked impacts of convergence will be upon financial services. These services are nearly all simply a means to an end, helping consumers to transact, save, protect or borrow. As digitally driven businesses become more customer-focused and seek to provide a total customer experience, so the boundary between finance and other consumer goods and services will blur. Insurer USAA has already taken steps in this direction with its broader non-financial offerings. In the UK supermarkets such as Tesco, Sainsbury's and Asda have already developed significant financial service capabilities. This raises the question of what business financial companies should, in future, be in. Should it be the provision of financial services or the facilitation of consumer lifestyles? The question indicates how far the boundaries are blurring for this sector.

This blurring also occurs at international and cross-cultural levels too. Software companies and customer service companies on the Indian subcontinent are providing important services to many different Western companies. It is also happening inside companies as

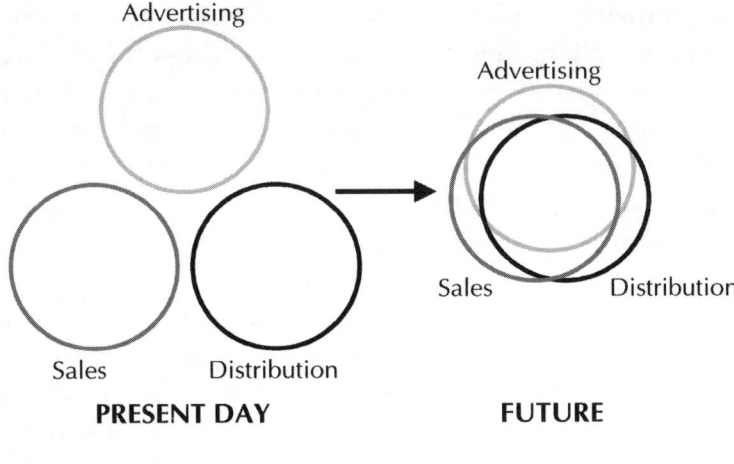

Source: Barnatt, 1999

Figure 3.1 The online convergence of business functions

previously separate roles and functions begin to merge. Christopher Barnatt illustrates just how this occurs in this network world. While surfing the Internet, a customer can click on to a banner advertisement, and be immediately taken to another website, with which the customer then interacts as a sales medium. Since many information-based products and services, such as software, music, legal advice and financial products can also be dispatched electronically to the customer via the Internet, the distribution process can then, in many cases, be completed online as well. The end result is that from the consumer's perspective the sales, advertising and distribution interfaces become one and the same on the Web (Barnatt, 1999) (see Figure 3.1).

The online convergence of business functions also poses quite a challenge for many organizations as Barnatt observes:

> The business implications of this inevitable consequence of moving advertising, selling and digital delivery on-line are clearly enormous. However, within many organizations, the inter-departmental political wranglings concerning which division ought to control on-line developments may perhaps be even greater. The thought that those who design advertising may, almost by default,

end up controlling the on-line sales and distribution interface, may for some prove quite a shock!' (Barnatt, 1999)

Network returns

Network dynamic definition
More value can accrue to all from more and more users – the more the connections (and the connected!), the more the value to every user. In effect a law of increasing rather than diminishing returns.

Network returns are the specific application of Metcalfe's Law to the new marketplace. This is where the network economy defies some of the fundamental principles of conventional economics, creating a law of increasing returns as opposed to the more familiar one of diminishing returns. As Kevin Kelly, former editor of *Wired* magazine, observes, 'The simplest version goes like this: the value of a network explodes as its membership increases, and then the value explosion sucks in yet more members, compounding the result.' Kelly explains it eloquently in greater detail:

> Networks have their own logic. When you connect all to all, curious things happen. Mathematics [i.e. Metcalfe's Law] says the sum value of a network increases as the square of the number of members. In other words, as the number of nodes in a network increases arithmetically, the value of the network increases exponentially. Adding a few more members can dramatically increase the value for all members. . . . This tendency of networks to drastically amplify small inputs leads to . . . a key axiom of network logic: the law of increasing returns. In one way or another this law undergirds much of the strange behaviour in the network economy. (Kelly, 1998)

The concept of dramatic increases in value to all members of a specific network is to do with achieving critical mass. Critical mass is the point at which all users actually perceive a real increase in value. John Hagel and Arthur Armstrong call this the 'inflection point'. As they explain,

... revenue will slowly ramp up until the inflection point is reached, and then revenue growth accelerates. Take the fax example. There is likely to be some minimal penetration threshold below which a fax machine has practically no value, but once the penetration threshold is reached, the demand for additional fax machines really takes off.   (Hagel and Armstrong, 1997)

With the launch of eSchwab in mid-1996 Chuck Schwab cleverly tapped this law. At the end of its first month of operation eSchwab had 25,000 users. By the end of the year, a mere six months later, the number of users had swollen to over 600,000. Jay Walker achieved the same with name awareness for his Priceline company. Within 150 days of launch Walker cleverly mixed offline advertising with online activities to create awareness of his company by over 60 million Americans. It is said that it took Coca Cola a hundred years to achieve the same.

The possibilities presented by network returns are particularly exciting. As the network expands, more value accrues to *all* users, even to the first persons who took up the product or service. Yet network returns does have a more universal business importance. This network dynamic does not apply just to information technology hardware or software, such as a fax machine or an e-mail application; it can be made to apply to any product or service that can benefit from a network effect. Take as an example a motor insurance portfolio. This is most successful if it contains the largest number of risks – risks being individuals with a vehicle. The more risks that there are in the portfolio and the more alike that the risks are – more people with similar automobiles who behave and drive similarly – then the more predictable become the losses and the lower relatively the premiums that underwriters can charge to their customers. At present when you insure a vehicle you are quoted a premium but know nothing of the other people or risks in the portfolio. If everyone in the portfolio knew the characteristics that the underwriter of the insurance was seeking and could recruit others with a similar risk profile, then the insurance premiums would gradually come down for everybody in the portfolio as the potential losses became more predictable. On the Internet this can be easily achieved. This is the application of the law of increasing returns to a non-IT product. Affinity groups already apply this principle in the physical world, known to insurers as beneficial selection. But then an affinity group, a club, an association or an action group is arguably a vestige of the earlier face-to-face network economy.

Network returns may at first seem counter-intuitive to the reader. A broader perspective of this network dynamic may therefore be of benefit. Brian Arthur, economist at the Santa Fe Institute, offers some additional clarity:

> Western economies have undergone a transformation from bulk-material manufacturing to [the] design and use of technology – from processing of resources to processing of information, from application of raw energy to application of ideas. As this shift has occurred, the underlying mechanisms that determine economic behaviour have shifted from ones of diminishing to ones of *increasing* returns. Increasing returns are the tendency for that which is ahead to get further ahead, for that which loses advantage to lose further advantage. They are mechanisms of positive feedback that operate – within markets, businesses, and industries – to reinforce that which gains success or aggravate that which suffers loss. Increasing returns generate not equilibrium but instability: If a product or a company or a technology – one of many competing in a market – gets ahead by chance or clever strategy, increasing returns can magnify this advantage, and the product or company or technology can go to lock in the market. More than causing products to become standards, increasing returns cause businesses to work differently, and they stand many of our notions of how businesses operates on their heads. (Arthur, 7/96)

The shift that Arthur describes reflects the growing impact that the network effect is having in Western economies, and it is the application of network returns to non-IT network products and services that suggests the real power of this competitive force. All of our e-champions are aware of this reality and are counting on it to a greater or lesser degree to sustain the value attributed to their companies.

■ Information over estimation

Network dynamic definition
Precision of information and accurate knowledge about customers' preferences and behaviours – rather than research, assumption or extrapolation – generating a basis for intelligence.

The deployment of networking technologies provides unprecedented opportunities for business organizations to learn about the preferences and behaviours of their customers to a degree of accuracy and value that has not before been possible in the physical business world. This can be achieved in two main ways: firstly, through remotely tracking the use of websites by customers; and, secondly, by developing interactive 'learning relationships' with customers. These are by no means the only options that can be pursued in terms of gaining customer-related information. Other methods include conducting online or e-mail surveys, observing comments made on bulletin boards or in online community discussions, examining online product or service reviews submitted by customers, and collating website feedback material.

The remote tracking of website usage offers one of the most effective methods for gathering behavioural information. It requires the deployment of what are known as 'cookies'. These consist of small text files that are temporarily inserted into a user's Internet browser whilst visiting a company's website. Once inserted, cookies can be used to track a user's 'clickstream' – that is, the sequence of mouse-clicks made by the user – and inform the company of what pages on the site were visited, for how long, in what order, and what transactions were made. Cookies can also be used for identifying the user during subsequent visits to that company's website, so that the user's general web access and usage, as well as interactions with the website over time, can be tracked. Most of our e-champions will use cookies in one form or another to enhance their knowledge of customers and of how they use their websites.

Until relatively recently interactive marketing technologies – such as cookies – have not been widely deployed. So, the potential to leverage fully the learning opportunities provided by interactive media has remained fairly limited. These technological marketing tools are now becoming more widely used and it is of growing importance for marketers to consider explicitly what are their consumer learning objectives in using these tools. Many businesses are finding that it is relatively easy to collect enormous amounts of data, but it is far harder to put that data to effective use. So, they must define what type of information may be of most value to them, how much is worth spending to acquire that information, and how best to leverage these Internet-based technologies to obtain it.

The development of interactive 'learning relationships' with customers is the other principal means of achieving precision of information about customers' online behaviour, needs and wants. John Deighton, Professor of Marketing at the Harvard Business School, provides a concise analysis of what is involved.

> The term interactive, as we interpret it, points to two features of communication: the ability to address an individual and the ability to remember the response of that individual. Those two features make possible a third: the ability to address the individual once more in a way that takes into account his or her unique response. Thus . . . interactivity as a tool . . . allows good marketing to become good conversation. (Deighton, 11/96)

Michael Dell's company is pretty smart at good online conversation. Order a PC online and you will find yourself at the start of a relationship that the majority of Dell customers value highly. Dell will use what they know about you from your order to develop a personal dialogue in which they will share with you information on upgrades and other relevant information about your PC.

Learning relationships are critically important in the network economy, as Dr Peter Wilton of the University of California's Haas School of Business stresses.

> There has to be a realization that dynamic learning relationships are the core strategic answer for a business [that chooses to go online]. . . . The core of the e-commerce platform is mass customization. It's based on a continuous loop of selective gathering of

more and more information about that one customer and feeding it throughout your operation to improve your value proposition for that one customer in real time. You're learning more about that customer every time they come to your site and every time you learn something more, you modify your value proposition for that customer. (McIntyre, 5/5/98)

As the network economy grows in influence, many more businesses will discover the pivotal importance of good conversation with their customers.

Immediacy

Network dynamic definition
The instant nature of intercommunication makes time a key element in consumer behaviour and how needs are served.

The critical nature of immediacy in the network economy is epitomized by the 'point-and-click' technology of the World Wide Web. This increases customers' expectations that the companies that serve them should meet their demands for goods and services at the click of a mouse-button. Online consumers have much higher expectations than they do when shopping in the real world. They are not prepared to sit around and wait for long periods of time before providers deliver ordered goods or provide customer service. Amazon has to depend upon postal services when it dispatches books to its customers, but it makes sure that it provides a faultless service by providing customers with immediate information as to status of order fulfilment and moment of dispatch. As Don Tapscott says, 'In an economy based on bits, immediacy becomes a key driver and variable in economic activity and business success. . . . The new economy is a real-time economy' (Tapscott, 1995).

Immediacy is about more than just the interface with the customer, it is about every activity from end to end of the value chain. It concerns procurement, manufacturing and product development as well as fulfilment, customer service, sales and marketing. In the late 1980s the telephone came into its own as an important tool in customer sales and service, yet it had limitations that the Internet overcomes. The Internet adds the benefit of 'zero-touch' services where information enquiries, application forms, address changes, orders, etc., can be completed by customers online without any direct involvement of employees. For Dell Computers, 'straight-through' processing of this kind is critically important to its ability to offer a completely personalized PC delivered to your door in a matter of days. Complete your order online and Fedex combines your order with others to aggregate the parts required. It then sources them from the component suppliers and delivers them to Dell for assembly. In other cases the fulfilment cycle may even be completed online, with the customer being the only human directly involved; for example, when it is a matter of information-based products and services, such as software or music.

Another facet of immediacy as a micro-reality is the rapid pace of change that the network economy promotes in every aspect of human life. Scott McNealy of Sun Microsystems created the idea that the 'Internet year' is only one-seventh the length of a normal year. Within the space of a decade the Internet has changed from being a computer network used by a small group of academics into a global medium for electronic commerce. Ever-decreasing product development cycles are a notable feature of the network economy, and they result from the interaction of rapid technological advances and growing consumer demands for better products and services. Since Jay Walker launched Priceline in April 1998 as an airline ticket system, he has added hotel rooms, cars, mortgages and groceries. Almost certainly there will be several more products and services in the pipeline. Egg has calculated that it will only achieve its long-term value forecasts if customers take up an average of around four products each. This will put a premium on rapid product development and launch. A savings account and online mortgage have now been followed by a credit card, and all in just over a year.

Immediacy presents significant organizational challenges for established businesses. A technology supplier advised a UK finance sector company that the advanced solution they required was available now, could be implemented and operational within months. The problem, the supplier went on to chide, is that it will take you two years to make the decision. Immediacy impacts upon every single aspect of business life. Nor is this hectic pace likely to relent, as Jeff Papows, President and CEO of Lotus Development Corporation, observes: 'Since information technology is deeply embedded in just about every business these days, rapid-fire technology cycles tend to accelerate non-technology business cycles as well. The effect only gets stronger as technology becomes more pervasive' (Papows, 1998). As businesses in every sector adapt to this competitive reality and recognize an urgent need for constant and systematic innovation, they would do well to heed the Silicon Valley motto: 'Speed is God and time is the Devil'.

Buyer ascendancy

Network dynamic definition
Because consumers can more easily and quickly acquire information about the market they can exercise a greater degree of control over the buyer–seller relationship. Market asymmetry realigns from provider-bias to buyer-bias.

Buyer ascendancy is the most powerful of the network dynamics and the one most feared by established businesses. The reason is quite straightforward: buyer ascendancy threatens to take control of revenue streams away from them. Probably the most respected of management gurus, Peter Drucker, long ago observed that customers, not products, are the source of profits. As competition has intensified across most industry sectors over the last decades of the twentieth century, management teams have sought to become more customer-orientated without sacrificing their sales-driven approach to business. By retaining a sales-driven business model they have wanted to remain in control of their fortunes. Adept marketers in successful businesses have managed to reconcile the incompatibility of customer orientation and the organizational need to achieve sales targets. Realization that the network economy will make that task much more challenging is a major factor driving the widely held belief that commoditization is an inevitable consequence of online business.

There is no doubt that the network economy shifts the balance of power away from the providers of goods and services towards buyers. There are four principal reasons. Firstly, the network environment increases the range of providers from whom a buyer can, without effort, choose to make a purchase. Secondly, the network environment arms the buyer with far more information about providers and their products. Thirdly, the interactive nature of the network environment encourages buyers to take a more participatory role in the whole buying process. Fourthly, the network environment enables buyers to communicate with one another about their prospective or past purchases. These are powerful factors that demand further consideration.

Instead of having to make a time-consuming tour of main streets, malls and stores on foot, buyers can use the Internet to access relatively quickly a large range of suppliers without having to move a millimetre. With competitors only a click away, providers must be able to develop immediate and effective relationships with customers. Consumers can also access significant amounts of detailed information from each potential provider within a short space of time that might otherwise require days to obtain from offline sources. Armed with this information, they can afford to be much more selective in their choice of supplier.

Navigability and really effective searching are shortcomings of the network that may reduce some of the impact of this micro reality in the short term. Search engines are forecast to improve significantly. In addition, the availability of intelligent agents and smart systems will carry out much of the work and make life even easier for the buyer. Shopbots – literally shopping robots – are already available to conduct searches on your behalf for the goods you want at the price you are prepared to pay. Like many other online intermediaries, Priceline conducts searches on behalf of its customers to find the supplier who will provide the service on the terms set by the customer.

The interactive nature of networks leads to consumers taking a much more active role in their interaction with suppliers. As John Gage, Chief Scientist at Sun Microsystems, comments:

The Web frees customers from their traditionally passive role of receivers of marketing communications, gives them much greater control over the information search and acquisition process, and allows them to become active participants in the marketing process. (Gage, 4/96)

Participation means control is very much in the hands of the buyer not the supplier as eminent business strategist, Gary Hamel, observes 'Online customers simply aren't going to be pushed around. For the online advertiser, the challenge is to educate, entertain, and entice for no one can be compelled to pay attention online' (Hamel, 7/12/98).

In the network environment buyers can also exchange views with one another, and they do, even though in the real world one would not think of standing outside a store where you had just made a purchase and asking fellow customers: 'How was it for you?' Our e-champions understand implicitly the critical importance of customers exchanging views as the comments of Chuck Schwab's young co-CEO, David Pottruck, reflect:

> No longer can a firm be unresponsive to its customers and ignore them, when customers not only have the ability to communicate back to the company but to communicate with each other. Customers have an opportunity to have enormously more control over the business. Listening to customers involves re-engineering the way you respond to customers, which is unlike anything that business has had to contend with for the past twenty-five years. (Skelly, 7/10/98)

In other words, the impact of buyer ascendancy is set to bring about radical changes. Raised expectations among consumers will mean that those businesses that fail to recognize and act on the importance of this network dynamic will quickly lose market share to those organizations that do match these expectations.

■ Provider equalization

Network dynamic definition
Size, corporate history, location and physical assets become less important factors for the conduct of business. This provides significant (and global) opportunities for new entrants in an environment where brand awareness can be quickly established.

'On the Internet no one knows you are a dog' was the famous caption of a cartoon in the *New York Times* that captures aptly the nature of provider equalization. The network economy provides the opportunity for relatively new and unknown businesses to compete on an equal footing alongside large and well-established companies in the global marketplace. As John Chambers, Chief Executive Officer of Cisco Systems, observes in more conventional terms: 'Perhaps the major business change will be the levelling of the playing field between big and small companies. Big companies will have competition like they have never seen before' (quoted in Tellzen, 24/11/98).

In the marketspace of the network economy, brand will remain important as a guarantee to the customer. As major real-world brands migrate their activities to stake their claim on the virtual prairie, one might expect this network dynamic to be a relatively weak competitive force. Yet it is clear that name awareness can be built quickly on the Internet, despite an absence of both major physical assets and an established track record. Virtual companies with a total obsession for delivering customer value find that name awareness rapidly converts to real brand value. Compelling evidence for this comes from a survey of US consumer awareness of Internet brands conducted in September 1998 by the New Jersey-based research organization, Opinion Research Corporation International (see Figure 3.2).

This remarkable data indicates the power and speed of the network economy. As James Dettore, President of the Brand Institute, observed. 'The Internet is giving rise to a whole new class of brands that have successfully crossed the 50-million "mega-brand" threshold.' What is particularly notable about these Internet 'mega-brands'

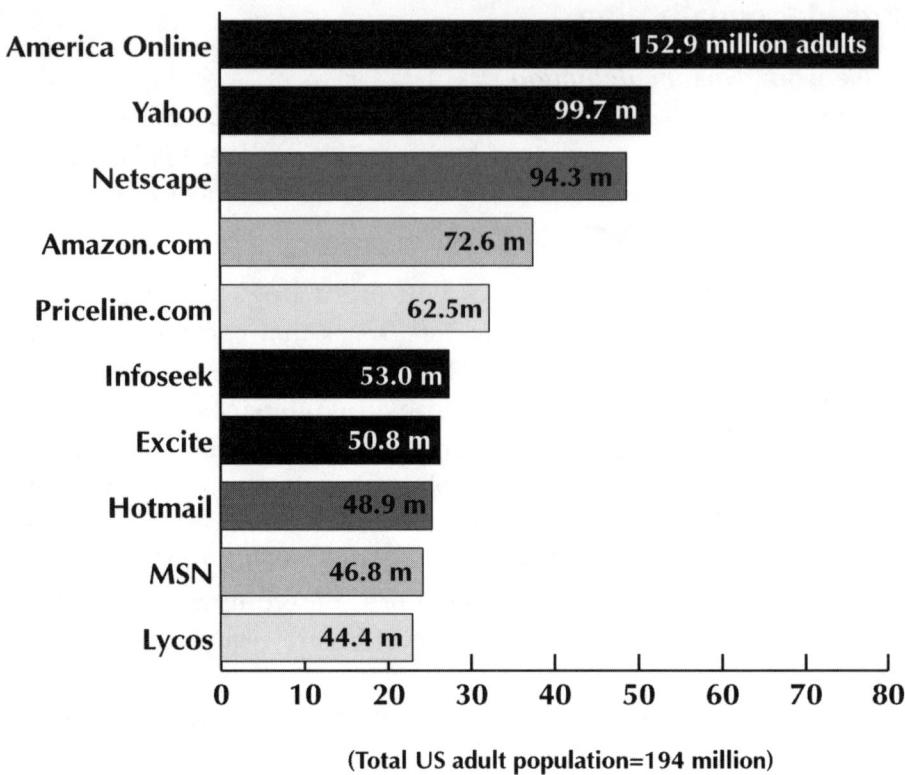

Source: Opion Research, 10/98

Figure 3.2 Internet brand awareness among all US adults

is the extremely short time with which all of them have achieved their level of awareness. Priceline is particularly outstanding among these 'mega-brands' for achieving the awareness of 62.5 million adults in only 150 days following its launch in April 1998.

The Internet does offer the opportunity for businesses to establish rapidly a new brand that can, if carefully managed, be sustained over the longer term. The enormous investment by new Internet businesses on building name awareness, using offline and online media, is witness to how important this is seen to be. With extensive reach to markets on offer – only otherwise accessible with major physical assets and infrastructure – the prize has to be worth the gamble.

Major real-world brands have been slow to take advantage of the opportunities on offer in the network economy, preferring to stick with the existing business models that are still the source of adequate profits. This attitude is now changing rapidly and we are beholding what some have called a virtual land grab as established businesses develop online strategies. At present it is unclear yet whether the advantage that these household names hope to secure will result in filling the virtual prairie and negating the competitive potential of the provider equalization network dynamic. The odds are that there will still be plenty of space in the market.

Buyer–seller re-engagement

Network dynamic definition
The network economy redefines the potential marketplace. It suggests new forms of buyer-seller interaction and new types of intermediation. Information can be assimilated for the potential buyer and offerings can be presented in a variety of novel and effective ways.

In the familiar physical marketplace, goods or services are typically offered at a marked price. The prospective customer assesses what is on offer and decides whether to purchase or not. In Western society, at least, the offer is usually on a take-it-or-leave-it basis. Sometimes, in circumstances defined by custom or practice, a customer might make an offer of a lower price to the seller, say, on a new car. If the price is too high or the bundle is insufficient, the customer will take his business elsewhere – physically visiting another store to get a better deal. Absurd and time consuming though this may seem, it is the process that is replicated millions of times every day among the world's consumers as they seek to get value for money.

The virtual world offers all sorts of new opportunities. Information can flow anywhere in the virtual marketspace providing a more efficient means for buyers and sellers to find one another, as well as offering all sorts of new ways for both parties to establish a contract. The low-cost direct connection between buyers and sellers made possible by the network economy has long been expected to lead to the decline of the middleman or the intermediary. Yet, the intermediary role looks set to go from strength to strength. The threat of 'dis-intermediation' is undoubtedly a serious one but a process of 're-intermediation' is much more apparent. As Internet researchers and authors, Larry Downes and Chunka Mui, have observed:

> Dire predictions have it that everyone from brokers to handlers, expediters, lawyers, wholesalers, and warehousers, as well as travel agents, insurance agents, and other remarketers will eventually be cut entirely out of the picture, or 'disaggregated'. But in many sectors these intermediaries have proven to be remarkably robust. Long chains are being taken apart, but they are also being put back together in new configurations. To paraphrase Mark Twain, reports of the death of middlemen have been greatly exaggerated. . . . We have worked with several traditional middlemen and come to the conclusion that dramatic changes are transforming but not destroying the business of many intermediates. (Downes and Mui, 1998)

They are right. A new generation of middlemen is being created, ranging from electronic shopping agents – shopbots – to services that bring together sources of information on a specific subject of value to a buyer. These 'infomediaries' use an acute awareness of irregularities or inadequacies in the flows of information in the network economy to add value for prospective buyers. Jeff Bezos launched Amazon as a bookseller, yet the more we see of how Jeff is building his customer-centric company and extending the range of services on offer to his customer, the more we see that Amazon is, in effect, an infomediary. On the Internet, it seems, every business must continually reassess how it adds value for its customers.

Re-engagement between buyers and sellers will open up many new opportunities for innovative and IT-savvy infomediaries. It will also put out of business those traditional intermediaries who do not add sufficient value. They are left with one of two choices, as Downs and Mui bluntly state: 'Add value or adios'. Beyond the intermediary role, buyer–seller re-engagement will lead to a re-evaluation of buyer–seller interfaces in ways not possible before the advent of the network economy. The most exciting of these new interfaces are auction-based, such as Jay Walker's Priceline and its reverse-type 'name-your-own-price' customer auction, and Pierre Omidyar's eBay and its person-to-person auctions. There are many other new forms of interface and the only limitation on what these might conceivably be is the capacity for creative imagination in the Internet business community.

Interconsumer collaboration

Network dynamic definition
Connection creates an environment that encourages consumers to become more interactive with one another. On the Internet discussion groups and e-mail are manifestations of the emergence of virtual community.

Above all, the network society and its associated network economy are about developing and sustaining connections between people. People who have grown familiar and comfortable with the Internet find the power to connect with others compelling. Visit the various chat rooms hosted by portal services such as Yahoo or AOL and discover people of diverse nationality, cultural and social backgrounds exchanging views on a wide variety of topics of mutual interest. Among the young these chat rooms have become an essential part of their lives. For many business people, online conferences and discussions are fast becoming an important means of finding out what the latest thinking is in their sector or professional discipline.

Interconsumer collaboration evidences a very real and perhaps surprising facet of the network society. This is the sense of mutuality that runs strongly through the Internet; it can be experienced in the widespread sharing of content and applications among users. Users who exchange views around a theme or subject are said to be members of a virtual community. In broad terms, a 'virtual community' is defined as any group of people who share a common bond, yet who are not dependent upon physical interaction and a common geographic location to sustain their group affinity. Why didn't this happen with the telephone? It is the capacity for one-to-many communications that enables individuals to feel part of a community in a manner never previously possible with the one-to-one limitations of the telephone.

One of the first online virtual communities to be developed was based upon a private dial-up bulletin board system (BBS) founded by Stuart Brand in the United States in 1985. Known as the WELL (the Whole world ELectronic Link), this online virtual community became widely known following the publication of Howard Rheingold's book, *The Virtual Community*. This book contended that the creation of similar communities using computer networks would enable the empowerment of otherwise marginalized individuals and groups in the face of physical, mental and political adversity (Rheingold, 1994). Yet, it has only been with the growth of the Internet that the potential for the widespread creation of online virtual communities has been realized. Now thousands of virtual communities are accessible over the Internet.

The implications for business and commerce of interconsumer collaboration are particularly significant. As Internet authors, John Hagel and Arthur Armstrong, identified:

> Virtual communities are more than just a social phenomenon. What starts off being a group drawn together by common interests, ends up being a group with a critical mass of purchasing power – based in part on the fact that in communities, members can exchange information with each other on such things as a product's price and quality. (Amazon.com website)

Many companies will feel really threatened by this network dynamic. Interconsumer collaboration reinforces the impact of buyer ascendancy in redefining the market. Few companies feel sufficiently confident about the quality of product and level of service that they provide to their customers to want to make it easier for them to talk to one another about their experiences. Customers who wish to air a grievance will find the occasion to do so and can use interconsumer collaboration to their advantage in this, as Intel found out at great cost. It failed to acknowledge the almost insignificant flaw in a chip, customers found out and used this competitive force to pressure Intel into a change of mind that almost brought the business down. Intel's experience on this count is far from unique in the business community.

Companies like Amazon and eBay actually want customers to share views with others and actively establish opportunities for this to occur. They have recognized that this network dynamic offers them the chance to know their customers better than ever before was possible, enabling them to interact with each other and with the company itself. As Hagel and Armstrong observe, 'Companies that organize virtual communities can use what they learn to create undreamed of customer loyalty' (Amazon.com website). Companies that have the imagination to explore the many ways in which inter-consumer collaboration can be applied to the benefit of their customers and target markets are likely to be among the winners in the network economy.

Summary

The competitive forces in the network economy are new and different from those in the familiar physical business world. Fail to understand them and it will be difficult, if not impossible to shape an effective business response to them. In this case your business may well succumb to price-driven competition and migration of customers due to remoteness of relationship.

The eight network dynamics – convergence, network returns, information over estimation, immediacy, buyer ascendancy, provider equalization, buyer–seller re-engagement, and inter-consumer collaboration – provide shape and form to the new competitive forces. These enable businesses to formulate the basis for success through an effective response to the powers of technology and the macro-realities of business performance, as Figure 3.3 reminds us.

Technology is undoubtedly the major impetus shaping the basis of future network-based business competition. Knowledge of the emerging customer dynamics that are fuelling consumer behaviour and expectations will be as important in shaping future success. The next step is to explore these customer issues before developing a

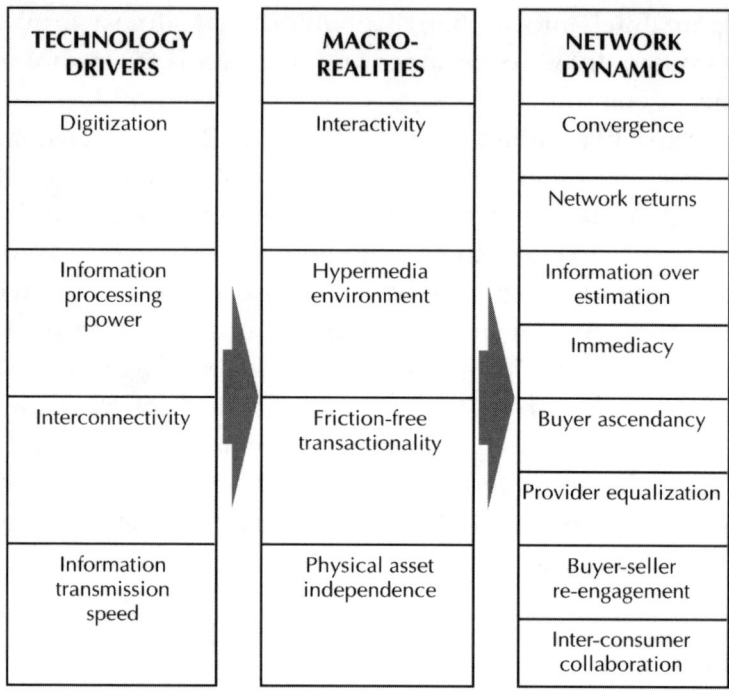

Figure 3.3 Determining the competitive forces of the network economy

framework for creating network-based value – the Value Levers. In the next chapter we will explore:

▶ Why successful internet entrepreneurs are preoccupied with customers
▶ The opportunities that the true application of marketing presents
▶ The realignment of markets from suppliers to buyers
▶ The collective power of individuals and how to harness it

Part Two
Customers to the fore

4

The rise of customer power

▶ A fresh perspective on customers, seeing them as our e-champions see them
▶ The importance of customer value and its implications for effective marketing
▶ A transfer in the balance of power from suppliers to buyers
▶ The real opportunities of the online purchasing and its impact on customer value perceptions, online and offline
▶ The insidious yet pervasive collective power of individuals in the network economy

A customer obsession

One factor above all others is common to the businesses of our e-champions, yet distinguishes them from their old-world counterparts. It is their total preoccupation with providing customer value. By conventional and familiar business standards, theirs is an obsession. For them lesser emphasis would be unthinkable. Schwab wants to provide customers with the most useful and ethical financial services in the world, while Bezos is intent on building the world's most customer-centric company. Dell doesn't underestimate his customers and knows just how smart they are, Pluthero is giving his company's service away to his customers, Harris has an absolute passion for customer service, and Omidyar's company is known for its fair-mindedness and social conscience. Are they all soft in the head?

Customer orientation may have become a subject of intense business interest in the last two decades as competition has increased, but few senior managers of established companies would go so far as to put customer value before shareholder value. This overriding customer value priority of our e-champions runs counter to accepted business thinking. Surely stock market analysts would bleat unhappily if customers were really put first – with a potentially disastrous effect on stock prices? Yet, investors in these seven companies, and in many more Internet-focused businesses, are accepting this declared behaviour, and are positively supporting companies with a customer fixation. They know that, in the long term, as investors, they too will win, and handsomely. Customer obsession is good for them and the source of long-term value creation, as well as good profits. But, where are the sales-driven business models that will generate revenues of x this year and $x + y\%$ next, and that can be converted into smoothed earnings to meet stock market expectations? Have investors taken leave of their senses? Or is it conventional thinking that is wrong? Maybe it's the network economy that turns custom and practice on its head?

■ Marketing and the customer

Peter Drucker, granddaddy of business gurus, is the man who reminded the business world that profits come from customers not from products. He also believes that the business community should be aware that the concept of marketing, as it is almost universally applied today by companies in the conventional economy, is not being employed as it was originally envisaged.

> The term was coined 50 years ago to emphasize that the purpose and results of a business lie entirely outside of itself. Marketing teaches that organized efforts are needed to bring an understanding of the outside, of society, economy and customer, to the inside of the organization, and to make it the foundation for strategy and policy. Yet marketing has rarely performed that grand task. Instead it has become a tool to support selling. It does not start out with 'who is the customer?' but 'what do we want to sell?'. It is aimed at getting people to buy the things that you want to make. . . . The question should be 'how can I make things that customers want to buy?' (Drucker, 5/10/98)

Other authorities share Drucker's disappointment. As long ago as 1960 marketing doyen Theodore Levitt postulated that too many businesses viewed marketing as just a tool for selling a business's output. Instead, Levitt argued, the seller should 'take his cues from the buyer in such a way that the product becomes a consequence of the marketing effort, not vice-versa' (Levitt, 7/60). His disappointment continues. Fellow experts have picked up the baton, joining in the general recrimination and continuing to chide businesses generally for their shortcomings. When it comes to the future, Peter Doyle, Professor of Marketing and Strategic Management at Warwick Business School in the UK, is clear about the future role of marketing: 'Successful companies of the future regard marketing as a philosophy of business – a belief that all the activities and processes of the company have to be oriented and co-ordinated around offering superior value to customers' (Doyle and Knight, 1998).

Without a doubt all of our e-champions' businesses fit Doyle's criterion, and precisely too! So why can they apply marketing almost to the letter of what it was originally envisioned to achieve, when established businesses have consistently failed? Are they following the customer cause out of some sense of altruism? The e-champions have recognized that, in the network economy, power passes almost completely to the customer. Understand the customer, develop a dialogue, meet their needs, deliver outstanding service and build a true relationship that will lead to a continuing source of value both to them and in due course to your investors. Quite simply, you cannot apply a sales-driven business model successfully on the Internet. You have to make customers buy continually from you, and not from your competitors, as author, Gary Heil, notes:

> The only business objective that [now] makes sense is a long-term relationship with each profitable customer. Today's customers have vast power to collaborate with you to build your businesses. . . . But if they're not happy, they will walk away faster than ever before – or [even] actively undermine you. (Heil, 1996)

Many established physical-world businesses are aware of their marketing shortcomings, and of their failure to achieve effective customer orientation. Customer relationship management (CRM) programmes have become the last real business frontier, and the natural response both to growing competitive intensity as well as to a gradual realization of the inevitability of the network economy's effects. International marketing consulting company, Frost & Sullivan, reports just how popular CRM is becoming. They predict that the value of the total CRM market will explode over the next few years, with revenues to CRM solution providers in Europe alone rising nearly tenfold to $6.81 billion by 2005. 'The most significant trend characterizing the CRM market has been the Internet. The Web has been acknowledged as instrumental to the success of the [CRM] market in the longer term' (Frost & Sullivan, 8/99). Rich pickings, indeed! Yet, for all their investments in CRM, established businesses are likely to find themselves falling short of fulfilling their customer-centric objectives. The reason is plain. A sales-driven, product-focused, shareholder value-biased business model is completely incompatible with delivering real customer value. Early reports of the CRM feeding frenzy from the UK tend to confirm this, as consultant Nick Hewson explains: 'People jump in far too quickly and buy [CRM software] products without having worked out where they are going' (Chappell, 6/99). Fellow CRM specialist, Stephen Izatt, puts his finger on the root cause: 'To be successful, any CRM project must be integrated with behavioural change across the business' (Dempsey, 3/2/99). There are dire warnings in this! Here be dragons!

Managing the transfer of power

While incumbent businesses grapple with the task of customer focus, the transfer of power from vendors to buyers continues apace as the forces of the network economy begin to bite. Buyer ascendancy is a technology-driven competitive reality that will have significant impact upon the business landscape. Customer power compounds the effect with an equally impelling force, as 'cyberguru' Esther Dyson confirms: 'You have to understand that the Net gives consumers more control, more power. It's a more competitive environment that tends to make good businesses better and weed out less capable ones' (Dyson, 6/98).

The principal implication of this shift in power is the pressure it puts on vendors and suppliers online to provide customer service that is both outstanding and consistent in its quality. 'Service can be a differentiating factor. Online customers desire the same one-on-one attention they would receive if they physically walked into their neighbourhood bank, all while sitting at their computer' (Cyber Dialogue, 22/6/99), says Mike Welsner of research firm Cyber Dialogue. However, many online firms do not recognize the critical importance of the service imperative and are falling short in the customer service they are providing.

> You need to establish a friendly dialogue and give the customer reason to stay on the site. Apart from anything else, if you look at log files on e-commerce sites, a large number of people give up along the way. But if you can give them help and answer their

questions you can have that personal experience, and have a customer at the end of it. (Venes, 8/7/99)

says Robin Grant of website strategy company Organic. A five-month-long study of consumer purchasing patterns at twenty-five commercial Internet sites in June 1999 by Net Effect Systems confirms this. It reported that just 5.75 per cent of visitors to electronic commerce sites begin the process of transaction. Sixty-seven per cent of those customers that do begin this process (by placing goods in their online shopping baskets) fail to complete the purchase due to poor or non-existent real-time customer support.

At stake is every online company's brand. Brand takes on an even greater significance online, yet its future lies almost entirely in the hands of customers. It is no longer sufficient to rely upon advertising, public relations and investor relations activities. Building perceptions, controlling corporate communications and managing brand awareness will have limited effect. What matters is the experience that consumers get when they deal with your company online. As Esther Dyson confirms, 'Another way to put it is that, even more so on the Web than in the real world, you build your brand equity by doing something of value for people, not by simply advertising something of value' (Dyson, 6/98). Customers are no longer the forgiving recipients of whatever is available or on offer, as once they were.

Changing behaviours

The experience of purchasing online appears to have a marked effect on overall consuming behaviour, whether online or offline. Experienced online consumers tend to be very committed to Internet shopping and will actively seek out other goods and services that they can satisfactorily purchase over the Internet.

As offline consumers we have all become accustomed to frequently indifferent quality and variable consistency in our regular, day-to-day and face-to-face purchasing experiences. But it seems that, all too often, we take these for granted with few questions asked. Online consumers tend to develop a much more precise expectation of how vendors must meet their needs. They are now taking those raised online expectations and experiences back to the physical, offline world and are developing a critical eye to all their shopping experiences in the mall, on the main or high street – in fact, anywhere. There is contradiction here. The prevailing wisdom is that online interfaces, used by vendors to interact with their customers, are inherently less effective than many of those more familiar offline real-world customer interfaces. In fact, quite the reverse is probably true. Stop to think about how just effective your last shopping trip was. How long did you have to line up or queue? Did you get precise information from sales assistants every time you asked? How long did it take you to find the goods that you were seeking? How quickly could you have established whether there was more choice or a better deal available in town for those new clothes, that new stereo or car? Now, can you imagine a company offering those same levels of offline real-world service in the online world, and being successful?

When it comes to purchasing online, the challenge is not to overcome the limitations of the interface, but to exploit the opportunities of greater speed, convenience, accessibility, and the provision of more personalized goods and services that the online interface offers. 'The legacy of e-commerce will be the way in which, in the early 21st century, it focused business attention on the immediate customer (sales) interface', reflects Internet and futures research author Christopher Barnatt (Millennium Group, 11/99).

Businesses reluctant to embrace the network economy can still take some comfort in the fact that numbers of consumers and volume of business-to-consumer trade are relatively small. But both the number of consumers and volume of trade are growing fast. More alarming for reluctant businesses will be the fact that once consumers overcome their hesitancy to purchase online and make their first purchase successfully, they seem to undergo an almost religious conversion to online purchasing. Evidence from a variety of sources also indicates that once consumers start to use the Internet they begin to spend less time shopping in physical stores and outlets. Almost one-quarter of online consumers said that they would spend less money in bricks-and-mortar shops, and more in virtual shops in the

Product or service purchased	Offline customer	Online customer
Books	US$112	US$190
CDs	US$80	US$128
Leisure travel	US$800	US$1306

Source: KPMG, 7/99

Figure 4.1 Average spending per UK consumer per year

following six-month period, according to a survey conducted by research firm, NFO Interactive. Online consumers also spend more than they would in an offline environment. Twenty-four per cent of Internet users said that the amount they spent on products and services in a given year increased when they shopped on the Internet (NFO Interactive, 5/99). This trend appears universal with online consumers in the UK as equally prepared as their US counterparts to spend relatively more online (see Figure 4.1).

Behaviours may change but there will be many occasions when a real-world shopping experience will remain unbeatable – as a leisure activity, as a social occasion or as an opportunity to touch, feel or try on merchandise before you buy. Over time these occasions will become fewer and fewer for more and more people. The offline experience just won't compare.

Collective power of individuals

For so long businesses have controlled the consumer's experience. It's a hangover from the mass markets of the industrial era when business was about selling product, and success was about selling product harder. All this is now in the melting pot as the experiences and achievements of the e-champions so amply demonstrate. For businesses familiar and able in the cut-and-thrust of the familiar physical world the challenge is daunting. As time progresses these firms will feel as though they are being held to ransom, not by some identifiable group with whom they could negotiate, but by the power of millions of individuals, behaving individually as consumers but acting with a collective effect and authority.

As time progresses the classic sales-driven, product-oriented, shareholder-value-first business model will seem more and more outmoded. The sceptical manager will continue to maintain that marketing, as Drucker and others envisaged it more than fifty years ago, can never be applied in its pure form, preferring not to acknowledge the evidence of Internet-based businesses whose success has been based upon the sort of customer-centricity that marketing gurus exhort. What that manager will also overlook is that the network economy provides the perfect substitute for a sales-driven approach – the law of increasing returns. Build relationships with your customers and let them do the selling for you as they interact with other prospects and customers in the network environment. Whoever thought that the familiar, but often maligned, practice of pyramid or multi-level marketing from the real-world would find its true place in the network economy?

So far we have explored the issue of customer power from a business perspective and established that its influence is inescapable for all companies, offline and online. Yet the scope and scale of this growing customer power is much more insidious. Throughout the last decades of the twentieth century we have witnessed major social change. What is remarkable is the way that some of the key social trends and influences shaping western society today conspire to provide additional impetus to the network economy. This remarkable nexus of forces will deliver over the next decade the revolution of historical proportions that Manuel Castells had earlier forecast (Castells, 1996).

■ Summary

In this chapter we have considered the new and dominant role that the customer enjoys in the network economy, noting that our e-champions are at the vanguard of the 'customer power' movement. We have noted that this realignment of market roles reflects the application of marketing principles as marketing gurus Peter

Drucker and Ted Levitt first envisaged them. We have recognized that customer value thresholds are raised through online purchasing experiences and questioned whether companies that adhere rigidly to sales-driven business models will be able to do well in digital business.

In the rest of Part Two we will evaluate the key social trends and then develop the consequent customer dynamics. This will then pave the way for us to evolve a value-based approach to digital business that leverages both customer and network dynamics. Specifically, in the next chapter we will explore:

▶ The six social trends that influence consumer behaviour in network society
▶ Their distinctive characteristics and particular effects upon people and business
▶ How these trends conspire to amplify the effects and influence of the emerging network economy

5
Society calls the tune

▶ Network society and network economy
▶ Key social issues shaping Western society and their distinctive impact on the network economy
▶ The six trends that are core to this process: 24/7 society; flexible working; social fragmentation; self-determination; beliefs erosion; and metamedia consumption
▶ Definition and evaluation of those trends, their principal aspects and underlying issues
▶ How others see these issues and interpret their impact

A nexus of social trends

We are beset by rapid change all around us. Gone is the static world of the agrarian era and the slow-moving but evolving world of industrial times. The third wave of the information age is now metamorphosing rapidly into a network world around us, where society and commerce take on very different characteristics. The key to comprehending fully this evolving network economy, and its impact upon business and commerce, is to build an understanding of the network society as a principal factor in the plot.

The evolution of developed human society is driven by the interaction of social trends, some weak, some strong. In recent years the advancement of information technology has exercised considerable influence, amplifying some of these social trends and magnifying many of the interactions between them. Exploring and evaluating the principal trends at work here will provide the principal clues to gaining a handle on the workings of this network society. Six major social trends hold the key: 24/7 society; flexible working; social fragmentation; self-determination; beliefs erosion; and metamedia consumption. Let us now explore each of them in turn.

24/7 society

> **Key facets of the 24/7 society trend**
> 24-hour, seven-day-a-week access
> Location independence
> Real-time services
> Instant gratification
> Commercialized everything

Say hello to the 24/7 society

Consumers today demand both accessibility – the ability to get whatever they want whenever they want it – and convenience – the ability to get whatever they want through whatever access channel they prefer at the time. These demands are driving much of the developed world towards a society actively engaged in consuming

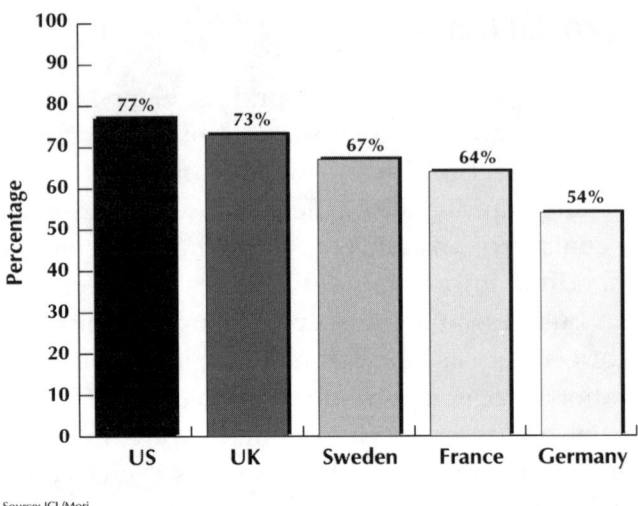

Figure 5.1 'I find it useful to shop outside normal opening hours'

behaviour twenty-four hours a day and seven days a week, as Figure 5.1 illustrates.

Demand in other major European countries will shortly match US and UK levels as the full force of this trend is more widely felt. A more detailed study of the UK's experience by the Future Foundation reveals just how strong that demand is for out-of-hours services. Eighty per cent of people believe that companies should provide telephone-based customer care during non-office hours; 38 per cent of people believe that 'life would be easier if everything was open all the time', and 35 per cent of people say they would like the opportunity to 'shop around the clock' (Future Foundation, 1998).

Many consumers are already taking advantage of extended opening hours. Twenty per cent of consumers regularly shop after 6 p.m. (34 per cent do so occasionally); 50 per cent of consumers shop at a convenience or liquor store out of normal hours, and 35 per cent have done so at a department store, service station or pharmacy (Future Foundation, 1998). 'Time has become increasingly important in our personal lives and convenience is now king', say the Future Foundation. Other commentators agree. 'A real demand for a 24-hour society is growing, and soon it will be possible to get your suit dry-cleaned, have a hair cut or a tooth filled at any time of the day or night' (Jones, 8/1/99). For the urban US consumer many of these activities are already a reality.

Growing time pressures

The increased time pressures of daily life experienced by consumers in the developed world are a prominent factor in the rise of this 24/7 society. Across Europe 49 per cent of adults believe that 'they never had enough time to get things done', according to The Henley Centre, a social and consumer research organization. Time-related pressures are a particular burden in the UK, where 59 per cent of adults claim they have insufficient time to get things done, and 21 per cent claim to be 'very concerned about the amount of free time I have' (Henley Centre, 1998/9). Confirming the time-starved nature of UK society, half of consumers agreed with the statement that 'I'm often under time pressure in my everyday life', with this figure rising to over three-quarters for working couples with children, according to the Future Foundation (1998).

Changes in the workplace have contributed significantly to increasing time pressures and the growing demand for out-of-hours service. Here, the increasing adoption of flexible working practices – in combination with the tendency for the length of the average employee's working day to increase – have acted as a significant push towards this 24/7 society. Reflecting this fact, 40 per cent of US citizens and 35 per cent of UK citizens believe that their working hours will become more irregular in the future (ICL, 1998). This also demonstrates how two identified social trends – 24/7 society and flexible working – interact and compound one another.

Time after time

The 24/7 society also demands fresh thinking and action. Businesses that can save time for busy and pressured customers will clearly gain a significant competitive edge in the marketplace. 'We . . . expect an increasing proportion of consumer spending to be channelled into time-saving devices and leisure pursuits as consumers search for ways to salvage valuable free-time or escape the hectic pace of everyday life', comments Rob Nicoski of Piper Jaffray (*Business Wire*, 1/4/98). The implications are clear. Consumers may want a 24/7 society to match their varied and hectic lifestyles but they also want help in how they manage their way through it. 'The challenge is to match time-based products and services with the appropriate consumer moods,' observes The Henley Centre (1997), 'Value for time is the overriding imperative'.

As the 24/7 society develops in the network economy, so time will play and increasingly important role in companies' marketing and operations.

■ Flexible working

> **Key facets of the flexible working trend**
> Fewer jobs for life
> Changed work patterns
> Erosion of home/work divide
> Portfolio careers
> Job insecurity/uncertainty
> Longer working hours

The rise of flexible working

Virtually every part of the developed world has seen a trend towards increasing levels of job flexibility, a principal driver of which has been the growing impact of globalization and the emergence of a truly global marketplace. Rises in part-time work, temporary jobs and self-employment are regularly registered, while the incidence of multiple jobholding and frequent job change increases. Significant staff losses flow from widely adopted 'downsizing' and 'rightsizing' strategies, confirming to employees their growing suspicion that the concept of a job for life is a thing of the past. Job insecurity is now prevalent in many workplaces. As Charles L. Schultz of the Brookings Institute observes:

> Two decades ago, [US] workers entering new jobs in established firms could look about and see that most of their older and more tenured fellow workers had climbed a fairly steep wage ladder and appeared to enjoy a relatively high degree of job security. Over the past twenty years intense media attention and some dramatic

downsizing among large companies have created a widespread perception that corporate layoffs among senior workers, at all skill levels, have seriously eroded the prospects for job security as a reward for long service. (Schultz, 10/99)

Changes in the global economic environment have had major repercussions upon both employment practices and the lives of employees throughout Europe too: 'In the European Union, as in the rest of the industrialized world, various forces are responsible for the pace and extent of change that is dramatically reshaping the way we live and the world around us', ponders the Demographic and Social Trends Panel Report of the European Commission,

> In the economic realm, globalization of markets and business operations, of capital and investment flows, hyper-competition, and rapid technological progress, impact heavily on the world of work – increasing job flexibility and precariousness, skills obsolescence and unemployment – with knock-on effects on lifestyles and social conditions beyond the immediate work environment. (Gavigan, Ottitsch and Greaves, 4/99)

The concept of the 'contingent workforce' – one where current active employment is conditional upon available work – originated in North America and subsequently became a significant feature of government and business thinking in many other countries around the world. But it is in the UK that flexible working practices have probably so far had their greatest impact. Rapid growth in part-time work has occurred in the UK over the last two decades, with part-time employment rising from 16.4 per cent to 23.2 per cent of total employment between 1980 and 1993 (the comparative figures for the US were 16.4 per cent and 17.1 per cent) (OECD, 1994).

Bellwether nation

To appreciate the scope and scale of the wholesale change that is going on, the UK provides ample illustration. 'Work is redefining itself, [and] Britain has been going through a labour market revolution. This revolution is not complete . . . [and] there is further,

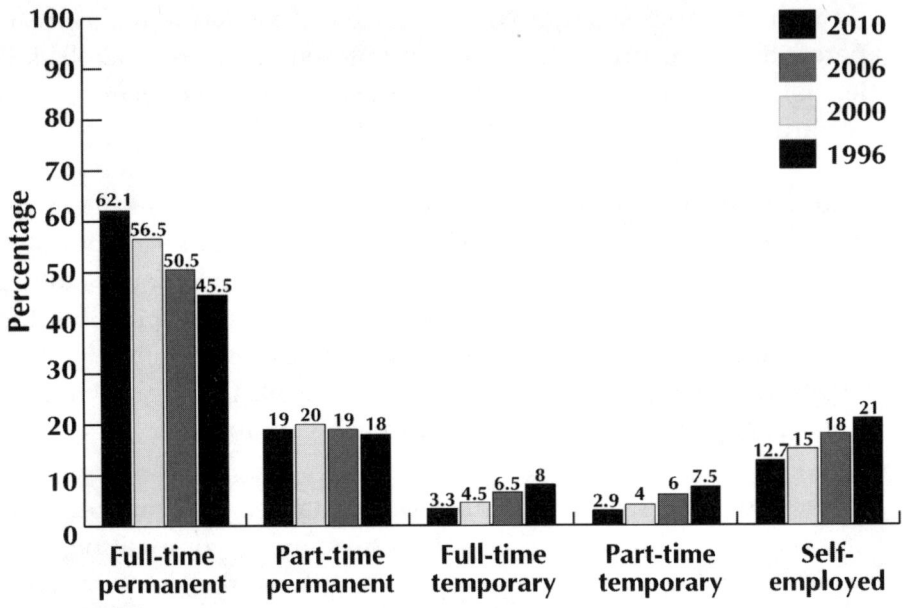

Figure 5.2 The changing structure of UK employment

massive change to come, from forces we can already see', reasons an authoritative independent report (RSA, 1998). The scale of the UK's continuing 'labour market revolution' is shown in Figure 5.2, which records the UK's employment figures for 1996 alongside forecasts for the years 2000, 2006 and 2010 by The Henley Centre. Between 1996 and 2010, non-permanent forms of work are predicted to rise from 18.9 per cent to 36.5 per cent – almost a doubling in the number of people in non-permanent forms of employment.

The growth in self-employment represents a major shift for the UK. Forecast to make up over 21 per cent of the workforce in 2010, this is more than 230 per cent up on the figure a half-generation before (9 per cent in 1981). In part it reflects a transition to the concept of 'portfolio work' – the practice where individuals develop a set of personal skills and a knowledge base that they then sell to other individuals and companies. Professor Charles Handy, the man who coined the phrase, explains:

> More and more individuals are behaving as professionals always have, charging fees not wages. . . . They find they are 'going portfolio' or 'going plural' . . . [This] means exchanging full-time employment for independence. The portfolio is a collection of different bits and pieces [of work assignments] for different clients. The word 'job' now means a client. (Handy, 1994)

This is what the trend monitoring division of advertising agency Young and Rubicam refers to as the 'Me, Myself and I Incorporated' job market trend.

The forecasts referred to above may well underestimate the growth in UK self-employment as more and more companies become network economy literate and begin to outsource on a major scale many of their corporate functions. 'Entrepreneurship will be more pronounced as companies . . . outsource many of their corporate functions', predicts Professor Richard Scase, 'At the same time, a more self-reliant and 'independent' culture among those who are technically and intellectually expert will reinforce this trend . . . [so that] people's working lives will become more varied' (Scase, 1999).

The challenges posed by flexible working

Flexible working takes its toll, imposing adverse effects upon many members of a country's workforce. 'The pace and extent of change in society in general, and in work in particular, have been dramatic over the past twenty years', says organizational psychologist Professor Cary Cooper,

> We have moved from the 'entrepreneurial 1980s' to the 'outsourcing and downsizing 1990s' to an emergent 'flexible and short-term contract' culture. This has meant longer hours at work, intrinsic job insecurity and an increasing lack of balance between our work and our home lives. (Cooper, 8/99)

These comments add to the growing body of evidence that the rise in flexible working, together with increasing working hours, has had a negative impact on the psychological and physical welfare of many in the working populations of both the USA and the UK.

There seem to be two main causes for this. Longer working hours have reduced the amount of leisure time that people can spend relaxing and with their families. The average leisure time of a working US citizen has decreased from 26.2 hours per week in 1973 to 19.8 hours per week in 1999, according to a series of Harris polls (Harris Poll, 6/99). Secondly, flexible working practices for workforces overall have tended to encourage higher levels of work-related anxiety. In the UK, worries over job insecurity are very common among employees, with around 30 per cent of workers expressing some degree of concern that their job would not be secure over the next twelve months (Henley Centre, 1998).

The trend towards flexible working is such an important one for today's consumers. It affects every aspect of their lives: how they work, how they consume and how they play. With such a widespread impact it is a dominant influence on customer behaviour in the network economy.

Social fragmentation

Key facets of the social fragmentation trend
Loss of family/community ties
Decline of the nuclear family
More people living alone
Economic inequality
Disparate values
Lifestyle diversity

The rise of social fragmentation

In the last half-century, much of the Western world has become socially diverse in nature. Developed countries have witnessed a growing profusion of household structures. A significant decline in the traditional 'nuclear' family – two parents plus child or children – has led to an increase in the number of single-parent families and one-person households. Increasing numbers of couples choose to cohabit rather than to marry, and the divorce rate has increased significantly in many developed countries over this period. In addition to these weaker familial and social ties, there has also been a

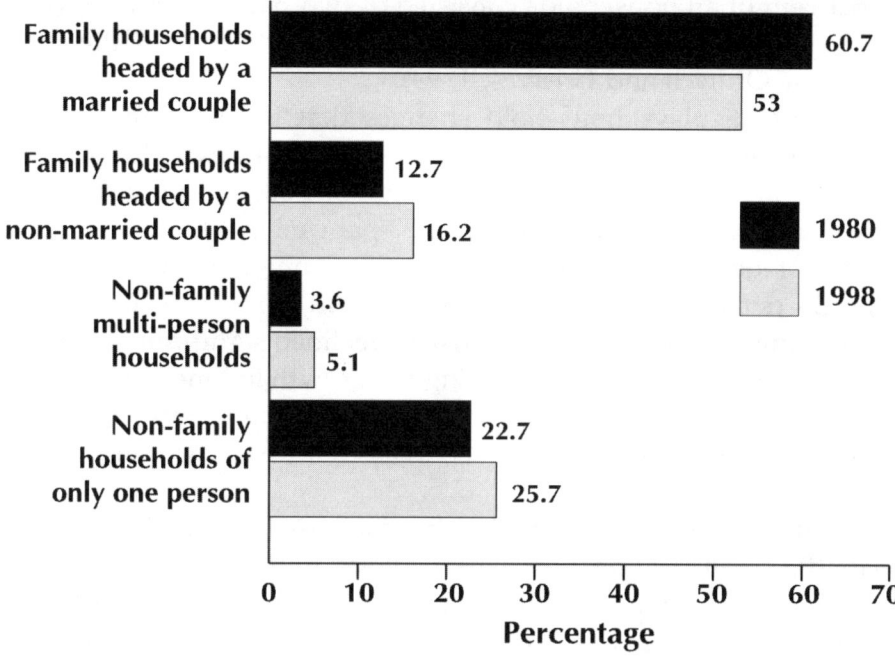

Figure 5.3 Changing households in the USA

notable rise in economic and social inequalities within and between countries, with the rich getting richer and the poor getting poorer. This is due largely to unfettered market forces.

In the US the average household fell in size from 2.76 in 1980 to 2.62 in 1998. This fall is largely accounted for by a decline in family households headed by married couples, and by a corresponding increase in non-family households headed by an unmarried person, or composed of one individual (US Census Bureau) – as Figure 5.3 indicates. The diminished number of families headed by married parents has much to do with the high rate of divorce in the US – as many as one in four adults are currently divorced.

European Union (EU) experience is much the same. The average household size fell from 2.8 persons in 1980 to 2.4 in 1994. By 1999, the decline in the 'traditional' EU nuclear family meant that only

40 per cent of all households consisted of two-parent families, while single-person households accounted for 30 per cent of the total (Gavigan, Ottitsch and Greaves, 4/99).

The UK displays household changes that illustrate the overall pattern of experience across the EU. Average household size fell from 2.7 in 1981 to 2.4 in 1996. The number of 'traditional' households fell from 31 per cent in 1981 to 23 per cent in 1996, matched by an almost identical increase in the number of one-person households from 23 per cent in 1981 to 29 per cent in 1995. The underlying causes, however, are various. Marriage declined significantly, yet the divorce rate grew markedly, fuelling the growth in lone parent families. Cohabitation increased, while more women were opting to delay having children or remain childless (Office for National Statistics, 1999).

Social fragmentation in the UK has increased markedly in recent years. Personal relationships – particularly those between partners, and between parents and children – are weaker and less enduring today than they were a quarter of a century ago. This has had important consequences for UK society as a whole, and especially for children. Family breakdown has a strongly negative impact on the attitudes and behaviour of children. Research shows that girls from divorced families are twice as likely to become teenage parents, and that children from divorced or lone-parent families are more likely to suffer poverty or become involved in crime than children of married parents. It may therefore be no coincidence that the country with the EU's highest rate of divorce – the United Kingdom – also has the highest rates for teenage pregnancies, juvenile crime as well as drug- and drink-abuse by youth and under-age smoking (Gavigan, Ottitsch and Greaves, 4/99; Johnston, 15/6/98; Morgan, 7/99; Office for National Statistics, 1999; Patton, 14/5/99).

The growth of inequality

The steady rise in social and economic inequality also contributes strongly to fragmentation and growing diversity of consumer needs and lifestyles in today's world. 'Global inequalities in income and living standards have reached grotesque proportions', stated the 1999 United Nation's Human Development Report in condemnatory tones (UNDP, 1999). In support of its censure the UNDP observed that the three richest men in the world held total assets greater in value than the combined GNP of the world's forty-three least developed countries, which together comprise over 600 million people. Diverse factors contribute to global inequality, they report, ranging from diminishing restraints upon the free play of market forces through burgeoning stock market investments to cuts in welfare provisions of many states. Over the last thirty years the impact of these inequalities has been felt most keenly in the developing world, yet developed countries have not been spared.

It may seem hard to imagine but, in the world's richest country, the benefits of economic growth have not been enjoyed across the population as a whole. The per centage of persons below the poverty line in the USA increased from 11.7 per cent (26.1 million people) in 1979 to 13.7 per cent (36.5 million) in 1996, according to US government statistics. Contemplate the poorest 20 per cent of US households and the richest 20 per cent to discover a stark contrast. Share of national income enjoyed by the poorest fifth declined from 5.3 per cent in 1980 to 4.2 per cent in 1996, while that enjoyed by the richest fifth rose from 41.1 per cent to 46.8 per cent (US Census Bureau, 1/10). Consider, then, just the top 1 per cent of US households to unearth a degree of disparity yet more marked. In 1998 their net worth was 2.4 times the combined wealth of the poorest 80 per cent. Take it a final stage further and examine just one household to discover that Microsoft Chairman and CEO, Bill Gates, owned more wealth than the poorest 45 per cent of US households (representing around 100 million people) (Gates, 5/99). For the greater majority of US citizens the American dream will surely remain just that, and nothing more!

With a welfare state now fifty years old, the UK surprisingly paints a similar, if not quite so exaggerated, picture. It experienced an 'unprecedented' rise in income inequality over the last two decades of the twentieth century, following three earlier decades of steadily falling disparity. By 1997 the richest 10 per cent of the UK population held as much income as all households in the bottom 50 per cent, while all measures of poverty had significantly increased since 1979, according to the Institute of Fiscal Studies (1997). 'The increase in inequality is probably the biggest social change we have experienced in the last twenty years', declared Paul Johnson, author of the IFS study. 'With no apparent chance of higher social security benefits, higher taxes or better earnings prospects for the low paid, this change with all its consequences is here to stay' (Balls, 28/7/97). The wealth gap is set to increase further, so that by 2010 the wealthiest 10 per cent of the UK population will be ten times richer than the poorest 10 per cent (Salvation Army/Henley Centre, 1999).

A world of individuals

'There is no such thing as society: there are only individuals', postulated long-serving British Prime Minister, Margaret Thatcher. This has become more of a reality during the course of the last three decades in much of the developed and developing world. The weakening of traditional family structures and the declining strength of social relationships have led to spreading physical and emotional isolation among individuals. From this has sprung a growing diversity of lifestyles, encouraged further by social and economic disparity. It remains a matter of continuing concern, as a recent report by the European Commission observes.

> In terms of individual lifestyles . . . there will be variety in both personal relationships and in patterns of living. Each of these will be characterized by a greater degree of transience than in the past. Feelings of personal and emotional insecurity will be more fragile and life histories will be more discontinuous, fragmented, adaptive and chaotic than in the past. (Gavigan, Ottitsch and Greaves, 4/99)

There are important implications for business in this fragmentation so aptly described in this EU report. 'Overall consumption itself will become a more individualistic activity due to changes in personal, family and household relationships. Consumers will seek products and services that reinforce their sense of individuality and non-conformity', predicts Professor Richard Scase of the University of Kent in the UK, 'Their preference for these types of purchases will be fanned by the plethora of new media and growing exposure to more diverse international cultures' (Scase, 5/97). It is almost uncanny that the long-running trend of social fragmentation needs the newly arrived network society and network economy to help resolve its more challenging manifestations.

Self-determination

Key facets of the self-determination trend
Diminished welfare state
Increased self-provision
Strong consumerism
Intolerance of poor service
Greater self-awareness

The rise of self-determination

The end of innocence is the moment in time when a child becomes an adult and realizes that he or she must take responsibility for his own actions or her own future. No longer can they expect parents to make decisions for them, or automatically to provide for them. In Western society today this rite of passage has a newer and more far-reaching context: it applies to adults. Individuals in society are experiencing a creeping awareness that they must take charge of their own destinies. Over the last half of the century just gone they have looked to the resources provided by governmental institutions. In this last stage of the industrial era, developed societies assumed a collective sense of responsibility for the wellbeing of the individual – providing for welfare, healthcare and retirement needs. The degree of provision varied from society to society, and was less comprehensive in the USA compared to Europe, where typically the solution was an extensive welfare state. In the industrial era mass production meant choice was also limited. Consumers purchased happily whatever products were available, accepting any shortcomings with few questions. There was a universal sense of almost parental oversight by government and business.

In the last decade this has been changing. Today's consumers are waking to an environment in which they have to exercise more self-reliance, and where the affluent enjoy the opportunities to demand and purchase offerings that more satisfactorily meet their needs. Both the risks and the opportunities faced by today's consumers are becoming broader in scope, and they must adapt. Yet, there is almost a contradiction in this simultaneous extension of choice and risk, as a report by EU sociologists acknowledges:

> The society unfolding between now and the year 2010 will offer to a significant part of Europe's population a rich and unprecedented variety of chances and opportunities for self-fulfilment and accomplishment. These possibilities, however, may well present themselves to the individual in a way that is analogous to standing aloft on a narrow mountain ledge with the permanent insecurity of a never-too-far-away chance of a slip and fall into marginalization. (Gavigan, Ottitsch and Greaves, 4/99)

The pressures on the welfare state

The concept of universal welfare is but fifty years old. In the UK, for instance, the welfare state was born in 1947 after the Second World War. The burden of universal provision on governments grew throughout the following decades, as they assumed more and more risk on behalf of their populations. It could not continue indefinitely. Changing demographics and the growing impact of market forces put governments under increasing pressure to find ways to shift the burden of welfare provision away from the state and back towards the individual. This has been a dilemma faced by the majority of European and North American countries since the late 1970s. The problem has yet to reach its peak. Throughout most Western developed nations, the dual impact of increased longevity and a declining fertility rate means that the proportion of people over sixty will almost double between 1990 and 2030. Unless significant changes are made in many government policies, many of these nations will shortly find themselves in a situation – popularly referred to as the 'pensions time bomb' – in which a diminishing number of people of working age are available to support a growing number of retired people.

According to Michael Mazarr of the Washington-based Center for Strategic and International Studies, the decreasing ratio of workers to persons of pensionable age will ensure that 'aging and its associated economic and social challenges' will soon become 'the developed world's number-one demographic issue' (Mazaar, 1997). Certainly in the case of the USA, this can be seen in the series of major national debates that have taken place with regard to the future of social security and medicare. As longevity increases, many suggest that the retirement age should be raised, but this is not a solution that will win votes among the most influential members of electorates, the 'baby boom' generation of the post-war era. The suggestion of a raised retirement age has also been put forward as a serious option to EU governments, based on a recent report by Merrill Lynch. This predicted that – on the basis of current trends – the ratio of workers to pensioners in the EU will fall from around 4.8 in 1990 to 2.6 in 2030. It concluded that the situation could in large part be remedied by gradually increasing the age of retirement from sixty-five to sixty-nine over the next forty years (Mantle and Bowers, 14/10/99).

The UK government's awareness of the problem associated with the 'pensions time-bomb' has led it to exhort UK citizens to make provision for their own future welfare rather than to rely upon the resources of the state. Significant sections of the UK population are now heeding this message. In 1997 a majority of consumers accepted for the first time that they, rather than the various state agencies, were primarily responsible for providing for their old age (Henley Centre, 1997). 'The message of self-provision as a future inevitability has now been absorbed by a large proportion of the public', concludes insurers Swiss Re (Swiss Re Life & Health, 1998).

The rise of the 'vigilante consumer'

As the industrial society gave way to the information society, so production for the masses succumbed to increasing competition and the provision of variety and choice. This in turn gave rise to the self-assertive or 'vigilante consumer', a phrase coined by North American marketing consultant Faith Popcorn. Popcorn reasoned that businesses would confront a new breed of 'vigilante consumers', who recognized and were prepared to exploit their new-found power (Popcorn, 1992, 1996):

Ever watchful. That's the consumer of today. Sleeping with one eye open. No more wool pulled over those peepers. We're out to protect our interests, and pity the poor company or group that tries to pull a fast one on us. We're on our toes, in wakeful attention. It's not just the angry few who are protesting with raised fists. Vigilante Consumers are everywhere. . . . Vigilante Consumers translate feelings into action and wallets into weapons. Shopping is war. The enemy is any entity that doesn't meet our needs. . . . Woe to the corporation or group who gets in the way of the Vigilante Consumer. (Popcorn, 1996)

Nor is it just a US phenomenon. UK consumers too are demonstrating this facet of self-determination. Cynical attitudes among consumers towards companies rose significantly in the last decade of the recent century.

In a world of increasing variety, choice and assumed risk, 'self' becomes the dominant concept for the consumer. It requires the emergence of the network economy to provide consumers with the means for its full expression.

Beliefs erosion

Key facets of the beliefs erosion trend
Loss of faith in established institutions
Decline of shared moral/ethical norms
Trust vacuum
Cultural diversity
Fluid lifestyles

The rise of beliefs erosion
Towards the end of the twentieth century many social commentators claimed that human society was entering into a 'post-modern' or 'late-modern' era, in which the trustworthiness and validity of established conventions, institutions and thought-systems are no longer accepted unquestioningly by large swathes of the population. There are many contributory factors to this altered state. Among them are the end of the ideological certainties of the Cold War, the splintering

of the traditional family, the increasing absence of well-defined male/female roles, the endless spin-doctoring of politicians and the well-publicized acts of violence carried out by disaffected youth or 'road-rage' aggressors. All have contributed to a sense that we have entered a 'phase of Western history' which looks set to be 'dominated by anxiety, irrationalism and helplessness' (Waugh, 1992).

'Trust no one' is the advice of the popular *X-Files* television series. This strikes a chord with today's younger consumers, many of whom feel that they can only really have faith in themselves. 'Individuality has become the only doctrine to which young people seem fully committed.... Fundamentally, the 1990s are seen as a confusing time in which to be growing up. A vacuum exists, where ideology and dogma once lived', pronounced Sean Pillot de Chenecey of international youth marketing agency Informer Interactive Research. His astute observations are a powerful warning.

> The collapse of [trust in] institutions which provided the framework within which people organized their lives is keenly felt. The lack of certainties in these fundamental concerns has left this generation bereft of benchmarks against which to assess day to day life issues. This can be felt across virtually every aspect of modern life.... When there are fewer signposts, and those which exist are increasingly difficult to rely on, the young cherry-pick ideas, beliefs and motivations. (Pillot de Chenecey, 21/5/99)

The absence of hard-and-fast certainties encourages the rise of a multitude of lifestyles that are both strongly individualistic and highly eclectic in nature, as The Henley Centre, affirms. 'The essence of our "post-modern" age is the denial of a single Truth, along with the assembly and adoption of different influences in an experimental "pick 'n' mix" fashion' (Salvation Army/Henley Centre, 1999). Nothing, it appears, is viewed as being inherently wrong or right, and today's consumers can make their choice from a vast menu of lifestyle and behavioural options. But, at the same time, there seems an absence of sufficient external criteria to help them make their choice. Consequently, many of today's consumers feel as though they are lost at sea without a compass to guide them.

A sense of moral decline

A prevalent sense of moral decline in many parts of the developed world cannot, therefore, be a surprise. For the majority of US citizens the decline in moral values presents a far more serious social issue than race relations, the environment, the economy or national defence, according to a survey conducted by Shell Oil. When questioned on the strength of ten important moral values, the majority of respondents said that US society had become weaker on eight of them. Notably, these eight values were: respect for authority, commitment to marriage, respect for the law, respect for other people, personal responsibility, good citizenship, the work ethic and belief in God. Only 'tolerance for people who are different' was thought to have become stronger (PR Newswire, 3/5/99).

The sense of moral decline is evident in other developed countries. In the UK, 40 per cent of the population in 1998 believed that 'Britain, as a place, is getting worse.' Since the UK economy was generally performing well at the time, and most people's incomes were improving, this seemed to reflect a collective sense that the moral and social fabric of the UK was gradually coming apart at the seams.

Consequences of diminished trust

Allied to the sense of moral decline has been a growing disillusionment with traditional institutions. In the UK, for example, there has been a dramatic fall in the level of confidence that individuals place in traditional institutions over the course of the last twenty-five years.

The deep and worrying nature of this trend, as illustrated in Figure 5.4, drew the following comments from The Henley Centre's researchers:

> Trust is an increasingly fragile value in contemporary society. Faith and confidence in traditional authority and institutions have declined over the past twenty years, with the pace of this decline noticeably speeding up as we move towards the end of the twentieth century. This collapse in trust reflects the extent to which the old rules, values and systems are no longer seen to be relevant or

meaningful in an age of globalization, technological revolution and social transformation. (Henley Centre website)

These declining levels of trust are having a deleterious impact on the 'social capital' of many developed states. That is the judgement of Francis Fukuyama. He is in no doubt as to the consequences that we face. 'A society dedicated to the constant upending of norms and rules in the name of expanding individual freedom of choice will find itself increasingly disorganized, atomized, isolated and incapable of carrying out common goals and tasks' (Fukuyama, 1999). The outcomes are not pleasant, with meteoric rises in the incidence of juvenile crime just one of the manifestations. In the USA a rise from

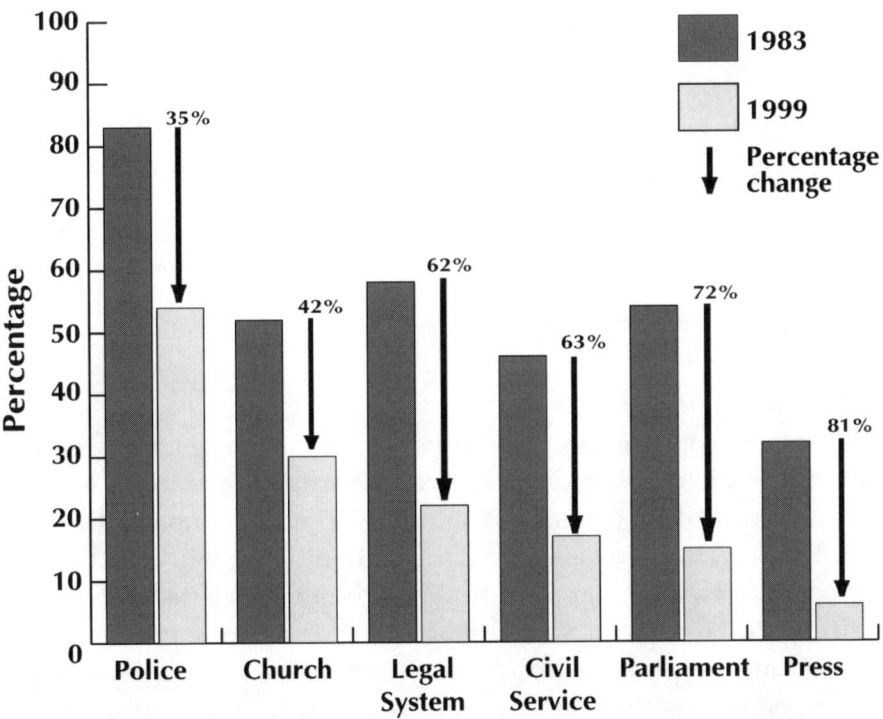

Source: The Henley Centre/Salvation Army

Figure 5.4 Fall in confidence in traditional UK institutions

120,000 arrests in 1992 to 250,000 by 2010 is predicted by Michael Mazaar (Mazaar, 1998), while the UK experienced a threefold increase in juvenile crime over the last half of the twentieth century (Hall, 14/1/99).

The rise of the risk society

The trust vacuum and erosion of beliefs inevitably give way to what influential German sociologist Ulrich Beck calls a 'risk society'. 'Society has become a laboratory where there is absolutely nobody in charge', notes Beck alarmingly (Beck, 1992). Clearly, we live in a society where, despite the presence of relative prosperity, the future for many appears incoherent and uncertain. Few, if any, have yet factored in how the network society and economy may exert a positive influence.

■ Metamedia consumption

Key facets of the metamedia consumption trend
Technology acceptance
Technology transparency
Multiple channel literacy
Multi-sensory familiarity
Experience-centricity

Technology meets society

Metamedia consumption is the key to the emergence of both the network society and the network economy. It is the trend in which technological driver meets social development, enabling the interface between human beings and the technological marvels they have invented, creating a panoply of almost boundless possibilities.

In the last decade or so, falling costs of computing processing and data transmission have led to the burgeoning availability of various forms of information technology in working and living environments. The consequences for developed society are a significant rise in our use, acceptance and ability to manage a variety of forms of communication, whether they come in image-, sound- or text-based

Time frame	Knowledge media	Examples
Past	Single channel media	Spoken language *or* the written word *or* pictures
Present	Multi-channel media	Text *and* sounds *and* still pictures *and* moving images
Future	Metachannel media	The World Wide Web *and/or* interactive television *and/or* computer generated virtual reality, *and/or* controlled reality environments

Source: Barnatt, 1997

Figure 5.5 The broadening of communications media

forms (Figure 5.5). But this adoption and spreading fluency in electronically mediated forms of communication exchange has not resulted in the abandonment of earlier forms of information exchange – the spoken word or writing. Rather, the most significant occurrence has been the progressive addition of new forms of media, so that we use multiple modes of information exchange at the same time where in the past only one mode of information exchange was used at once. Christopher Barnatt calls this the 'metamedia revolution' – the changing use and experience of communication media by human beings over time as technology has advanced (Barnatt, 1995).

'In future we are moving towards the development of an environment in which the use by humans of meta-channel media or "metamedia" will become increasingly commonplace", says Barnatt. The adoption of computer-generated forms of virtual reality and the rapid evolution of the Internet into a multi-sensory information exchange environment attest to this. It is the conveyance of experiences as well as the conveyance of information that truly distinguishes the mode that now drives us towards the full achievement of a network society.

The coming 'net-powered generation'

Maturing adoption of information technology tools foretells universal acceptance and, with it, pervasive influence upon the lives of those in developed societies as well as, ultimately, those in third world societies. The remarkable diffusion of mobile telephony through the third world is clear evidence of this. By 2003 there will be more than 1 billion mobile phones on the planet, one for every six men, women and children, even though half the world's population has yet to make a telephone call. The rate of take-up has astounded even the experts. In 1982 AT&T reportedly asked consultants McKinsey & Co. to forecast the total global market for cellular (or mobile) telephones. In McKinsey's view at that point in time, the total demand would never exceed 900,000 units. Remarkably this is now the number of new mobile phone subscribers going live globally every three days (*Economist*, 9/10/99)! Mobile telephony and other access devices such as interactive TV will outstrip PCs as the means of participation in the network economy and will ensure truly global diffusion of information technologies.

The most striking effect of this general adoption of technologies is likely to occur when a generation that has grown up with these newer forms of technology enters the mature and productive phase of its individual lives. There are notable differences in the way in which the adults and children currently engage with Internet technologies.

> Adults consciously adopt Web technology . . . and the concept of [technology] adoption works since they have lived decades without the Internet and must now fit it into their lives. Adults have to consciously append the Web to their pre-established routines and behaviours, and then opt to change how they do things like shop, invest, and communicate . . . whereas young consumers internalize the Net

comments eminent Internet research firm Forrester Research. 'Born into a world replete with connected computers, young consumers more easily integrate the Net throughout their lives. Why is internalization so important? Because when a generation of consumers internalize a technology, its dissemination becomes self-sustaining and pervasive' (McQuivey, 8/99).

This internalization of Internet-related technologies will have a radical effect on the expectations and behaviour of today's younger generation as consumers. 'Deeply aware of the power of information, young consumers will expect to find deep and accurate information anywhere at anytime' is Forrester's evaluation. 'With access to ever more suppliers and the information to make better decisions, young consumers will grow up expecting every supplier to offer a wealth of combinations and configurations. For them, excuses like out-of-stock and one-size fits all will not compute' (McQuivey, 8/99).

The experience-oriented consumer

As consumers become yet more adept at using multi-sensory capabilities to interpret and assimilate diverse pieces of information reaching them through a variety of technological media, the whole nature of the consumer–network economy interface will become more oriented towards conveyance of experience, not just information.

Capable consumer goods and services marketers have long known that there is a strong emotional component to consumer behaviour. This may even override rational considerations in a purchase decision. In the network economy with its burgeoning consumption of metamedia, the adoption of a business philosophy that recognizes both emotional and rational elements to consumer behaviour will become mandatory to success. 'Post-modernists' arrive at this same conclusion, that rational judgement is not of itself sufficient, from a different and less empirical perspective. North American theologian, Stanley Grenz, makes the case. 'In postmodernism, the primary assumption is that truth is not rational or objective. In other words, the human intellect is not the only arbiter of truth. There are other ways of knowing, including one's emotions and intuition' (Tapia, 12/9/94).

Non-rational ways of knowing are likely to become very important factors in influencing the consuming behaviours of a 'net-powered generation'. Businesses ignore them at their peril.

Summary

Throughout the last decades of the twentieth century we have witnessed major social change. Key social trends and influences are shaping Western society today and are conspiring to provide additional impetus to the network economy. In this chapter we have defined and evaluated the six key trends: the 24/7 society; flexible working; social fragmentation; self-determination; beliefs erosion; and metamedia consumption. The advance of information technology is exercising considerable influence, amplifying some of these social trends and magnifying many of the interactions between them. Metamedia consumption plays a pivotal role providing the network interface for humans, and the lens to magnify the interaction of the other social trends. Over the next decade this remarkable nexus of forces will deliver the social revolution of historical proportions earlier forecast by Manuel Castells (Castells, 1996). There is real advantage to be gained by businesses in understanding these forces in society.

In the next chapter we will:

▶ Develop further the theme of rising customer power and the confluence of social trends
▶ Explore the more direct impact of these trends in the form of emerging customer dynamics
▶ Investigate how these dynamics will inform business conduct and performance in the new economy

6

New customer dynamics

▶ A guide to consumer behaviour in digital business
▶ The specific influence and blend of social trends in shaping emergent customer dynamics
▶ Experience richness, attention scarcity, individualism, now mentality, active participation, trust deficit, access freedom and affinity gap
▶ Definition and evaluation of customer dynamics, and how they inform business conduct and performance in the new economy
▶ Evidence of application by e-champions and the contribution made to their own success

Customers and the network economy

As members of human society we are, above all, consumers in one way or another. Our behaviour as consumers is fashioned by social norms to which we adhere. These standards are not static; they evolve about us, driven by the pressures of social forces interacting with one another. As a network society engulfs us, so our consuming behaviour responds to the particular pressures created by this exciting new environment. The challenge in this for business is to understand, embrace and adapt to these changing social norms and the consequent new behaviour they engender among both current and prospective customers.

The purpose of exploring the six key social trends in the previous chapter has been to furnish a broad understanding of the forces that are driving the emerging network society. A deeper evaluation of those trends reveals that they do reinforce one another to create new standards for consumer behaviour. The task now is to make sense of the interactions between the various trends and define the consequent new customer dynamics that are core to Internet-based business success (see Figure 6.1).

In identifying these distinctive customer dynamics, it has become clear that the e-champions have been sensitive to them in developing their own businesses, so their experience can once more help to guide our own. There are eight principal new customer dynamics that are central to future business success: experience richness, attention scarcity, individualism, now mentality, active participation, trust deficit, access freedom and affinity gap. Let us now explore each in turn.

Experience richness

> Virtually everything has been commercialized and is available on tap at almost any time of the day or night. Time-pressured individuals with diverse lifestyle needs demand personalized content, easily and quickly accessible. Evolution from the spoken and written word to a multimedia environment is creating a society fluent in multisensory

assimilation. The richness of experience is now an important expectation from all consumer activities.

We are not passive observers of society; we want to be actively involved. As consumers, our expectations have been raised, and in turn we express our demands to the companies that serve us. We are also quite different from one another with diverse backgrounds and upbringings. We don't want messages and images shaped for others, we want them fashioned to our own distinct needs. Our time is limited, so we also want those messages in a form that we can rapidly grasp. We have also become fluent in assimilating messages from different media and in various formats. The richness of our experiences becomes an important facet of our consuming lives.

The concept of supplying experiences to consumers has already undergone some development in the conventional and familiar offline economy. Marketers have long recognized that emotion plays an important role in the purchase of goods and services. Consequently they have built brands around images that communicate some sense of experience. Yet this has presented them with a challenge. In a world of one-way broadcast media, marketing messages alone cannot convey a true sense of experience to the consumer, without purchase and utilization of the product. Broadcast messages are anyway a hit-and-miss affair, since communication is unlikely

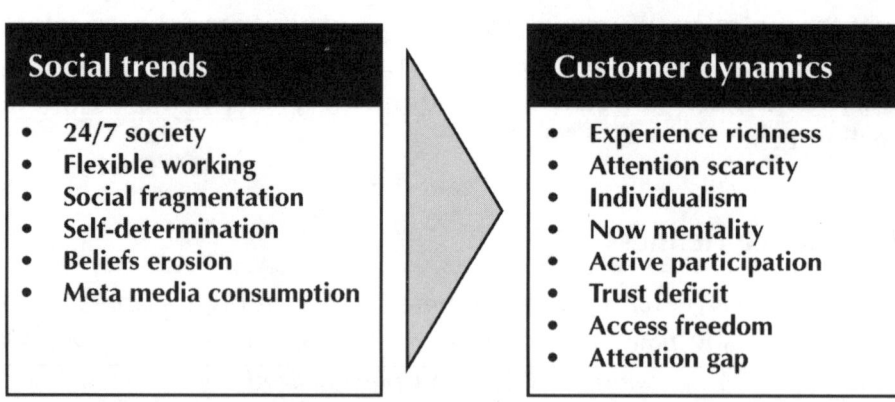

Figure 6.1 Social trends and new customer dynamics

to be sufficiently targeted or personalized to each and every prospective customer. So, in the pre-network economy, it requires internalization of images, perceptions and probably enjoyment of the good by each consumer to create a truly rich experience. As authors Joseph Pine and James Gilmore identify. 'While prior economic offerings – commodities, goods, and services – are external to the buyer, experiences are inherently personal, existing only in the mind of an individual who has been engaged in an emotional, intellectual, or even spiritual level (Pine and Gilmore, 7/98).

Personal transportation is one area where the emotional content of the offering can be absolutely critical to purchase and continuing customer satisfaction. So, customer experience is of paramount concern to auto or motor manufacturers. The Harley–Davidson motor cycle is world-renowned, and marketers in the company have deliberately sought to build on this reputation by suggesting that the ownership of a Harley–Davidson opens up a whole world of pleasurable experiences. As authors Stan Davis and David Meyer indicate, 'customers who buy a Harley feel they're getting much more than a motorcycle; they're buying into a lifestyle, an attitude, an image' (Davis and Meyer, 1998). Harley–Davidson's CEO, Richard Teerlink, confirms this reality: 'There's a high degree of emotion that drives our success. We symbolize the feelings of freedom and independence that people really want in this stressful world' (Lieber, 23/6/97). With profit margins higher than many of its competitors, Harley's experience-rich-based approach is obviously working.

Yet it is in the online world where the limitations of experience richness are overcome, and its full potential can be realized. As Pine and Gilmore observe, a business environment is emerging in which, rather than just delivering products and services to customers, companies will seek to stage 'memorable experiences' for their customers. Contrast the approaches of booksellers Barnes & Noble and Jeff Bezos's Amazon towards providing 'memorable experiences'. Book-loving consumers have pleasant associations of book-reading experiences involving sitting in a comfortable environment with a cup of coffee, perhaps sharing favourite passages with friends. Barnes & Noble recreated this for them by installing coffee bars in its bookstores, providing comfortable chairs and giving greater opportunities to browse its bookshelves. As a result, Barnes & Noble has found that its customers no longer view its chain stores as just a place to buy books, but as somewhere they can go to for a pleasurable experience.

Amazon has managed to transfer this experience to the virtual world, much to Barnes & Noble's concern, as Leo Sheiner of Global Market explains.

> When you shop at Amazon.com . . . you can find books by almost any kind of criteria. When you have found one that is appropriate, you can ask to see more that are similar in content. And you can see what other readers have had to say about those books. As soon as you search for a book with[in] a given subject area, you are within a micro-community with people of similar interests, and you can benefit from their judgement. . . . To sum up, [Amazon provides] a rich experience [which] makes the user want to return. (Sheiner, 10/98)

What is more, you can create this personalized experience for yourself wherever and whenever suits you, at home, say, with your own cup of coffee and easy chair if you like! While Barnes & Noble have responded with their own online bookstore, Amazon has reportedly considered its own real-world stores in strategic locations. Access freedom – giving customers the choice of online and offline to suit their immediate preferences – looks equally important as a customer dynamic, as we shall see later.

Chuck Schwab identified the importance of experience richness in his vision for the future of financial services on the Internet. 'It is as simple as turning on your computer', observes *Fortune* magazine, 'and right there are all the pockets of your financial life on the screen' (Gunn, 7/12/98), . Chuck's company has held true to his experience-rich vision by offering Schwab customers online access to as broad a range of reliable information services as possible, together with a very large selection of financial products. Pierre Omidyar, too, realized the importance of this dynamic in his formative thinking on eBay, when he realized that the Internet could be used to establish a centralized market forum, where people could buy and sell unique items, as well as meet other users with similar interests. For John Pluthero, providing richness of experience to his Freeserve customers is essential to keeping them loyal in the highly competitive world of free Internet access. He provides his users with over thirty different content channels on topics such as news, business, entertainment, careers, cartoons, shopping and sport so that they can create their own personalized bubble of content.

It requires the online world to create the truly personalized rich experience. It provides the medium for the critical connection of social trends, blending diversity of lifestyles with desire for twenty-four-hour access, the immediacy imposed by time-pressured existence and a fluent multisensory online ability.

Attention scarcity

The changing nature of work lives constrains available time for the majority. Consumerism inherent in the 24/7 society brings an ever-growing range of offers. Self-determination increases the span of issues in life to which consumers feel they have to give attention. Time, and attention capacity, have become among the scarcest resources.

Busy, busy, busy are the consumers of today. Working lives are no longer ordered and simple, but more often hectic and frequently chaotic. As others in society do less for us, so we have to do more for ourselves and take on more tasks and responsibilities. With so much to do and so little time in which to do it, our whole existence has become frenetic. What time do we have to consider the new, when we know at least what the familiar will provide, even if it's not totally satisfactory?

Businesses today are finding it ever more difficult to gain the scarce attention of consumers. Analysts calculate that, in any one day, UK consumers are exposed to more than 2,000 marketing messages in one form or another, and in the USA that figure is as high as 3,000. The challenge, then, is first to get consumers' attention, and that is no mean feat. The majority of consumers lead increasingly time-pressured lives and have a limited span of attention for any marketing message. Having climbed a mountain to gain their interest, there then ensues yet another challenge for business: to get consumers actively to change their behaviour and try the product or service. Confronted by an array of almost limitless choice, as consumers in developed societies are, this challenge presents a second mountain to the business, of no lesser severity. One way to climb that second mountain is initially to give the product away. Where frequent repeat purchases may follow, free samples are thus used to encourage behaviour change.

In the online world the challenge of gaining consumers' attention is further magnified by a plethora of competitors, many of them only a click away. Here, the idea of giving away the product or service has already become mainstream. For digital television in the UK, it involves giving away free set-top boxes in order to get consumers to try inaugural interactive digital television services. In the first four months following the launch of its free set-top box offer in June 1999, News Corporation's BSkyB estimated that the number of subscribers to its Sky Digital service had increased from 685,000 to 1.8 million. By spring 2000 this had increased to 3.4 million. According to BSkyB, 45 per cent of the take up of its digital service – representing nearly 1 million people – had been to new subscribers, while the remainder has been to existing analogue subscribers upgrading to digital (*Marketing*, 21/10/99). The set-top box give-away was a major high-risk investment for BSkyB. By October 1999 BSkyB had acquired more than 80 per cent of the total UK digital market, putting it well ahead of its rivals. Commenting on BSkyB's plans before the June 1999 launch, investment analysts at Morgan Stanley proclaimed:

> Should this strategy succeed, the by-product will be a larger subscriber base with which to negotiate key content rights going forward ... [while] a greater subscriber base will lead to enhanced revenues from PPV [pay per view] and interactive revenues.

Indeed, Morgan Stanley analysts estimated that Sky Digital's subscriber base will be over 6.1 million by 2003 (*Cable Europe*, 12/05/99).

Getting consumers' attention is one thing that Jay Walker has most certainly achieved with Priceline, a feat that has earned him the respect and admiration of marketers the world over. To enable potential customers, who have put in offers that are just too low to experience the name-your-own price service, Priceline has reportedly often made up marginal differences between a consumer's bid and the price that airlines or hotels are prepared to accept. Priceline's purpose in this is to encourage sustained behaviour change and further usage of Priceline by the customer. Consumers will only do this if they get to experience the service in the first place, so Priceline sometimes invests to get them started, and to encourage them also as satisfied Priceline customers to give word of mouth and word of mouse referrals.

Until late 1998 take up of the Internet in the UK had been much slower than in the USA. The cost of local calls plus the cost of Internet access had put off many consumers. John Pluthero changed that at a stroke. When customers sign up for Freeserve, they get unlimited free access to the Internet via a browser that is automatically configured to bring up the Freeserve portal website. Nor did Freeserve have the challenge of having to get a retailer to stock its product – parent company, Dixons Group, is the UK's leading electronics retailer. For Pluthero the cost of customer acquisition was the cost of burning a CD-ROM and getting it to the retail outlets. Customer acquisition cost is reported to be less than $50.

For Mike Harris at Egg the task may have seemed even more daunting: consumer interest in financial services is notoriously low. By offering a savings rate that initially exceeded even the base rate at which banks in the UK were prepared to lend money, Harris achieved his five-year target of half a million customers and £5 billion of savings in less than seven months. As parent company Prudential Group's Finance Director stated on Egg's launch 'Rather than acquire a company and expensing the goodwill, we are building a new organization and charging the investment to earnings' (Regulatory News Service, 5/10/98). With a bank costing upwards of several billion pounds, Egg's strategy looks very sound.

Yet when it comes to overriding the shortfall of consumer attention in the online world there is an important additional factor that needs to be taken into account – the competitive dynamic of network returns. In the network economy the law of increasing returns can bestow a remarkable influence on the take up of a product or service once it has reached critical mass. All you need is to overcome that attention scarcity in the first place.

■ Individualism

> *Fragmentation of family and community creates a growing cohort of self-dependent adults. A sense of 'self' impels even the most reluctant and less capable to seek what feels right to them personally. Erosion of societal beliefs and values raise questions and doubts that lead to a creeping knowledge that 'self' is paramount. Consumerism has educated society and created expectations of personalized product and services.*

Social fragmentation isolates individuals who are ever more aware of the need to provide fully for themselves in a world of growing self-determination. Erosion of belief in society reinforces the sense of isolation and the feeling that one's own advice and decisions are likely to be the right ones. Consumerism creates battle-scarred and hardened consumers who are no longer tolerant recipients of flawed goods and services. Individualism is a potent customer dynamic.

Today, consumers are very different from one another; they have diverse backgrounds, attitudes and lifestyles. Awareness of 'self' leads to a sense of uniqueness and an expectation that vendors and suppliers of their needs should treat them as such. As consumers' confidence in their own power grows, businesses are discovering that business strategies and marketing techniques developed for mass markets are increasingly inappropriate to today's marketplace.

Recent technological developments make it easier for companies to provide customers with offerings that are tailored to their particular needs and aspirations. Yet it is the development of interactive relationships between providers and customers that supplies the means for truly individualized products and services. Such interactive relationships allow vendors to engage in dialogue with their customers, and match offerings precisely to needs. But for this company-customer dialogue to be effective it must exceed the envelope of immediate needs being served. Fluidity of lifestyles and steady erosion of the work–home divide means that it is now hard for people to separate their lives into neat, self-contained compartments. Because every part of a person's life is becoming connected to every other part, successful businesses are taking a more holistic approach to their customers and to their needs. 'For contemporary consumers, product satisfaction is linked inextricably with life satisfaction, and companies must attend to both these dimensions if they expect to win', affirm marketers Susan Fournier, Susan Dobscha and David Glen Mick, writing in the *Harvard Business Review*. 'True customer intimacy – the backbone of a successful, rewarding relationship – requires a deep understanding of the context in which our products and services are used in the course of our customers' day-to-day lives' (Fournier, Dobscha and Mick, 1/98).

This holistic approach to customer lifestyle is fundamental in the online network economy. For Chuck Schwab it is elemental, as his vision attests: 'Right there are all the pockets of your financial life on the screen.' But it is through interactivity and dialogue with customers that Schwab truly taps the customer dynamic of individualism. 'On Schwab's website you can look up real-time quotes, news, historical financial data, or use sophisticated software tools', observes *Fortune* magazine reporter Eileen Gunn. 'You can customize the home page to see your personal account when you log on. You can set up your own asset-allocation model, screen for the best-performing mutual funds that fit that model, and then buy the funds through Schwab. Who needs a broker?' (Gunn, 7/12/98).

For Jeff Bezos and Amazon the foundations for addressing the individual book-buying needs of his 17 million customers in more than 160 different countries start with the range of titles on offer. The British website offers more than 1.5 million titles, including all British books in print and 200,000 US best sellers, while the biggest real-world UK bookstores stock around 150,000 titles.

As Jay Walker and his Priceline CEO Richard Braddock expand the number of products and services available through Priceline, customer individualism is high on their list of priorities. Braddock believes that the Internet offers tremendous potential for the deployment of one-to-one marketing strategies: 'It's the ultimate leverage point in what I see as the evolution toward targeted marketing and the ability to treat your customer on virtually a one-by-one basis', says Braddock. 'Marketing is all about information and knowledge of the customer. We create a basis for a longer-term relationship. Over time we'll be able to offer you [other] things [and] cross-sell [to] you' (Jaffe, 17/5/99).

With the network dynamic of buyer ascendancy being arguably the strongest competitive force in the network economy, individualism is a dynamic factor absolutely critical to future success.

Now mentality

> *Consumerism has led to widespread expectations that all needs and wants can be fulfilled in the present. Growing awareness of 'self' fuels consumers' expectations and demands of their suppliers. Time pressure from changing work patterns underpins the search for instant satisfaction.*

The time pressures of busy work and leisure lives lead consumers to seek 'anytime, anyplace' access to goods and services. Self-determination breeds a confidence and a growing demand for immediate satisfaction. Over the last decade instant gratification has been a growing trend in the conventional physical economy powered by increased competition between companies. As time becomes ever more critical in people's lives, consumers become ever less willing to wait on the leisure, or tardiness, of the companies that serve them. Gradually, society is awakening collectively and individually to the consumer power that it wields. 'Now mentality' is a facet of modern consumer lives to which the instant intercommunication of the network society gives a new impetus.

The digital world unleashes the full power of this customer dynamic. Online it is now possible to complete the full cycle of raising awareness, completing purchase and delivering service. 'Check out this simple scenario', suggests Radikal Communications,

> a user's interest is aroused by a banner ad; this results in a click-through to the advertiser's web site. On this web site, the user is informed about a specific product or service. Within the same course of action, the user decides to purchase the presented prod-

ucts or service. If the product is electronically deliverable, it will be delivered almost instantaneously. Deal closed. (*Online Marketing Tips*, 1/2/99)

For pure information-based services such as software, investment, personal finance and even travel, the full purchase process can be delivered online in this way without the need for any subsequent physical delivery. Even the music industry can be added to this list with the escalating application of MP3 – a data compression format that allows near-CD quality music to be accessed over the Internet and then quickly downloaded. Pioneers in the retailing of MP3-formatted music over the Internet include US companies MP3.com and Emusic, as well as UK-based Crunch. Spreading popularity among the young Internet-savvy generation has resulted in MP3 recently becoming the most searched-for topic on the Internet – until then it had been pornography!

Recognition of the relevance of now mentality and the pace of change towards a real-time environment has inevitably been slower in industries that require physical deliveries. This is not the case among e-champions who have recognized that, although they may not be able to control fully the physical delivery process, they can at least apply outstanding service and continuing customer communications that minimize consumer concerns about this aspect of the purchase process. So, Amazon may not be able to deliver instantly a book in hard-copy format, but it will advise customers before they order how long despatch will take, by what means and what delivery options are available. Amazon will advise how quickly it will take for a given order to arrive and will then confirm despatch of that order. Twenty-four-hour delivery is Amazon's target for in-stock books. Dell Computers cannot deliver a computer manufactured to full personal specification immediately, but it aims to do so within three days if possible. Like Jeff Bezos's company, Michael Dell relies upon outstanding customer service and excellent communication to minimize any impact of the physical delivery process on the overall customer experience.

One Internet-based business that has put now mentality at the core of its business model is the New York-based start-up, Kozmo.

Kozmo allows customers to choose from a range of 30,000 products on its website, from CDs and videos to food and other groceries. For a premium, Kozmo then promises to deliver the selected goods to the customer within one hour. So far, using a combination of massive warehouses, sophisticated computer planning technology and a very efficient dispatching service, Kozmo has found that it can meet its delivery promises and make money at the same time. By late 1999, Kozmo's customer base was growing by 35 per cent a month, and plans had been put in place for Kozmo to expand to thirty or more US cities by the end of 2000 (Green, 31/8/99).

'Value for time is the overriding imperative' notes The Henley Centre (1997). Maximum value to customers in the network economy will therefore be derived from minimizing the time taken to meet their needs.

Active participation

> *Growing confidence and technological competency fuel an expectation of greater involvement in the service experiences of consuming activity. A developing sense of self-identity and confidence compound the desire for a more participatory role in shaping that experience.*

Active participation is primarily a function of three social trends. Self-determination encourages consumers to take a far more proactive stance in their affairs. More active involvement in the online world of the network economy requires fluency in that multisensory capability and network interface that stems from metamedia consumption. Finally, a desire to play a more vigorous role in shaping one's own consumer experiences is a manifestation of the creeping erosion of one's belief in society or in established social institutions. Consumers have lost confidence in the ability of others to shape and deliver their consuming experiences to them. Rather than just sitting back and watching the future unfold, consumers have become ever more interested in shaping that future for themselves. 'A watchdog culture has encouraged customers to be more proactive', reasons The Henley Centre, 'even when they sense improvements, they continue to complain because they feel that they are part of a positive feedback loop which they wish to perpetuate' (Henley Centre website).

The stimulus that beliefs erosion has given to promoting active participation can be traced back, in part, to the postmodernist concept that the world is a place to be experienced rather than just analysed, and that participation takes priority over rational reflection. As Professor Bernard Cova of the L'Ecole Européenne des Affaires explains:

> In post-modernity, the consumer may be finding the potential to become a protagonist in the customization of his world. That is why . . . marketing has to include the consumer not as a target for products, but as a producer of experiences. The essence of postmodern experience is participation; without participation, the consumer is merely entertained and does not experience. (Cova, 1996)

To the postmodern consumer the interactive nature of the network economy is critical. It enables online offerings wherein they can shape their own experiences and participate jointly in the creation of a new future for themselves. The provider's role shifts from being a mere supplier of products or services to the creator of the environment in which experiences are shaped.

There is a strong linkage between the two customer dynamics of experience richness and active participation. Rich experiences, full of content and personalized to the individual, require also a strong and active participatory role. Toyota's online presence illustrates the point. The Toyota website personalizes and provides visitors with their own homepage. As visitors provide information about themselves, the site automatically feeds them with appropriate articles and targeted offers every time they return. Visitors can enter a virtual showroom in which they become users, building their ideal auto by selecting the model, colour, engine, size, interior trim and so on. The completed vehicle can then be saved in a personal online showroom alongside other models consumers choose to create. Users can then show their own range of creations to their families and friends. Once users have decided that they would like to purchase a vehicle, they can e-mail their specification to their preferred dealer and arrange a test drive. In future, Toyota plans to have set up its systems so that customers can order their customized autos and get behind the driving wheel three days later.

To our e-champions, active participation is essential to their customer-centric focus. Imitation, it is said, is the sincerest form of flattery, as E*Trade Chairman Christos Cotsakos illustrates. E*Trade is an online brokerage house based in the USA, and the second largest behind – and some way behind – market leader Schwab. 'The old traditional brokerage model assumes people are dumb. They get charged a lot of money for the advice and counsel', says Cotsakos, 'Our model is: people are inherently smart. We liberate you with information, charge a value-added price, let you become self directed and have you handle your [own] financial services.' Schwab and E*Trade both truly believe their customers are smart. They also know their customers would prefer to conduct most, if not all, of their trading activities themselves, and that they are capable of doing so. Few organizations in the old real-world economy attribute such ability to customers. All too often they engender a provider– customer relationship that is 'parent–child' in transactional mode rather than the 'adult–adult' mode that most customers would prefer.

Customer-obsessed Jeff Bezos actively encourages his customers to put forward suggestions about how Amazon's website could be further improved, and to comment on any shortcomings they happen to experience in Amazon's services. He also provides the means for customers to take their active participation one stage further. They can become members of Amazon's Associate Program – its affiliate sales network. Amazon pioneered the concept of syndicated selling on the Internet, and by mid-1999 well over 200,000 people and organizations had joined the ranks of affiliates. The programme involves individuals or organizations seamlessly linking – for free – their own websites to Amazon using a simple piece of downloaded software. Affiliates subsequently receive a 5–15 per cent cut of whatever is spent by visitors clicking through to Amazon from their own websites.

Michael Dell, too, knows his customers and he knows that they are proactive in their purchasing behaviours:

The World Wide Web provided a way to link our customers with all the information they needed to buy and manage their computers, and do it in real time. It worked for everyone; no matter what software platform they used. Even better, there was an almost instantaneous alignment with our customer base; the Internet immediately attracted knowledgeable users, to whom Dell primarily sells. We knew that our customers – and potential customers – would be there first. (Dell, 1998)

The readiness with which Dell customers have embraced Dell's Internet-based sales development is testimony to Michael's awareness of their desire for active participation. By late 1999, the company's sales over the Internet exceeded $35 million a day, up from $12 million a day in late 1998, representing more than $13 billion on an annualized basis.

As a customer dynamic, active participation will snowball. As more companies recognize their customers to be fellow adults, and as they adapt their internal processes such that customers can play a greater role in fulfilling purchase transactions, so consumer confidence and self-assurance will increase.

Trust deficit

Education, sophistication and unfulfilled expectation have led to widespread questioning of the institutions and cornerstones of society. Insecurity and uncertainty driven by the changing nature of work and societal fragmentation amplify the concern. A vacuum remains to be filled.

The erosion of belief in society and institutions is the predominant social trend that drives trust deficit, but there is a wide range of pressures that help to fuel this negative customer dynamic. The breakdown of the family, the rise of lone-parent families, the explosion of single-person households of all ages and a more general feeling of alienation are social fragmentation factors that undermine the inherent trust in society fundamental in earlier generations.

Recent work-related changes have also contributed to a lack of well-being. Where once there was a strong sense of certainty and security in employment, now there is little. Paternalism in employment is a value that few organizations can afford to retain in today's highly competitive and cost-conscious world. Where it does exist, younger generations value it little, and trust it even less. Self-determination is another social trend that (sadly) contributes to trust deficit. As individuals find they can no longer rely upon governments to provide for them when they are ill, out of work or retired, the realization that they must rely more upon their own provision contributes to this lack of trust in others.

What, then, fills this vacuum left by the decay of social structures, the decline of paternalistic employers and the degeneration of society? Individuals look increasingly to the role that brands play in their lives to provide pillars of certainty and guidance in life, as The Henley Centre affirms: 'As popular trust in institutions declines and individuals feel they are faced with ever more choices and ever less time in which to make them, consumers are seeking new partners to help them confront, share and manage the risks that they face in their everyday life.' In this situation, say Henley, 'brands are ideally positioned to fill the vacuum' (Henley Centre, 1998).

It is the manner in which brands function to fill the trust vacuum that indicates just how deep is our collective uncertainty and insecurity. 'Brands are playing a larger role in helping us to define and articulate our values', says Dorothy MacKenzie of creative marketing consultancy Dragon:

> Now that our individual identity is derived less from what our position in society, or family, or our religion may be, the role of brands has become increasingly important. Brands provide some means of reliable contact with the rest of the world – and so have become a surrogate source of authority.   (MacKenzie, 25/4/97)

These pressures have been mounting for some years, long before the network economy and the Internet achieved any level of visibility. The Internet brings almost infinite access and, with it, wide choice for consumers. Its influence is to intensify the impact of this customer dynamic. Many believed that the role of brands in the network economy would diminish. Trust deficit indicates just why that will not be the case.

Our e-champions have built their initial success on the knowledge that a strong brand will be essential to their continuing success. Jeff Bezos's preoccupation and obsession that Amazon should be the ultimate customer-centric company can only be achieved by consistent and outstanding customer service. Providing a cornerstone of assurance upon which Amazon customers can always rely is at the core of the relationship which he is building with his 17 million customers in over 160 different countries. Trust is central.

Jay Walker is committing major amounts of capital investment into very effective brand development, where consistent delivery of customer experience enables the Priceline brand to build on pure name awareness. Jay increased his marketing spend of $24 million in 1998 to $64 million in 1999, even though Priceline incurred a loss of $112 million in 1998 and that loss is likely to have increased to over $200 million for 1999. This boldness turns accepted business practice on its head. Few senior managers of established businesses would be allowed to continue to commit that level of marketing spend without evidence of payback. Walker is sensitive to the customer dynamic of trust deficit and knows his company must win his customers' trust in order to succeed. Analysts expect Priceline to break even in 2001 on revenues of between $500 million and $1 billion.

The world of personal finance is significantly devoid of trust, and particularly in the UK. The mis-selling of pensions in the late 1980s and accusations of unreasonably high costs charged by banks and insurers to UK consumers are just two factors that contribute to the sector's poor image. Mike Harris knows he has an uphill struggle to implant in his customers' minds that Egg is not just different, but will deliver better products and service consistently. His passion for customer service indicates that he has the right credentials. Expect to see ongoing major investment in brand development as Egg continues to blaze a trail apart from the negative image of UK financial services.

Trust deficit is a negative customer dynamic that the workings of the network society may do much to resolve. Many of the social issues that combine to drive this customer dynamic are deep and seemingly insoluble. The beneficial influence of the network society will be welcome, although the nature of the remedy may come as a surprise.

Access freedom

> *The 24/7 society enables reformation of traditional mindsets about consumption, liberating consumers from the constraints of time and physical location. Metamedia consumption provides society with a fluency in assimilating knowledge and developing experience. Self-determination creates an emergent 'can do' attitude.*

There are rising expectations and demands of consumers in the 24/7 society for ready and convenient access to commercial offerings. Social fragmentation and the disparate nature of people's lives bring diversity to lifestyles, and the swelling sense of self-reliance breeds consumer activism and a desire for freedom of enjoyment. The arrival of the network economy fuels this already strong pressure from customers for access to products and services whenever and wherever. The 'marketspace' of the Internet and its capacity for instant intercommunication remove the constraints of time and physical location.

Yet access freedom is about more than when and where we purchase; it is also about how. With a wealth of information now at the consumers' fingertips and a plethora of choice, there must be better ways for them to make their purchase decisions. Western society is used to a simple offer. This good is on offer at this price. Take it or leave it. If discovering an alternative takes time or requires some physical effort, such as a journey to another store, then the price requested may be high and the value poor, but the options are limited – so you buy! The network dynamic of buyer ascendancy recognizes the potential for realignment of the market from buyer bias to customer bias. The customer dynamic of access freedom creates the demand to activate this technologically driven competitive force.

Consumers are now discovering that their demand for a fresh approach to how their needs are met is being addressed in the online world. New technology is leading to the development of new types of market forums that empower them to locate and conduct price comparisons on products and services from an ever-expanding range of providers. Shopping comparison websites, such as CompareNet and BottomDollar, are well-established in the USA, and more recently European-based operations, such as DealPilot in Germany and ShopGuide in the UK, have picked up the consumers' challenge. There are web-based businesses that use aggregated buying power to forge better deals for the consumer, such as Mercata in the USA, Adabra in the UK and LetsBuyIt in Sweden. Rather than starting with a product and looking for customers, these organizations start with customers and then find them the products they want. They achieve this by negotiating deals with a range of suppliers, so that the more customers buy a given product or service, the lower the price becomes. 'In the Seventies, aggregated buying meant ideologically sound co-operatives', comments *Revolution* magazine. 'In the nineties, the Internet has changed it into plain good business sense' (Burgess, 10/99). And it's only good business sense because customers want it!

As business folk begin to believe that the constraints and conventional wisdom of business-to-consumer commerce in the old real-world physical economy need no longer apply, so they begin to apply their imaginations in search of all manner of new ways to meet consumer preference for freedom of access. Shopping comparison sites and aggregated buying are only two of the myriad ways in which it is possible to reshape markets, reorganize buyers and even reorganize sellers in the pursuit of access freedom.

Our e-champions are sensitive to this dynamic, too. Priceline's approach to business, where customers name their own price and vendors have the opportunity to decide whether to make them an offer or not, is very simple. 'Priceline . . . is successful because it manages to simplify what could be a complex process. Here you can buy cars, airline tickets, hotel rooms, mortgages and more – you make an offer and Priceline sees if anyone is prepared to do a deal for that price', comments the *Financial Times*.

Take cars. Priceline takes you through a step-by-step process during which you choose your motor[car] – model, engine, upholstery, colour, extras. At each stage you are told not only the recommended price, but also what the dealer would pay for it – so you know his margin. Priceline then suggests a price (somewhere between retail and wholesale) which you can adjust. Click on a button, and within a day the company tells you if a dealer is prepared to agree to your price. It costs you $25 (£15), but you have saved a couple of thousand. (Bowen, 17/9/99)

Chuck Schwab's complete approach to stock trading provides access freedom in every respect, whenever, wherever and however. Charles Schwab Corporation started as a discount brokerage house in 1971 and was immediately blazing a trail that most of the established full service brokerage houses considered ill advised. By the time he launched eSchwab in mid-1996, the business had over 200 (now over 300) retail outlets across the USA as well as telephone-based trading and a dial-up service for PC users. The addition of eSchwab provided another means of access for Schwab customers to choose from as suited their needs at any time. But it went beyond just offering unlimited choice as to time and location, eSchwab created a new type of marketspace for online trading. Customers could become investment experts in their own way. You can set up your own asset allocation model and screen for the best-performing funds that meet that model. You can get real-time quotes, historical data and use sophisticated software tools to help you make decisions. Access freedom in the Schwab mould is about making the customers into their own broker, if that is what they want to be.

John Pluthero tapped the customer dynamic of access freedom strongly with Freeserve. By launching the first free Internet access service, he made 1.5 million friends in the UK in only a few months. Interest in the Internet had been growing but the combination of local call charges and service provider fees had made Internet access an expensive option. Not only did Pluthero's success inevitably spawn a whole host of imitators – in the UK alone there are now dozens of free access services, even the major and established service providers such as BT, Demon and Worldcom's Pipex have had to respond to his challenge. As Pluthero and his colleagues add more and more services to the Freeserve portal, they continue to tap this dynamic.

Access freedom is a strong customer dynamic. It is clear that the only bounds to its influence will be defined by the extent of creativity and imagination in those business people who are bent on digital business success.

Affinity gap

Community and family are fundamental to human society. A new, more flexible work environment, disparate families, pressures of time, pace of change and erosion of beliefs are conspiring to create a void – an absence of affinity that needs to be filled.

A broad alliance of social trends correlate to drive the last of the eight identified new customer dynamics. Affinity gap has a negative influence upon customer behaviour, and, as with trust deficit, the network economy provides the means to mitigate, if not resolve, this dynamic over time. The decline in physical communities, whether family or social group based, is a leading feature of social fragmentation. The changing nature of work patterns and organizations are undermining the important social stability inherent in long-term employment. The social dimension is one of the less obvious aspects of the flexible working trend, yet is has an important, if undesirable, impact. A key facet of the social trend of beliefs erosion is declining faith in established social institutions. Together, these particular elements combine to create an absence of a sense of affinity among individuals

Maybe we don't need community any more? After all, in the primitive network economies of the agrarian era, limitations of travel and reliance upon the spoken word as the means of communication reinforced the local communities of the day. With the industrial era, more widespread migrations and travel, together with education and the increased use of the written word as an additional method of communication, gave us an independence that we learned to value as individuals. As the information era metamorphoses into a network society, we enjoy a greater sense of freedom from the constraints of time and space, and as individuals we feel more liberated from the need to rely upon one another. Yet there exists within today's society a strong yearning for a restored sense of community. It is what Geoff Mulgan of the UK-based think tank Demos calls the 'connexity dilemma', wherein the more independent humans try to become, the more interdependent they realize that they actually are (Mulgan, 1997). Many technological and social developments have taken place in the last two centuries, and their effects have seemed progressively to reduce the constraints put upon human freedom by a simple sustenance-driven and primitive network economy. Nonetheless, human beings still cannot live without one another if they are to lead happy and fulfilled lives. So, affinity gap is a very real, if disagreeable, customer dynamic that social trends have been stoking up for some decades, long before the new technology-based network society became a reality.

The potential solution to the problem now lies in this new society, as The Henley Centre confirms:

> Historically, we have always longed for the perfect community; and this communal yearning is high at present. In the past, community was defined by geography – where you lived signified a lot about who you were, what you did for a living, your beliefs. But, now, traditional neighbourhoods are under pressure as people spend more time at work and more time in the home, making it difficult for them to be able to invest in their local communities. So which communities are people yearning to be in today? . . . People are more likely to search for a sense of networked individuality and identify with others with whom they have something in common. . . . [In other words, there is a] shift towards communities of interest. (Henley Centre website)

Networked individuality leads to online, or virtual communities. These are the communities of interest that exist in the cyberspace of the Internet and that have begun to address the affinity gap. There are major online communities that seem like a circle of wagons on the uncertain and dangerous wilds of the Internet prairie. Geocities, TheGlobe and Tripod are some of the best known. TalkCity is also highly valued by its users, and is arguably the best example of an online community. Members of its large network of users provide most of its website content, and the amount of time spent by the average TalkCity user in one of its online communities is at least one and a half times the equivalent figure for any of the other most popular community sites. According to TalkCity, the reason for the burgeoning popularity of its services is that they 'satisfy consumers basic social need for communication in a convenient manner that is not limited by . . . time and geographic constraints' (TalkCity website). Created in early 1996 from the remnants of Apple Computer's abandoned eWorld online service, TalkCity currently focuses on providing home-page and real-time chat facilities to its rapidly-expanding customer base (comprising over 2.6 million in June 1999). By summer 1998, the TalkCity site included twenty topical categories, over fifty themed communities, fifty co-branded partner communities, and thousands of user-generated communities. To moderate its real-time discussions, TalkCity employs a large number of staff, as well as a large team of trained volunteers. It is also a strongly family-oriented online network, and operates a strict code of conduct, supported by the use of software programmes that automatically detect and then block the use of profane, racist or other offensive forms of language. A particularly popular service provided by TalkCity are the chat facilities that enable users to listen to online audio broadcasts of sports matches, and then exchange comments in real-time with other listeners as the match progresses. TalkCity earns its revenues through a variety of activities: marketing, sponsorship and co-branding deals with major companies; designing and developing customized communities; conducting online market research; and facilitating online meetings for businesses, their clients and suppliers.

Smaller 'niche' communities exist in abundance. UK-based CharlotteStreet was launched by a national newspaper, the *Daily Mail*, in October 1999. It is a modern, lively and informative community-oriented site where women are able to share views, advice and experiences, as well as get access to a diverse range of information services that are of interest to them and their families. According to Nicola Davenport, CharlotteStreet's editor,

> CharlotteStreet isn't about telling women what to do. It's about providing information, support and advice for women when they need it, at a place where they can share their experiences with other like-minded individuals in a uniquely personal way. Today's woman is often juggling a career, relationships, a home and children. Somewhere along the line she will need some advice or information, whether it is the best mortgage deals or the latest health and beauty tips. CharlotteStreet is about providing women with an environment that will enable them to make decisions in all areas of their lives. (*M2 Presswire*, 28/10/99)

The website comprises seven information channels covering leisure and free time, work and money, love and marriage, babies and family, and home and shopping. There is also an extensive message board area where advice and help is on hand from online experts and other site users about the issues that are affecting women in their everyday lives.

Among our e-champions, too, the affinity gap is being addressed. Pierre Omidyar describes eBay as the world's largest personal online trading community. Community runs through eBay as letters do through a stick of rock candy. 'Our historic strategy has been focusing on developing a personal trading community, and what that means is enabling individuals and small dealers to do business with one another', reflects Pierre's CEO, Meg Whitman. 'And the really important part of that has been the community that has developed out of that. We started with commerce, and what grew out of that commerce was community.'

Jeff Bezos's quest to create the most customer-centric company could not be achieved without providing opportunity and means for customers to be able to communicate with like-minded individuals. Bezos offers services such as chat rooms and bulletin boards to bring together people sharing common interests. As Amazon's own person-to-person auction capabilities develop, so the emphasis on community is likely to be even further enhanced.

Affinity gap may be a negative dynamic, but the promise of the network economy to address and help resolve this sad feature of current society is a very exciting prospect.

Summary

In this chapter we have explored the issue of rising customer power in depth. We have identified specific customer dynamics that evolve distinctively from the social trends we reviewed in Chapter 5. These dynamics also provide a background to consumer behaviour in the network economy and will be crucial to successful business conduct and performance in the new economy. Our e-champions are clearly also sensitive to these dynamics in developing their own businesses, and have used them to underpin their respective successes. We should draw on their experience to guide our own (see Figure 6.2).

We now have a comprehensive appreciation of the customer dynamics that are defining consumer behaviour. We also have a detailed understanding of the technology-based network dynamics that are shaping the competitive environment. We can now move on to ascertain what these social and technological factors tell us about business in the digital age.

In Part Three we will develop the Value Lever framework to help

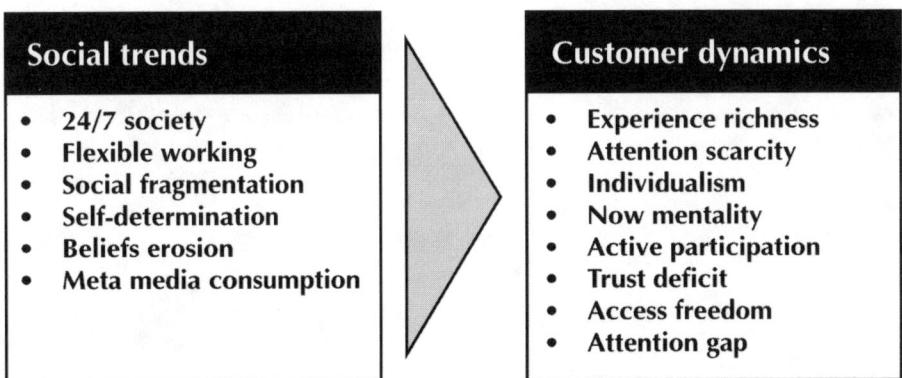

Figure 6.2 Social trends and new customer dynamics

you underpin your own digital success. But first, in the next chapter, we will consider:

▶ The need for fresh thinking, new mindsets and open minds
▶ The principal differences between conventional and digital business
▶ The importance of action over analysis and the benefits of first-mover advantage

Part Three
Doing business digitally

7

A fresh approach required

▶ Making the case for fresh thinking, new mindsets and open minds in the digital age
▶ How digital business is different to conventional business
▶ Why fast decisions and actions are important for digital success
▶ Discovering that price competition in the network economy is avoidable unless deliberately employed

■ A whole new ball game

Now to turn this knowledge of new competitive forces and emergent customer dynamics into a method to underpin successful business in the digital age. There is limited benefit to be gained in applying business techniques developed for the old physical offline economy. As UK industry body and e-commerce campaign group InterForum categorically states, 'traditional ways of business will have no place in the networked economy' (InterForum, 1998). Quite simply, we need new thinking, new tools and new techniques.

For businesses established before the arrival of the Internet, the challenge now is to appreciate the scale of what must be done to ensure survival, let alone future success. As the pervasive influence of the Internet has spread beyond the boundaries of the USA, so business communities in developed economies have come to recognize the extent of the task that confronts them. More than 90 per cent of global business leaders currently believe that the Internet will transform their physical marketplaces by 2001, according to a worldwide survey conducted jointly by The Economist Intelligence Unit and consultants Booz Allen Hamilton (BAH/EIU, 1999). Recognizing what is going to happen and, knowing how to remain a winner while this evolution takes place around your business, are two very separate matters. There is much commentary about the digital world, but as yet little really practical guidance.

■ New mindsets needed

The majority of commercial organizations are reluctant to embrace change, remaining wedded to old thinking and old business practices, applying yesterday's thinking to today's changed commercial environment. But the writing is clearly on the wall for all to see, and the dangers of complacency are writ large. 'Preparing for the e-business market requires more than technology investment; it requires an entirely new mindset' is the unequivocal opinion of IBM and The Economist Intelligence Unit in a recent joint research paper. 'Believing the Internet to be just a new communications channel, most companies are guilty of clinging to worn-out procedures and merely adapting their business thinking and processes' (IBM, 1998). Damning though this may seem, it does reflect the reality of what is going on as a generation of technophobic senior managers tries to deny what is happening about them.

Acquiring a fresh mindset in a long-established company may be a challenge but it isn't impossible, as two of our e-champions readily demonstrate. Mike Harris required more than just sponsorship from the then Prudential Group Chief Executive, Sir Peter Davis. Mike required complete buy-in to what he was proposing when launching and developing Egg. Without that support the 'anything can change but the status quo forces' inherent in a large financial institution would have surely have retarded, if not negated, his efforts. John Clare, Chief Executive of Dixons Group, may have found it difficult to accept instantly the concept of free Internet access service for his customers, but he bought into the proposal quickly when John Pluthero explained the case. The respective successes of Harris and Pluthero will be that much greater for the fact that so many of their competitors will continue to adhere to entrenched attitudes and narrowness of thinking. 'Managers can't avoid the impact of electronic commerce on their businesses', says respected Chairman and co-founder of software company Open Market, Shikhar Ghosh, 'They need to understand the opportunities available to them and recognize how their companies may be vulnerable if rivals seize those opportunities first' (Ghosh, 3/98).

If you lack the practised eye and experience of management in an established business, then pause for a moment and reflect that this may not be the drawback you have always feared it might be. You have no baggage of obsolete knowledge and you have nothing to unlearn before you can absorb new methods and concepts. You start with a fresh mindset. You can always obtain the help of others for the more mundane tasks of planning and business operations. It's time to put your ideas into action – your lack of experience may even be an advantage. Don't underrate your chances. Neither Pierre Omidyar, nor those who know him, expected the success of eBay – and he's a very modest billionaire!

	Business	
	Conventional	**Digital**
Nature	Largely static	Dynamic and transient
Environment	Primarily physical ('Atoms')	Primarily virtual ('Bits')
Discipline	Primarily analysis	Primarily imagination
Time frame	3 or more years	6 or less months
Key tools	Porter *et al.*	Value-based
Business focus	Return on investment	Return on intuition
Priority	Shareholders	Customers

Adapted from Downes and Mui, 1998

Figure 7.1 Differences between conventional and digital business

Understanding the difference

So, the emergence of the network economy necessitates a different emphasis to the business plans of tomorrow. This is 'digital strategy', say respected Internet authors Larry Downes and Chunka Mui (Downes and Mui, 1998). The unpredictable challenges posed by the network environment are quite different to those more familiar and comfortable to business managers in the old physical economy, as the contrast in Figure 7.1 illustrates.

The primary tenet of conventional business thinking is that, in a physical world that is largely stable, managers will perpetually focus on refining the way their businesses operate to position them better, and to make them more effective or more efficient than their competitors. In this world, analysis is the name of the game, and plans are laid typically for a three-year period with expected returns on investment over that period. It is a continual process of making the existing business model run better, and doing things right rather than reappraising whether they are the right things to do.

When it comes to 'virtual' business thinking, the distinctive features of the virtual environment dominate the physical one. Creativity and the application of imagination become more important to business success. Literally anybody can take advantage of this unfamiliar and very open competitive arena to launch new initiatives and ventures that are rapidly accepted and speedily assimilated by the consuming public. Even the conservative UK business community had to accept this reality when John Pluthero's Freeserve changed the behaviour of over a million consumers in only four months. In this volatile climate it is not just return on investment – central to thinking and plans in the old highly researched and planned business environment – that matters, it is also the preparedness to bet on new ideas and take calculated risks that counts. Return on intuition rather than merely return on investment is what really counts. Informed Internet investors understand this, which is why Jeff Bezos still holds the interest and commitment of the majority of important Amazon investors, even though in 1999 Amazon reported continuing losses. Ultimately, Bezos will have to achieve profits that will justify the stock price bestowed by the market. In the meantime, the sustained support of core investors indicates they believe Jeff can pull it off in a big way, and that Amazon is not an overrated flash in the pan.

■ Getting first-mover advantage

There is an additional and very important advantage that accrues to firms that bet boldly and act rapidly on sound and creative business ideas appropriate to the network economy. They are likely to secure a real edge from being early, if not first into their respective markets. Customers are creatures of habit for whom ease of access and convenience are important benefits. Unfreeze their behaviour once to migrate them to a new offering, a new way of purchasing or maybe simply away from a competitor, and inherent laziness will ensure that their behaviour refreezes shortly afterwards. If customers then have confidence in the new product or service experience, they will stick with it and remain loyal.

Gaining consumer attention is only the first step. It is the impact of one of the new competitive realities, network returns, which confers the early-mover advantage here. Gain critical mass among your customers with your new offering and then let the network effect act as a booster rocket to your efforts. Word of mouth and word of mouse will multiply your customer base rapidly. It happened for Freeserve in four months. It has happened for Dell as it rapidly overhauled market leader Compaq. It happened for eSchwab as it moved from 25,000 users at the end of its first month in mid-1996 to over 600,000 five months later. It is happening for Egg.

It could be happening for your business, but it won't if you don't apply your imagination to a new development or business venture. Nor will it happen if you spend too long thinking about it, researching your idea and then refining the concept. Doing something quickly is an important prerequisite for digital business success. In a commercial world that bets on ideas and backs the application of intuition, action will be rewarded. The byword is 'Launch and learn, don't learn and launch'. First- (or early-) mover advantage comes from the application of speed. It took only eight weeks to check out adequately the Freeserve business model and get it up and running. eSchwab took less than six months to go from that fateful demonstration to Chuck to full launch. In the digital era the perpetuation of 'analysis paralysis', or the search for absolute certainty, is certain to prevent the immediate and decisive action essential to the success of that plan. Jack Welch, charismatic Chairman of General Electric, captures this thought. 'Any time there is change, there is opportunity. So it is paramount that an organization get energized rather than paralyzed.' True to his word, Jack is inviting all GE employees to help 'destroy the house that Jack built' in an endless search for an organization and business most suited to the vicissitudes of the new economy.

The quest for digital business tools

Knowing the difference between conventional and digital business is fine, and it's useful to know why rapid action is so important in the new economy. Time is of the essence, and at least four, if not seven, 'Internet years' will have sped by before the next calendar year is past, so good business ideas need to be rapidly executed while they are still valid. New rules apply and past experience is unlikely to be a guide to future achievement. Investors bet on good ideas that can be effectively implemented and rapidly scaled up, so being creative and applying your imagination to this exciting new commercial panorama are essential. The market realigns in favour of customers and customer value is paramount. It must be put before the interest of all other stakeholders in designing and executing business ideas.

But it still doesn't tell us how to proceed. What tools can we use to refine our ideas into workable business models? We need to be able to realize the potential, knowing that the fruits of our imagination will truly create value for customers, leading in turn to value for the owners of the business. The danger is, that if we don't get it right, then customer power will just drive prices down to a point where there is little or no margin for owners and investors ever to enjoy a true return. In a business environment where information flows everywhere, relationships seem more remote and customers have almost limitless choice and ultimate power, price-driven competition and 'commoditization' could be the ultimate outcome for our business ideas, however good they may be. The experiences of some of our e-champions do indicate that they compete on price, eroding margins and denying profit. There is a vital difference, though. These guys are using, or have used, price deliberately as a strategic weapon to gain consumer attention and market share, while building effective and broad relationships with their customers. Look a little harder and you will see that customer value is more important to them than mere low prices.

Chuck Schwab has always sought to offer the best value to customers, ever since he first launched his discount brokerage in 1971. When he put his successful eSchwab Internet business at the heart of Charles Schwab Corporation in January 1998, he gave all the company's customers access to a single price per trade. At a stroke he sacrificed $125 million of annualized revenue. In taking this enormous risk Chuck and his co-CEO, David Pottruck, were betting on their ability to provide unbeatable value to current and prospective Schwab customers whatever access route those customers chose – retail store, telephone, PC or Internet. In fact, Schwab offers such outstanding value that customers are prepared to pay a premium price of $29.95, i.e. 100 per cent or more higher than Schwab's nearest online rival, E*Trade.

For Mike Harris and Egg price was the key factor that got him to his five-year target in only seven months. Mike made an unbeatable offer to his customers with the high rate of interest that Egg was prepared to pay on their savings. Mike used price again when launching subsequent products – mortgages and credit cards. Now, he knows it will be customer value not price that will determine Egg's success as he builds rich relationships with his customers sharing margin with them and creating value for investors. But how can he be sure he can build lasting customer value?

'Free' is the ultimate in price competition, and that is just what John Pluthero anticipated was required to establish a large customer base rapidly. Advertising, and a share of the interconnect charges from customers' telephone calls when using Freeserve, helped to defray the cost of this free service, but they only made a contribution. Pluthero has always known that he needs to build true value-based relationships with Freeserve customers to generate significant revenue streams, if he is to justify the capital price of $4,000 or more that investors are ascribing to each customer. Now, customer calls to use Freeserve are free in response to aggressive competition in the UK Internet service provider marketplace. With the loss even of interconnect revenues, and no subscription fees to boot, the challenge that John and his team face in building a major business worth many billions of dollars is even more daunting. The jury may be out on whether Freeserve will achieve what is required, but investors have no doubt. They are remaining very definitely in.

So, what gives our e-champions the confidence and underpins their unswerving faith in what they are doing? They have a clear perception of the role of customer value in digital business and of how it leads, or will lead in turn, to profits and returns to investor.

Let's find out how to share their confidence in our own digital initiatives.

Summary

In this chapter we have considered the issues that confront the businessperson in this new digital age. Experience will count for little in a world that demands fresh thinking, new mindsets and imagination. Digital business is very different. It requires fast decisions and equally rapid action for large-scale success. Price competition and commoditization may well be essential in the short-term but customer value is the key to sustainable success.

In the next chapter we will:

▶ Grasp the full meaning of value and its implications
▶ Discover the linkage between network and customer dynamics
▶ Explore the consequent Value Lever framework

8

In search of value

▶ Appreciating the meaning of customer value and grasping the extent of the challenge it presents
▶ How evaluation of new competitive forces and customer realities leads to an effective framework for building lasting customer value
▶ The eight Value Levers of content integration; freeware; mass customization; real-time activity; prosumer involvement; agenting; new market forum and intercustomer relationship
▶ A detailed evaluation of the Value Lever framework and how each lever is constructed
▶ Relating Value Levers to events, experience and cases in the network economy

Whose value is it anyway?

'What is perceived as 'of value' is a very personal thing', observes Christopher Barnatt of the University of Nottingham Business School, grappling for a meaning of value that looks beyond the purely rational and monetary sense that economists and businesses have long ascribed to the word. Value is subjective, and what it is, or isn't, is determined solely by the viewpoint of the individual. No two individuals will attribute the same value to the same offering. As marketers have long known, but found difficult to grasp, value is a combination of rational and emotional assessment on the part of the consumer. Grab a consumer's interest with something relevant, make him or her an offer – this good or that service at this price – and the consumer will take a view. Does this feel right to me? Should I purchase? 'Value', observes Barnatt, 'is always something that any individual . . . would prefer to have rather than not have' (Barnatt, 1999).

In the network economy, so the conventional wisdom goes, consumers will exercise greater rationality as purchasers and users of goods and services. Confronted by infinite options and the opportunity to secure the lowest price, they will migrate from supplier to supplier. A sense of remoteness between customers and suppliers will preclude any opportunity to build relationships where added value can be demonstrated, higher prices charged and a better margin earned. But why should consumers change when they become active participants in the new economy? Emotional and rational components remain equally important in their online consuming behaviour.

The basic motivation of consumers may not change as they learn to purchase online. However, as they begin to flex their new network economy-derived power, consumers do feel the need to redress a lifetime of poor or indifferent service experiences on the high street, main street or in the mall. In the network economy consumers are less forgiving and have higher expectations. Their perceived value threshold online is generally much higher, and woe to any business that fails to recognize this. This presents perhaps the stiffest challenge for businesses since the vast majority have yet to offer even a satisfactory level of value to customers in the offline physical world, let alone begin to think of how to do it in the virtual one.

In creating value-based relationships with customers that are fit for the network economy, businesses, whether new or old, have to:

- ▶ stand out from the plethora of online options available to consumers generally, and overcome the propensity for migration to the lowest price at the click of a mouse;
- ▶ bridge that sense of remoteness that many businesses perceive exists between customers and themselves in any virtual interaction; and
- ▶ recognize that customers' perceived value thresholds have been raised for all time by a redistribution of market power from vendor to buyer

The business task is made that much harder for the fact that the rules of engagement have changed. 'The Internet has revolutionized the way businesses function', affirms Eric Marcus of US-based research organization Concours Group, 'The old ways cannot compete in a world where strategy and action come together. We have moved to a world that operates in Web time with new thinking, products, services and ways of doing business' (Marcus, 4/3/99). Yet, it need not be a superhuman task.

Competition, customers and value

Price, as Michael Porter observed, is the blunt instrument of competition. If you do not comprehend the competitive forces driving business behaviour and turn them to your advantage, then the only outcome will be to compete on price, leading to the consequent erosion of profits. Porter devised the technique for us to avoid this inevitability in the old stable physical world of business, but his methods now have limited value in a world dominated by virtual forces.

Online, consumers have limitless access to information and plentiful choices. This makes price-based competition and consequent

In search of value **161**

commoditization a much greater likelihood than it is in the physical world. To avoid this outcome we will need to take account of the new forces influencing the nature of competition in the network economy. These are the network dynamics that we isolated and evaluated in Chapter 3.

We also observed, in Chapter 5, how social trends merge to create a nexus of forces to impel the acceptance and prevalence of the network economy in society, and shape a set of distinctive customer dynamics. With the realignment of markets, from supplier bias to buyer bias, customer power becomes a dominant competitive force. So, the influence of the new customer dynamics will be strong.

If we can ascertain how the socially based customer dynamics interact with the technology-driven network dynamics, we can build a powerful framework to optimize propositions that will deliver outstanding value to customers, and produce in due course substantial returns for shareholders. What we will be doing is applying an explicit technique to match or even surpass that implicit understanding of value in the network economy that has earned our e-champions their remarkable successes.

Figure 8.1 illustrates the process for the generation of a framework of Value Levers. In the remainder of this chapter we will construct

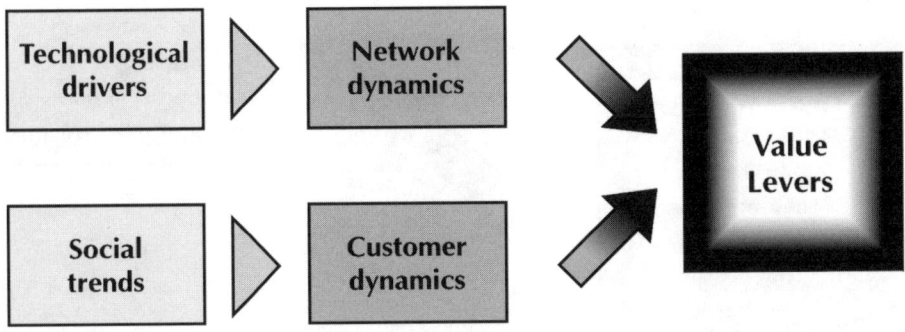

Figure 8.1 A framework for leveraging value

that framework and the basis for success in digital business, and in the following chapter we will examine how these levers work together in combination to generate maximum leverage, using the businesses of the e-champions to illustrate these remarkable tools.

■ The Value Levers

A closer evaluation of the eight network dynamics and eight customer dynamics reveals how these merge to build a powerful and distinct set of Value Levers – as illustrated in Figure 8.2. This Value Lever framework offers outstanding possibilities for building true value-based relationships with customers.

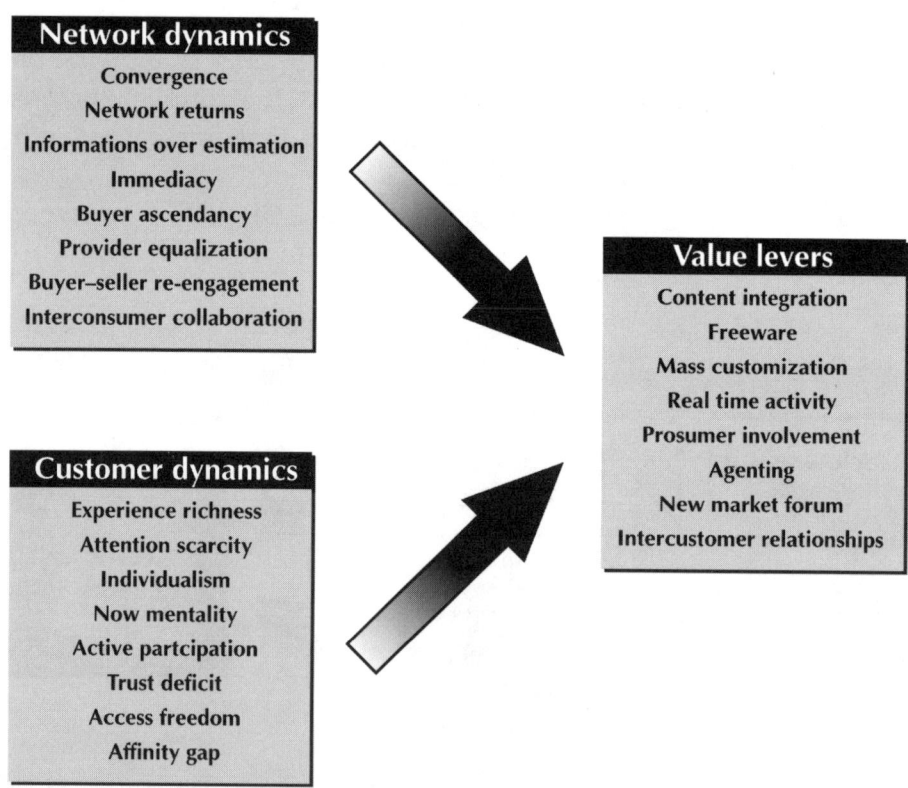

Figure 8.2 Customer dynamics, network dynamics and Value Levers

A description of each Value Lever follows with examples of their application.

Content integration

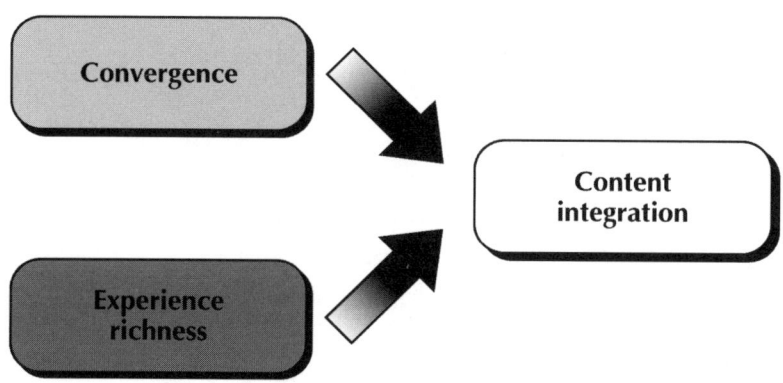

Characteristics of content integration
Bringing together information from many sources relevant to a context
Providing a rich bubble of experience to consumers
Impelling business towards a lifestyle role
Building value through differentiated content
Recognizing the importance of content to all businesses in the network world

'In every case, content plays a central role for companies conducting network commerce', concludes a report prepared for the European Commission by Cap Gemini. 'All businesses become content businesses as they move to the network world.' Information-based content in the form of text, audio and visuals in digitally based formats is fundamental to the workings of the network economy. It doesn't matter if the firm's product is physical, it can still be represented in digital format as a means to attract attention and interest potential customers. Core to the impact of the Value Lever of content integration is the fact that the cost of content reproduction and distribution in a digital environment is greatly reduced. 'Digital

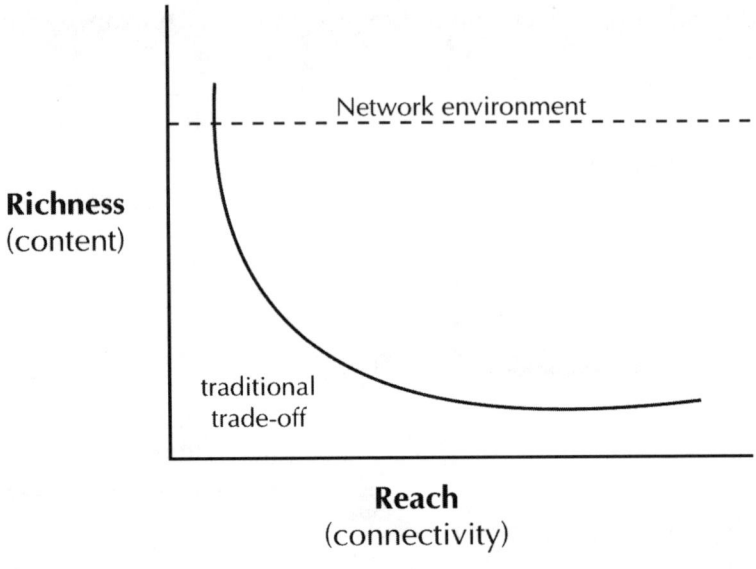

Figure 8.3 The reach–richness trade-off

networks dramatically alter the cost of content creation and distribution', continues the European Commission's report. 'Digital content can be reproduced at a fraction of the cost of physical content. Ever-increasing computing power continues to reduce the cost of creating and manipulating digital content' (European Commission, 1998).

Rich content can be assembled and distributed almost infinitely in the network environment. This has major implications for how a business communicates with its various communities of interest, and particularly with its current and prospective customers. Boston Consulting Group consultants Philip Evans and Thomas Wurster term this the 'reach–richness trade-off' (see Figure 8.3) (Evans and Wurster, 11/99).

In a non-network environment, physical and cost restraints make it difficult to reach a large audience and deliver a rich message at one and the same time. So, a salesperson can deliver a presentation and enjoy a powerful exchange with just a handful of people. To reach a really large market simultaneously will require, say, a broadcast advertising message. In this case, the number of people reached might be extensive, the content will be limited and there will be no interaction. The curve on the graph in Figure 8.3 shows the trade-off. So, *reach* refers to the number of people who can access the information, and therefore has to do with connectivity, while *richness* is to do with the amount or quality of information that can be provided. There are three elements of *richness*, say Evans and Wurster. The first element refers to the amount of information that can be moved between sender and receiver in a given time; technologists call this bandwidth. The second aspect refers to the degree to which information can be customized for the receiver, and the third refers to the extent to which the receiver can interact with the information being sent.

In a network world, with limitless one-to-many and many-to-one connections, the classic reach–richness trade-off curve ceases to apply. It then becomes possible to achieve almost infinite *reach* and deliver content *richness* at one and the same time. Network economy-literate vendors can deliver content-rich experiences to large numbers of consumers, drawing material in real-time from a wide variety of different sources. The facility do this is remarkably simple and is universally available to everyone. So, content delivered must be sufficiently compelling for the defined target recipients, and must also be differentiated from that of other providers. The straight line on the graph in Figure 8.3 demonstrates the impact of infinite reach without compromise of richness.

Content integration is a Value Lever used by many different providers on the Internet. Portal websites such as Freeserve, Yahoo! and Netscape Online provide relatively undifferentiated content to large numbers of users for them to customize to their own blends. Other sites provide more in-depth and context-specific forms of content. Travel sites such as Expedia and ThomasCook provide the capacity for consumers to experience the destination of their choice, in some case down to the view from the hotel room on offer. In addition consumers can access a full range of travel services to convert their virtual experience into a real one.

The importance of content integration as a Value Lever has been strongly emphasized by the merger between leading Internet portal company AOL and media giant Time Warner. Conscious of the ever-increasing bandwidth of the Internet and its potential for 'richness', AOL was looking for the ultimate source of content. Time Warner had its success rooted in the offline economy. Seeing the inevitable convergence of the Internet with broadcast media it wanted access to 'reach' that went beyond the limitations of broadcast media. The merger provides the solution for both and will precipitate more convergence and impel the issue of content yet further. For the consumer, expected increases in digital message 'bandwidth', to enable virtually unlimited content, including full broadcast quality video, will further intensify the richness of experience available.

Freeware

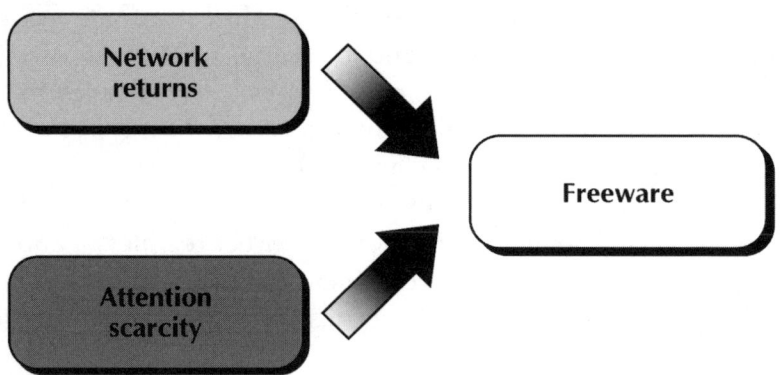

Characteristics of freeware
Creating demand when consumer attention is scarce
Giving away or discounting a key component of the offering to secure critical mass
Increasing value to all customers

There are two principles underlying the application of this Value Lever. One principle seizes consumer 'mindshare' to fuel market share, the other leverages that remarkable feature of the network environment, the law of increasing returns, which we described in

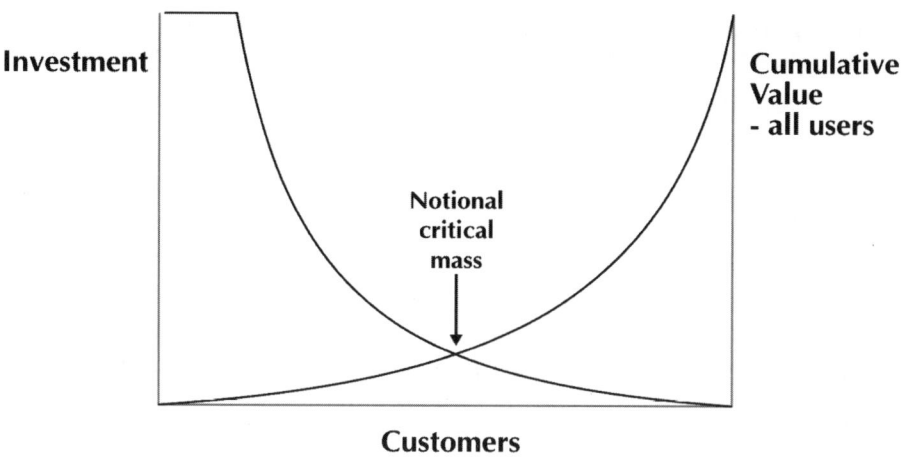

Figure 8.4 Leveraging network returns

Chapter 3. The two principles can be used to reinforce one another and make freeware a powerful business weapon.

Most consumers now live frenetic lives, and are bombarded with an ever-growing number of marketing messages. For vendors, catching the attention of potential customers is difficult, burdened as consumers are with a surfeit of information on a plethora of products and services. As Kevin Kelly observes, 'the only factor becoming scarce in a world of abundance is human attention' (Kelly, 1998). So, offering products or services for free can provide an effective means for vendors to capture a share of the ultra-scarce resource of human attention, or what marketers sometimes refer to as 'mindshare'. But, if a vendor gives away products and services away for free, how does that supplier make money? One trick is to develop multiple revenue streams, so that the main product can be given away, but profits can be generated from the selling of other products or services that complement the main product. Online brokerage E*Trade gives away free stock quotes, charts, investment information and news, but then charges for more sophisticated services such as online brokerage and portfolio management. In the UK, Egg's approach of providing almost unbelievable interest rates for savers is a variant on this. It is a loss leader to attract attention and gain customers.

The second principle underlying freeware is illustrated in Figure 8.4. The cost of reproducing a product or service made available across a network diminishes at an exponential rate as the number of users grows. As this takes place, the value of the product or service to every user and customer who has acquired that product or service increases at an exponential rate, in accordance with the law of increasing returns. In the reality of network returns in Chapter 3 we used the example of the online insurance portfolio to illustrate how people can be encouraged to recruit others to use the service to increase their own benefit.

At the intersection of cost and value in Figure 8.4, critical mass is notionally achieved. Beyond this point the network-based product or service will achieve relatively low costs and a relatively high value to both the supplier and to every user. The key here is for the supplier to ensure that it achieves a sufficiently high number of users for its network-based product or service to achieve critical mass. One way to help achieve this is, of course, to either give away a core component of the product or service for free or to give it away for free until such a time as critical mass is achieved. The achievement of increasing value to all users or customers will depend upon how adept the provider is at creating an implicit or explicit awareness of the role other customers play in the overall value proposition for each customer. This has the same basic principle as the technique of 'viral' marketing, which uses the network effect to achieve exponential reach with a message. It goes beyond that principle, however, since momentum is sustained and amplified by the ever-increasing value to all users from each additional one enlisted.

An extreme example of this is Alladvantage, which takes the freeware concept to the limit and actually pays consumers for their attention. Download a small application that displays advertising in a box on your screen while you are online, and Alladvantage will pay you $0.25 per hour and up to $40 per month. If you then introduce other users, you get an additional $0.10 for each hour they use Alladvantage, and so on. Quite simply, Alladvantage is applying familiar multilevel or network marketing from the physical world to the virtual world of the network economy. Value increases to all through more and more users, with the revenue supplied by advertisers. Some three months after launch in September 1999 Alladvantage reportedly had over 2 million users from a standing start.

Mass customization

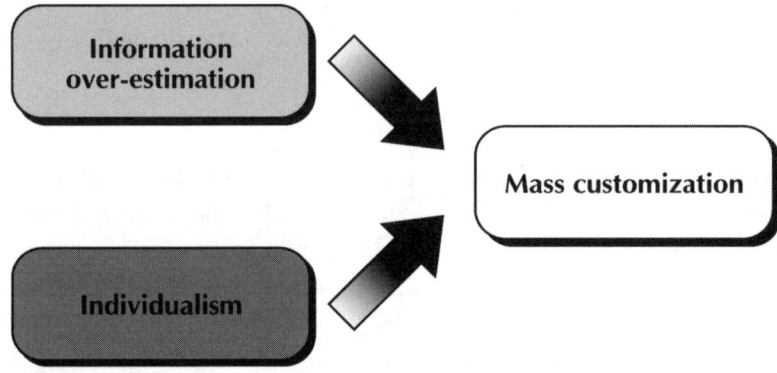

Characteristics of mass customization
Making an offering that is unique to each customer
Responding to individual needs
Creating perceived switching costs in the mind of the customer
Developing a real dialogue with the customer and getting it right every time

Three factors make mass customization vitally important as a Value Lever. Firstly, the acquisition by suppliers of accurate and detailed information about customers is far easier in the network economy. Customer data from virtually any type of communication can be recorded in a form that is digital or can be easily accessed and used digitally. Secondly, the use of digital technology greatly facilitates the personalization of products and services to individual customer need, as mass customization expert Joe Pine affirms: 'Anything you can digitize, you can customize' (Pine, 1992). Thirdly, customers want to be treated as individuals for many, if not most, of their consumer needs. 'Technology makes it possible to create, cheaply and consistently, a customer offering that is unique; not just one time, but every time', remark Larry Downes and Chunka Mui, 'and nowhere is it more viable than in cyberspace' (Downes and Mui, 1998).

Marketing consultants Don Pepper and Dr Martha Rogers of Marketing 1:1 Inc. distinguish between the production process of mass customization and the parallel marketing technique which they term 'one-to-one' strategy (Peppers and Rogers, 1997). Working with Joe Pine, Peppers and Rogers laid down the underlying principles.

> A company that aspires to give customers exactly what they want must . . . use technology to become two things: a mass customizer that efficiently provides individually customized goods and services, and a one-to-one marketer that elicits information from each customer about his or her specific needs and preferences. The twin logic of mass customization and one-to-one marketing binds producer and consumer together in what we call a learning relationship – an ongoing connection that becomes smarter as the two interact with each other, collaborating to meet the consumer's needs over time. (Pine, Peppers and Rogers, 3/95)

This learning relationship is the cornerstone of successful mass customization. The more time and effort that customers invest in responding to suppliers and enabling them to meet their particular needs, the less likely they are to switch to another vendor. An open dialogue between customer and supplier, through whatever access mechanism – physical or virtual – will build to create a mutual and respected understanding.

The effective application of the mass customization Value Lever will also have important implications for the way that managers interpret their business and its performance in the network economy. 'Share-of-customer' quickly replaces 'share-of-market' as a key business goal, illustrated in Figure 8.5.

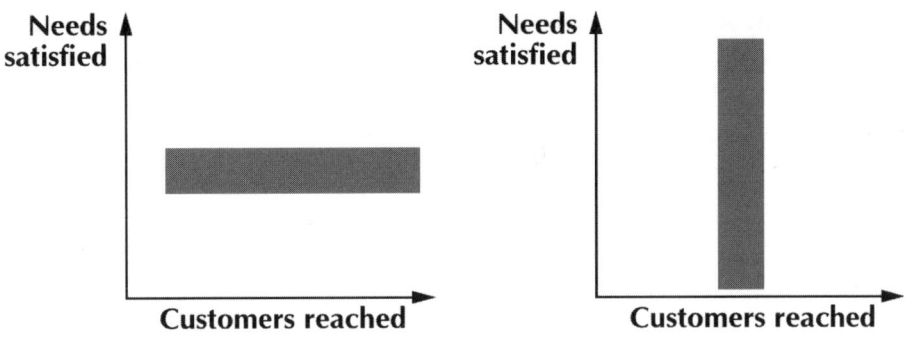

Adapted from Peppers & Rogers, 1997

Figure 8.5 Aggregate vs. one-to-one marketing approaches

The aggregate marketing approach is predominantly product driven. It treats all customers in any single market as the same, seeking to meet a common need with the same product. In contrast, the one-to-one approach is customer driven, aiming to sell as many products and services as possible to a given customer through a deeper relationship developed over time. The deeper relationship flows from the tailoring of offerings to meet each customer's needs. A company then repeats this process for every other customer who offers a similar prospect of profitable returns.

Mass customization is one of the most challenging levers to apply; it is also one of the most powerful. It requires an effective technology and organizational infrastructure inside companies to enable the development of learning relationships with customers. Having the right systems is only one part of the issue. Being able to store, sift through and use data from customer communications and transactions, in order to personalize responses and orchestrate purchases, presents a task in itself. Few organizations are yet doing it well.

Online grocery purchasing and delivery service Peapod, based in Skokie, Illinois, illustrates the potential. Peapod's online shopping service enables customers to search, compare, substitute, sort and categorize purchase selections from a wide range of supermarkets, This they can do on the basis of a variety of features such as brands, price, quantity and nutritional contents (e.g. calorific value, fat, protein, carbohydrates, cholesterol and sodium). Customers value this facility, which is also the basis of Peapod's mass-customization strategy. Peapod actively uses its record of all customer purchases to offer customized inventory recommendations and automated refill recommendations, using prompts such as: 'You normally order pasta weekly. You haven't ordered any for the last two weeks. You may want to consider ordering more before you run out.'

Our e-champions clearly find mass customization equally challenging and it is as yet used widely by only three of them: Schwab, Amazon and Dell. Amazon uses the lever in a fairly crude fashion, advising book or music customers what other products typically have been bought by people interested in the book or CD the customer is currently evaluating. Amazon also uses e-mail alerts to notify customers of new titles that are likely to fit their personal purchase profiles. For Schwab the provision of personalized information to investors is an important feature of setting them free from the need for advice and making them self-contained as their own broker. Order your computer online and Dell will keep you advised of important product data, possible upgrades and other information to help you manage your computer.

Of the seven e-champions, the two that have the most profitable businesses and are leaders in their respective sectors – Chuck Schwab and Michael Dell – are also the ones that are deploying mass customization to greatest effect. The significance of this probably also has something to do with the fact that their two companies are the longest established of the seven and owe much of their pre-digital success to a strongly personalized approach. For the more recently established businesses of the remaining e-champions, their preoccupation is to acquire customers as fast as possible in the search for real first-mover advantage. Mass customization is likely to feature more strongly as their businesses mature and competitive threats build.

Real-time activity

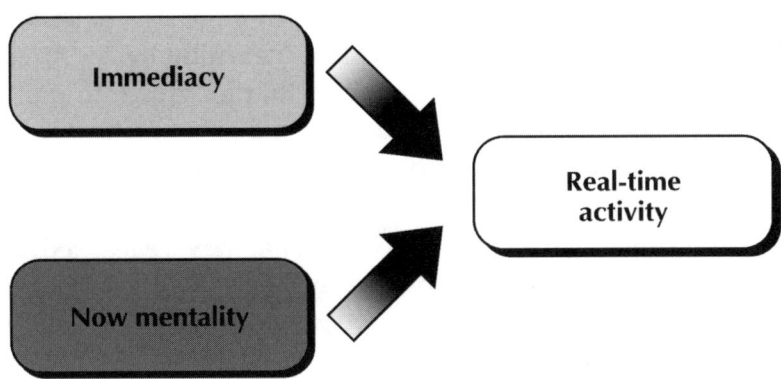

Characteristics of real-time activity
Responding to the instant nature of the networked world
Making speed an important component of the offering
Meeting customer needs satisfactorily in near-real time

Technological and social trends reinforce one another to make time a critical aspect of consuming behaviour and real-time activity an important Value Lever.

Consumers increasingly expect to have their needs met instantly. If a business fails to meet this almost universal expectation consumers will go elsewhere to competitors who can. 'You either move with speed or die. It's the converse of "speed kills"', says Richard McGinn, Chairman and CEO of Lucent Technologies (quoted in Gates, 1999). This desire for instant gratification means that customers automatically expect companies to respond quickly to their expressed needs. A real-time dialogue that provides marketing intelligence about customer behaviour requires a real-time response from businesses, and this is where the challenge arises. 'The new enterprise is a *real time enterprise* which is continuously and immediately adjusting to changing business conditions through information immediacy', agrees Don Tapscott (1995).

To become an effective real time enterprise places significant demands upon every aspect of a commercial organization's approach to business. 'All business operations – product development, processing, and strategy – need to occur in Web time', argues Eric Marcus of research organization Concours Group (Marcus, 4/3/99). Real-time activity needs to become a way of life if it is to be applied effectively as a means to leverage value. 'Learning cycles are much shorter on-line than off-line. Companies that are quick to try, quick to learn, and quick to adapt will win. Those that are fastest, and keep learning, will stay ahead', confirms strategist Gary Hamel:

> Companies that take months to assess what they've learned, whose internal processes don't run on Internet time, will get left behind. So it's pretty simple. If you don't believe deeply, wholly, and viscerally that the Net is going to change your business, you're going to lose. And if you don't understand the advantage of starting early and learning fast, you're going to lose. (Hamel, 7/12/98)

Gary Hamel's message is clear and unambiguous. Advantage can only accrue to companies that can think fast and act fast in the network economy. It requires alignment of every management process and organizational capability, or it won't work. 'Yeah, we have the systems, the people and processes to be able to respond in real time,' observed one client recently. 'The trouble is that it still takes us two years to make the decision.' Unless decisions speed up very soon the prognosis for his company is not good.

In the search for new business models time is a promising medium for the creative business person to consider and embrace. Time can be a key feature of a service and meet a real need for a large proportion of consumers. It can also be an important source of lost revenue among many service companies. Many service goods are perishable. What good is yesterday's unfilled airline seat or unoccupied hotel room? This has been an important factor underlying Jay Walker's business model for Priceline that invites consumers to bid for the seats or rooms that airlines or hotels know are less likely to be filled. Lastminute.com is a UK-based organization that applies a variation on this theme, taking advantage of the high levels of unsold inventory for ticket-based services in the UK and offering last-minute deals to consumers on a range of services including luxury holidays, flights and entertainment tickets. Lastminute's stated aim is to 'encourage spontaneous, romantic and sometimes adventurous behaviour' by offering customers 'the chance to live their dreams at unbeatable prices'. Given that approximately £2 billion worth of hotel rooms, £10 billion worth of flights, and £1.2 billion worth of entertainment tickets go unsold each year in the UK, there is a huge opportunity for Lastminute to exploit its business model.

All of our e-champions, not just Jay Walker, recognize the importance of speed and immediacy and account for it in different ways. For Schwab, speed is essential in every aspect of his company's operations to enable his customers to conduct effective online trading. For Pierre Omidyar, time is a key factor controlling the person-to-person auction model. For Dell, speed is what matters in the whole assembly and delivery of a computer that doesn't exist until a customer orders it. Delivery from Dell in Europe can take as little as two days from the moment the customer completes the purchase online.

Prosumer involvement

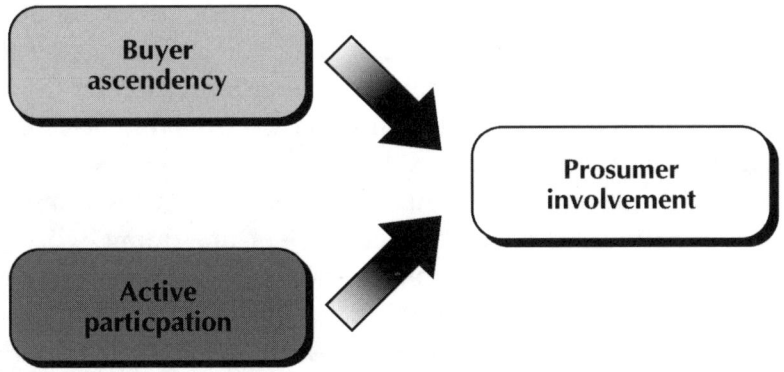

Characteristics of prosumer involvement
Enabling customers to create and deliver their own value
Making the customer an integral part of the value chain
Involving the customer in the production/administration process
Feeding customers' knowledge and ideas into new product development

Futurist Alvin Toffler coined the term 'prosumer' in 1970 in his book *Future Shock*. Toffler believed that the distinction between providers and consumers would become blurred as consumers became ever more closely involved in the production of the goods and services that they themselves consumed. As the network economy emerged, so Toffler's forecast has come true. Now we really are witnessing an increasing shift 'towards a much closer involvement of consumers in production' (Toffler, 1981).

What has made Toffler's forecast a possibility has been the growing use of Internet-based technology in computer networks inside organizations, known as 'intranets', as well as in the public environment of the electronic communications network linking people and organizations globally. Taking advantage of their intranets, companies have designed private external networks – extranets – that use the public Internet to enable external parties to access the company's internal systems and carry out directly many of the activities that employees would otherwise have completed. 'For a small investment, you can have the customer perform many of the expensive activities you can do today, including basic customer service, order entry and tracking, training, purchase order management, product configuration, and even product development', remark authors Larry Downes and Chunka Mui. 'The data you collect has far fewer errors because it has been handled only once, and then by the originating source. Cost savings on your end can come quickly and they are significant' (Downes and Mui, 1998). This is exactly what Schwab or E*trade customers and investors are actively doing when they trade online, or what Dell customers are doing when they specify their own computer configuration as they place their order on the Dell website.

What has made Toffler's forecast a reality has been the emerging customer dynamic of active participation and a growing desire for greater involvement among consumers in shaping and controlling their own service experiences. 'Customers are comfortable doing things themselves because it provides them with control and convenience. They don't have to rely on someone else to enter and read the correct information', confirms Evan Schwartz, 'And they can do all kinds of tasks whenever they want, without leaving their desktop – or their laptop' (Schwartz, 1997). So, the real power of prosumer involvement as a Value Lever lies in its potential both to reduce cost for the supplier as well as create value for the customer through an enhanced service experience at one and the same time.

Texas-based Garden Escape Incorporated demonstrates the outstanding potential of prosumer involvement. Also known as Garden.com, Garden Escape functions as 'a multi-dimensional garden resource' that provides 'the most comprehensive [source of] gardening information available in one place on the Internet'. Through its website, Garden Escape offers throughout the US more products (currently over 12,000) than any other gardening company in the world. The company's website provides many opportunities for prosumer involvement with its wide-range of interactive, garden-related facilities. These facilities include a 'Garden Doctor' service which allows customers to e-mail their questions to expert gardeners; chatrooms where customers can talk to other gardeners about gardening-related issues; an online garden notebook where customers can store their gardening notes, maintain an ongoing shopping list of garden supplies, and bookmark interesting product pages; a sophisticated 'Garden Planner' software application, which enables customers to design, redesign and save their own garden landscapes; and a plant-finding service that enables the customer to locate appropriate plants for their gardens in accordance with their personal preferences. Further prosumer-oriented facilities were added to the website in late 1998 with a service known as 'My Stuff', which enables customers to modify the website to match their own particular needs and preferences. The service also enables customers to review their own order history and order status with Garden Escape, and set up a gift registry and reminder service that can alert customers of impending birthdays, anniversaries or special events.

Agenting

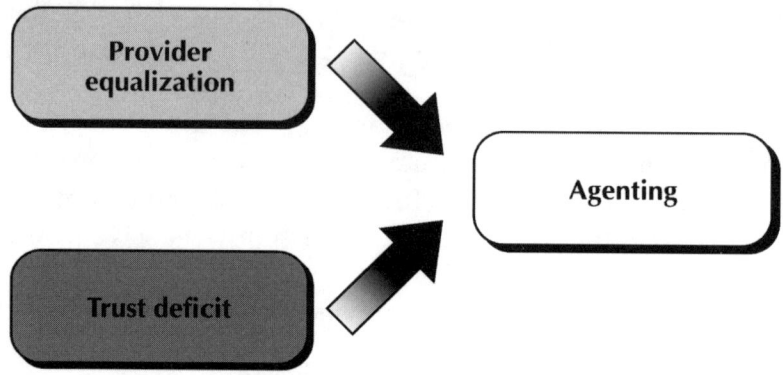

Characteristics of agenting
Helping consumers to make sense of the network environment
Providing a degree of certainty
Becoming a trusted guide
Facilitating access

Throughout the early growth of its public phase, the most prevalent search conducted on the Internet was to access pornography. It was only in late 1999 that the search for music in MP3 format took over the top search request spot. To a proportion of Internet users the Internet remains a questionable environment that raises concerns in their minds. For them at least the network world is an unmapped wilderness, a virtual prairie with occasional cyber habitation or other sign of digital civilization. European Internet users in particular still have high concerns about security, although this preconception typically falls away rapidly following a satisfactory initial online purchase. Still, levels of trust online are low.

But the Internet is not just about people, it's about businesses in countless forms with new, unfamiliar and indecipherable names, and that's even if you happen to speak English. The barriers to entry into any business sector in the networked world are low to non-existent, although success will require much more than just a virtual nameplate linked to some low-cost, third-party merchanting system for collecting the money. Brand becomes a guarantor for consumers online, and new brands can earn their spurs quickly in the network world if they have the right focus of effort and resource. So, a trusted guide plays an important role online and can be both an effective means of creating value for consumers and a source of revenue to businesses through commission earned on links to relevant and appropriate sites. The 'agent' role in the network environment seems to encompass three main tasks: enabling consumers to find their way around; providing them with access to the information they need or desire; and helping them to determine who can be trusted. Good examples of organizations conducting these agenting tasks are the operators of the better 'portal' websites.

As homes on the web for millions, portals now typically provide their users with an enormous range of online facilities. Arguably the leader of the portal pack is Yahoo! Founded in 1994 by Jerry Yang and David Filo, Yahoo! built its initial success as the Internet's leading search engine and website directory. Now the Yahoo! website offers an extensive range of services, including: personalized homepages; a news clipping service; various home-shopping faciles; online communities; free e-mail; online games; Internet chat facilities; and channel-based content covering a range of different topics of interest . Agenting is fundamental to Yahoo's! continuing success. 'It's all about extending, relentlessly, the navigational guide functionality of Yahoo!', says Yahoo! President and CEO Tim Koogle, 'and making it simple for users to come back to Yahoo!, help them navigate the Web and also consume things that are of value to them on the service' (Wilson, 29/6/98).

The challenge for the portal business is to extend continually its services to cater for a user base that is becoming ever more sophisticated in its online tastes and requirements. John Pluthero is capably demonstrating an ability to do just that as Freeserve's customer base continues to grow. He is well aware of the next major frontier for the portal business – rich multimedia and broadcast-quality video content made possible by almost limitless bandwidth. As the nature of the network evolves, so users will continue to need trusted guides and will value the role of agenting provided by portals.

The agenting role extends beyond portals and is vital to helping consumers everywhere optimize their online consuming behaviour.

Its presence is implicit in Jay Walker's Priceline, carried out automatically as part of the reverse auction process. Priceline customers submit the details of travel and the price they are prepared to pay. Agenting is applied by Priceline's computer systems in presenting customers offers to the accredited airlines linked to the Priceline network.

Agenting can become a fundamental part of any offering, and may also be used very effectively in conjunction with the content integration Value Lever to create a rich and rounded customer experience. Specialist sites like Mountainzone, aimed at people in interested in everything to do with mountains and mountaineering, and UK-based Simplyfood, with its copious coverage of all manner of food-, diet- and nutrition-related sources, are just two illustrations of how well this can be done.

As search engine capability improves, smart systems become more widely available and users become more familiar with the virtual world, agenting might lose a little of its edge as a Value Lever, but certainly not in the foreseeable future.

New market forum

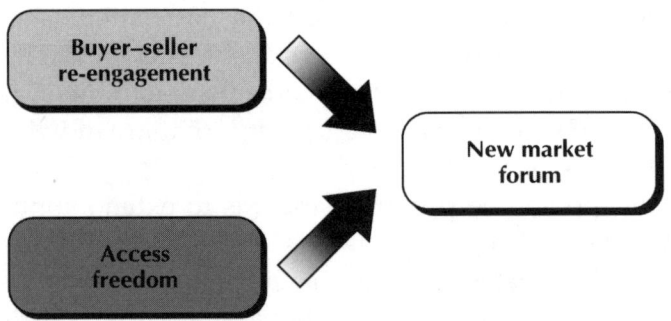

Characteristics of new market forum
Redefining buyer–seller interactions
Devising new approaches
Taking advantage of information asymmetries
Reverse-engineering markets

In the familiar physical world of Western society, the interaction between seller and prospective buyer is simple, clear-cut and almost universal in its application. The seller displays and offers goods at a price. The prospective buyer makes a value judgement and decides whether to purchase or not. The network economy offers all sorts of exciting possibilities to recast that exchange. Professors Shapiro and Varian attribute the potential to a digital environment that is 'a hybrid between a broadcast medium and a point-to-point medium' (Shapiro and Varian, 1999). But it is simpler than that. At the base level the potential is attributable to the network's capacity to offer infinite combinations for instant intercommunication – from one-to-one to many-to-many. Think of it as one big physical marketplace where countless thousands of businesses and countless millions of consumers can do business with one another – business to business, business to consumer, consumer to business or consumer to consumer.

Early views of the Internet saw a world where near perfect markets led generally to direct relationships between buyers and sellers and the elimination of large numbers of intermediaries and middlemen. Online consumers are certainly receptive to new and innovative means that enable them to make more effective comparisons, achieving even lower prices and better value where possible. However, they do not always resort to buying just the cheapest and cast aside the subjective and emotional elements of their purchasing behaviour. So, the Internet offers limitless potential for new ways of doing business that include all manner of opportunities for innovative intermediation as well as new and unfamiliar interfaces between buyer and seller. The possibilities are limited only by the bounds of applied imagination, as Internet author Walid Mougayar affirms: 'One of the key aspects of electronic commerce is to understand how buyers and sellers interact in the new digital markets, without being influenced by the preconceived notions of the physical world' (Mougayar, 1999).

Grasp the distinctive features of the networked world and it is difficult not to get caught in the excitement of new business possibilities. Think of information flowing though the network and recognize that every relevant source of information won't flow naturally or automatically to everybody who needs or wants that information. Identify where information does not flow satisfactorily, and you may discover the opportunity to provide potential buyers with an improved source that will enable them to leverage the stronger bargaining position that the Internet gives them. Or, you may devise a means to help sellers dispose of their wares more efficiently. So, the trick then is to perceive opportunities to rearrange behaviours in the network marketspace. Effectively, there are three main ways to do this and create new market forums – by empowering buyers, by organizing sellers, or by integrating marketplaces.

There are many possible options for reorganizing buyers. One option involves giving consumers power to aggregate their orders with other co-buyers to gain price advantage. 'The beauty of the idea is that it's totally consumer driven', says founder of Letsbuyit John Palmer, 'Potential customers simply tell us that they want to participate in a co-buy for a certain product. If we don't already have the item, we source it and negotiate an agreement with the manufacturer, We then post it on the site and aggregate the consumers. When we have enough of them, we close the deal and tell our customers by how much we've been able to drop the normal price.' Reportedly this leads to discounts of between 20 and 60 per cent. John Pluthero empowers Freeserve customers by giving UK consumers the opportunity to access the Internet in an affordable manner. Previously UK consumers had had to pay a subscription to an Internet service provider as well as pay local call charges to connect. John set them free – well almost – with an engaging portal service that continues to set the pace. Freeserve presents the market with a very powerful cohort of buyers.

Reorganizing sellers has proved to be a more problematic approach to new market forums. There is a list of failed virtual malls that did little to create customer value. IBM's WorldAvenue and Barclaysquare are two at the top of that list. They did a good job in linking sellers but failed to organize them in a way that was appealing to consumers, largely because they did little more than try to replicate a physical marketplace in marketspace. Among our e-champions, Jeff Bezos reorganizes sellers very effectively in every category that Amazon adds, as it transforms from Earth's Biggest Bookstore to Earth's

Biggest Selection. Michael Dell has now added an online superstore to the Dell offering. Gigabuys.com reorganizes sellers through a catalogue of over 30,000 computer-related products.

When it comes to reorganizing the marketplace, our e-champions provide excellent examples of what you can achieve. In turning his customers into their own brokers, Chuck Schwab created a business model that redefined the investment marketplace, supplying investors with personalized information at no cost and empowering them to make their own decisions. Pierre Omidyar realized that the Internet could be used to establish a centralized market forum where people could buy and sell unique items, as well as meet others with similar interests. The success of Pierre's radical concept can be evidenced in the fact that eBay is the world's most popular website in terms of time spent, with 10 million registered users spending an average of 105 minutes per month on the eBay site by the end of 1999. However, Jay Walker's Priceline must be the outstanding example of the application of the new market forum Value Lever. Priceline is based upon the completely novel concept of letting buyers name the price at which they are prepared to fly, buy a car or occupy a hotel room, and finding a match for that price. The Priceline model seems almost obvious if you accept the reality of customer power in the network economy – it seems alien and contrary if you don't

Imagination is the only constraint in discovering new ways to reorganize buyers, sellers or the market itself.

Intercustomer relationships

Characteristics of intercustomer relationships
Facilitating the development of a community of relationships
Enabling customers to share ideas and experiences with like-minded individuals
Empowering customers before someone else does
Providing a compelling environment

'The Internet is above all a medium that connects human beings together', reflects Egg's Mike Harris, encapsulating the notion that

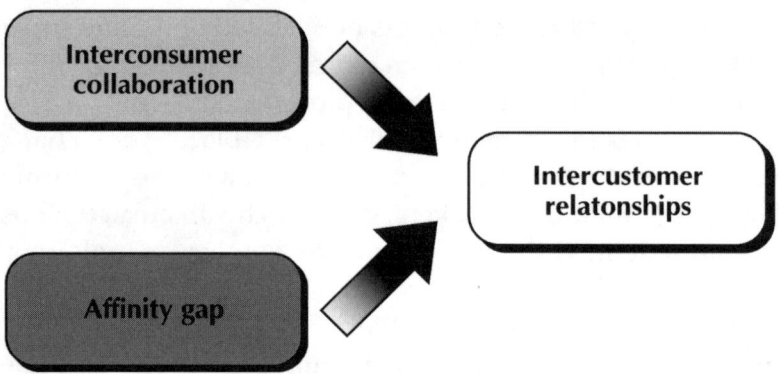

the network society is what matters, not the network economy. The Internet has the potential to alleviate, if not resolve, so many of the social trends that undermine developed society today. There is also a great sense of mutuality and preparedness to share information and content among Internet users. Yet for all this sense of humanity the network is an electronic and technological invention. 'It is far more important to realize that for all of its techno-wizardry the Internet is about people, not components', agrees Internet author Chuck Martin, 'Where there are people there is always the need for community. While some say that cyber community isn't real, it in fact has been a fundamental element in the development of the Internet from the beginning' (Martin, 1997). Maybe we don't yet really appreciate the power of the networked world to remedy the absence of affinity in present-day physical society.

With such powerful human and social factors in play, businesses bent on success in the network economy will have to acknowledge the important role that community-based relationships play in shaping the virtual environment. This means taking into account the possible impact of intercustomer relationships, and recognizing that they may be almost as important as the management of direct customer–vendor relationships. As customers become accustomed to the power that the network economy affords them, so they will look more and more to the opinions of other customers in helping them to shape their consuming experiences.

The significance of intercustomer relationships and their importance in reshaping the relationship between buyers and sellers in

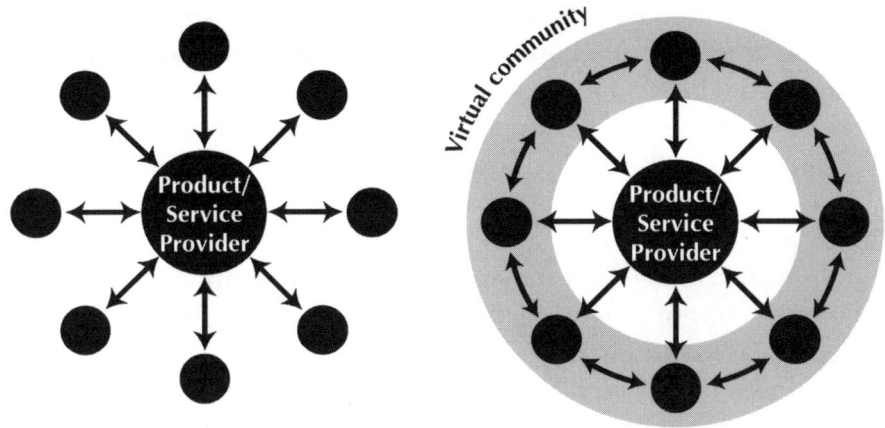

Figure 8.6 From relationship marketing to virtual community facilitation

the virtual environment have received much attention, due largely to the well-publicized work of two McKinsey consultants, John Hagel and Arthur Amstrong. In their view virtual communities – the facilitation of a network of relationships between customers – represented the first serious value-creation business model for the Internet, and they believed its adoption would lead to a paradigm shift in the way business is conducted.

Hagel and Armstrong suggested that a business should aim to facilitate relationships between its customers – not just with them, as Figure 8.6 suggests. This, they believed, would lead to virtual communities evolving into branded, first-port-of-call interfaces with which many consumers would develop lasting affinities. Consequently, they argued that those companies that were able to organize popular virtual communities could come to dominate business transactions over the Internet (Hagel and Armstrong, 1997). They were right in their logic and persuasive in their argument, to such an extent that many established businesses have considered the creation of online affinity groups to be deceptively easy. The inevitable result is that few businesses have had much success so far.

The reasons are clear. Businesses whose success springs from the physical world are unable to develop a sufficiently rich social environment in which a virtual community can flourish, preoccupied as they are with their own business needs. They are also concerned typically to exercise control over their defined communities. Communities have an existence of their own and cannot be controlled. Businesses have to enter into a true people-oriented community-minded consciousness if they are to succeed in online communities. Like other important things in life you just can't fake it and not expect to be found out.

Only two of our e-champions have overtly applied the intercustomer relationship Value Lever. Most successful in this has unquestionably been Pierre Omidyar and his community-minded eBay. The people who come to eBay's website do more than just buy and sell. Through the bulletin boards and online chat facilities provided at the eBay Café, users can get to meet and know each other, discuss topics of mutual interest, and petition one another for information. For many users, eBay becomes an integral part of their lifestyles, and a number of individuals have built up successful businesses as a result of selling items on eBay. The sense of community created by eBay has also extended to the offline environment, with groups of eBay users frequently planning events and vacations together. Members of the community also organize grassroots movements to improve the environment where they work or play. Online the eBay community is self-policing, so that users often form 'neighbourhood watch' groups to help guard against misuse or violations of website etiquette. 'We started with commerce, and what grew out of that commerce was community', says eBay CEO Meg Whitman, 'So we think of ourselves as sort of a community-commerce model. And what we've basically done is put in place a marketplace, a venue, where people can be successful dealing with one another' (*Business Week Online*, 21/5/99).

The other e-champion with a mind to intercustomer relationship application is Jeff Bezos. Amazon is keen to help its customers develop the sense that they belong to a community of like-minded individuals, and offers services such as chatrooms and bulletin boards which seek to bring together people sharing common interests. If you search for a book in a given subject area, you are effectively within a micro-community of people with similar interests, and you can benefit from their judgement if you want to. This philosophy will remain integral to Amazons' thinking as it extends its service to auctions, flea markets and beyond.

While other e-champions have not tapped intercustomer relationships explicitly, they have done so implicitly, relying upon word of mouth and word of mouse to fuel spectacular growth rates. For Chuck Schwab, the growth of eSchwab required customer engagement and involvement to achieve the remarkable quarter on quarter growth through 1997, 1998 and 1999. Visit just one of the 300 or more Schwab retail outlets across the USA to experience just how strong that implicit intercustomer relationship can be in the physical world. Perhaps for Freeserve the application of this Value Lever is slightly more tenuous, even though it will have contributed to its spectacular early growth. But what is clear is that Pluthero's sustained success and achieved target of 5 million users in five years will have to rely upon an ability to embrace intercustomer relationships whole-heartedly and with a strong underlying social perspective.

Few companies have really succeeded in applying the Value Lever of intercustomer relationship well. This only goes to indicate the scale of the opportunity that is still there to be seized. Perhaps more than any other Value Lever it requires the development of an application that is uniquely sensitive to the network society.

Summary

The means of achieving success in the digital business world owe little to the methods that previously delivered success in the physical business world. A fresh mindset is required together with new tools and techniques suited to the digital environment. Businesses that fail to understand the implications are unlikely to succeed in this changed business landscape. They are likely to find themselves prey to endless price-based competition as their customers desert to better options, whatever those may be. By understanding how the socially based customer dynamics interact with the technology-driven network dynamics, we can build a powerful framework of

Value lever	Definition
Content integration	Bringing together information from a variety of different sources specific to a context. In the network economy, all businesses have to become content providers, but value only accrues through differentiated content. Content impels businesses towards a lifestyle role.
Freeware	Creating demand in a competitive environment where consumer attention is a scarce resource. Giving away a key component of the offering, and then selling the add-ons and wrap-around content.
Mass customization	Making an offering that is unique to each customer. Responding to individual needs and creating perceived switching costs in the mind of the customer. It's about making it easy, creating a real dialogue and getting it right every time.
Real-time activity	Responding to the instant nature of the networked world. Making speed an important component of the offering. Meeting customer needs satisfactorily in (or near to) real-time.
Prosumer involvement	Facilitating customers to create and deliver their own value. Making them part of the production of administration process. Using their knowledge and ideas in the product specification and/or product development process.
Agenting	Becoming the trusted guide, facilitating access and providing a degree of certainty. Agenting is about helping consumers to make sense of the network environment.
New market forum	Creating new ways to redefine buyer–seller interactions and how these are achieved. Auctions – single, double sided and reverse, competitor price comparisons, quote services are some options.
Intercustomer relationships	Developing community of relationships. Enabling customers to share ideas and experiences with like-minded individuals. If you don't empower and enable customers, they will empower themselves – or others will help them.

Figure 8.7 The Value Lever framework

In search of value **189**

Value Levers to optimize propositions that will deliver outstanding value to customers, and produce in due course substantial returns to shareholders (see Figure 8.7).

In the next chapter we will:

▶ Explore the application of the Value Lever framework
▶ See how combining Levers amplifies advantage
▶ Review our e-champions business from a Value Lever perspective

9

Digital value profiles

▶ Appreciating the extent of the Value Lever framework's powers
▶ Discovering how levers combine to confer greater advantage
▶ Understanding the seven e-champions' companies through summary case studies
▶ Building digital value profiles of their businesses
▶ Assessing their implicit application of Value Levers

Combining Value Levers for advantage

In the previous chapter we explored the eight Value Levers and the distinctive impact of each of them upon successful businesses in the network economy. Understanding their influence one by one falls short of conveying the power that the Value Levers impart when combined selectively to amplify the core customer value proposition at the heart of a business model. In this chapter we will explore how our e-champions' businesses stand up to scrutiny of their implicit application of the Value Lever framework.

For each e-champion business we will develop a Digital Value Profile. This is an appraisal of the intensity with which each business appears to have applied the Value Levers in achieving their respective successes.

Before we consider those seven profiles we will review briefly how particular pairings of Value Levers can work together almost naturally to strengthen and amplify the benefit of one another in many circumstances.

How Value Lever pairings can make the net work for you

Prosumer involvement and mass customization

Think of these two Value Levers as being at either end of a continuum. Personalizing to the needs of a customer depends upon having enough relevant data to be able to refine the service, product or experience to his or her needs. How do you get that data? It may come from previous transactions captured in the physical world, or from purchased third-party market research data that tells you something about that person. Whatever the source, you need to know a fair amount about the customer to ensure that mass customization is truly creating value, and is not applied in a vacuum with negative effects. Prosumer involvement – enabling consumers to create and deliver their own value – can work hand-in-glove with mass customization to provide the basis of a mutually beneficial learning relationship. The proactively involved consumer is directly engaged in shaping his or her own experience. Prosumer involve-

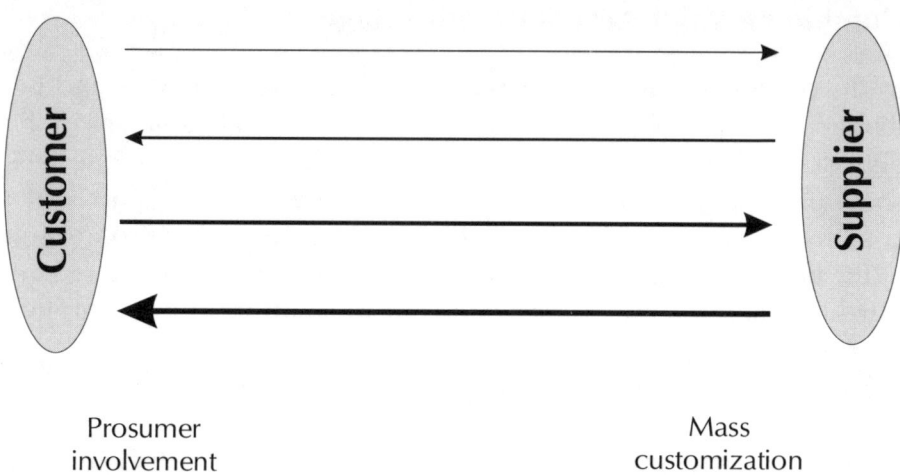

Figure 9.1 The prosumer–customization continuum

ment provides the data for effective mass customization to be applied in a subsequent response that triggers further prosumer involvement, and so on (Figure 9.1).

Real-time activity and new market forum

One thing above all distinguishes the network economy from the earlier industrial one: the capacity for instant intercommunication with anyone and everyone wherever, so long as they are connected. It is this simple fact that underpins the really successful applications of new market forum. Thinking in real time is difficult enough for most business people; doing in real time presents an even greater challenge, particularly for their organizations. Yet, developing the capacity for real-time activity will help to create the fresh mindset required to conceive new business models and the potential for applying the new market forum Value Lever. It also follows that where there is a really good new business model, the capacity for real-time activity will almost certainly exist. Remember that it is not just at the customer interface that real-time activity is required, it is almost certainly necessary in every element of the business process that exists to serve that interface.

Content integration and agenting

In the network economy every business becomes a content provider. The web enables us to cater for the demand among consumers for rich experiences and bring together all manner of content to help create a personalized bubble of experience. Content integration involves bringing the content to the point of interface with the consumer. For some elements of the process you may need to create the illusion of bringing the content to the interface, and that is where agenting comes in. Using the power of connectivity you may need to direct the customer to visit other websites in order to locate, in real time, elements of the total experience. In this way agenting supports content integration. Agenting has the distinct purpose of fulfilling the role of the trusted guide. Know which lever you are using and why. If you send someone from your site through agenting without embedding first a reason for that person to return, such as to continue a personalized content integration-defined experience, then you may lose a prospective customer.

Freeware and intercustomer relationships

Essential to the successful application of freeware is the achievement of critical mass for the network-based product or service in question. Beyond the point of critical mass, the number of users confers sufficient incremental value to each and every user that the network expands of its own accord. Word of mouth – the physical means of intercommunication – and word of mouse – its electronic equivalent – are pivotal to reaching and exceeding the critical mass threshold. Leveraging intercustomer relationships may fulfil an important role in underpinning success here. This is about understanding human nature and using that knowledge to seed communications that will flow between existing customers and to prospective ones.

■ Digital Value Profiles

To make Digital Value Profiles of our e-champions' businesses really useful we will need to consider not just which Value Levers have been utilized, but also the relative strength with which each has been applied. We have added a scale of one to five for this purpose in the following seven assessments. The Digital Value Profile for each business is portrayed graphically followed by a short background to the business and then an explanation of why that business has apparently earned that profile on a lever-by-lever basis. These profiles should then provide you, the reader, with the additional knowledge, and confidence, you need to begin to apply the Value Lever framework to your own digital activities.

Charles Schwab Corporation

Value Lever	Intensity
Content integration	▬▬▬▬▬▬▬▬▬▬
Freeware	▬▬
Mass customization	▬▬▬▬▬▬▬▬
Real-time activity	▬▬▬▬▬▬▬▬
Prosumer involvement	▬▬▬▬▬▬▬▬
Agenting	▬▬▬▬▬▬
New market forum	▬▬▬▬▬▬▬▬
Intercustomer relationships	▬▬

Background
Founded in 1971, the San Francisco-based Charles Schwab & Company emerged to prominence in the late 1970s as a result of its cheap and convenient 'no-frills' share-dealing service, which established the company as the pioneer of discount brokerage in the USA. In more recent years, Schwab has broadened its approach to develop a 'full-service investing experience', which involves giving consumers access to a similar range of facilities to those offered by the traditional brokerage houses, against whom Charles 'Chuck' Schwab 'rebelled' more than twenty years ago.

Schwab grew very rapidly and took advantage of its increasing revenues to invest heavily in technology, including in 1985 a number of PC-based offerings. The company introduced PC-based share-trading using a proprietary system in 1993 and launched automated phone dealing the following year, but the company's entry into the world of Internet-based trading occurred almost by accident. In late 1994 a small research team wanted to demonstrate an experimental form of software developed to enable Schwab's different computer systems to talk to one another. The project engineers chose a simple web-based stock trade as a quickly thought-up means to demonstrate the software. Chuck Schwab was so astounded – 'I fell off my chair' comments Schwab – that he quickly set up a new electronic brokerage unit called eSchwab to learn about, develop and implement an Internet-based trading capability.

By the middle of 1996, the eSchwab team was ready to deploy its newly developed online facilities for customers via its website. With little marketing effort, the new service was an immediate success with customers. Within two weeks of launch eSchwab had signed up over 25,000 customers, which had previously been set as the target for the end of the year. By 1996 year-end Schwab had over 600,000 active online accounts with $42 billion in online customer assets. By 1997 year-end Schwab had 1.2 million active online accounts with $80 billion in online customer assets. The success of eSchwab forced a pivotal decision upon Schwab management. In early 1998 they decided that the new electronic brokerage arm should be integrated into the rest of the organization, so that the Internet-based operations would provide a core component of the business as a whole. This decision was the cause of much soul-searching, since it meant that all customers – no matter what channel they were using – would have access to eSchwab's lower, Internet-based pricing structure.

In making this decision Chuck Schwab correctly guessed that he would have had to do so anyway sooner or later, and that it would be much harder – and more costly – to make the move later, rather than sooner. He also realized that cannibalizing his own business could be managed and controlled, while letting someone else eat up his business would be far more destructive. 'What it came down to was, if you don't eat your young, somebody else will', commented Piper Jaffray analyst William Burnham (Flynn, Summer 1998). The initial impact of Schwab's move cut revenues at a stroke and the stock market cut its valuation of the company, which fell 9 per cent on the announcement of the revenue drop. But the outcome was to vindicate fully Chuck's bold move. By the end of 1998 Schwab had 2.3 million online investors with $174 billion of online assets, confirming Schwab as the market leader in online brokerage. Schwab is now one of the largest electronic commerce businesses in the USA, and arguably represents 'the most successful embrace of e commerce by any major corporation outside the technology industry', providing 'an object lesson in how the Net can transform an entire enterprise' (Gunn, 7/12/98).

Today, Charles Schwab & Company forms part of a group of companies owned by the Charles Schwab Corporation, whose overall aim is 'to provide the most useful and ethical financial services' to consumers. By December 1999, the Charles Schwab Corporation was entrusted with more than $725 billion in client assets, and was serving 6.6 million active investor accounts. Schwab is now also one of the top three mutual fund distributors in the USA, and its OneSource mutual fund marketplace offers more than 800 mutual funds from 120 families (including its own proprietary funds).

Content integration
In Schwab's view, the future rests with organizations that give their customers the most freedom to make their own informed decisions, so relevant information is vital to the process. In offering customers access to a very broad range of reliable information services – research, charts, historical data, analysts' reports, software tools and economic trends, etc. – in a very accessible fashion, Schwab believes it will win both loyalty and a larger share of customers' assets. 'Price is not the transforming event', says David Pottruck, President and co-CEO, 'The transforming event is the ability to deliver personalized information to the customer in real time, at virtually no cost' (Gunn, 7/12/98).

Freeware
When Schwab launched its internet trading service, eSchwab, in mid-1996, it attracted 25,000 customers in the first month. Six months later at the end of 1996 it had over 600,000 active customers

and well over a million by the end of 1997. Investors generally prefer markets with a large numbers of participants, are less volatile and are more liquid. This preference can lead to a herd instinct. This human tendency may well have enabled Schwab to tap this Value Lever and secure significant first mover advantage as well, with all customers gaining from each and every additional eSchwab user.

Mass customization
For customers to be their own brokers they need information that is relevant to them and their portfolios. For Schwab, providing personalized information is fundamental to making people self-directed but it is not the strongest Value Lever application in the profile.

Real-time activity
Real-time is elemental to online brokerage success from a customer perspective. David Pottruck sums up Schwab's real-time philosophy and capability: 'The key to our success is how we melded the Internet into the middle of who we are and what we try to do for our customers. . . . We obviously don't have any idea where the Internet is going. We only know it's going very fast and flexibility is very important' (Skelly, 7/10/98). Every aspect of the Schwab operation is real-time, including the decision making!

Prosumer onvolvement
'On Schwab's website you can look up real-time quotes, news, historical financial data, or use sophisticated software tools. You can customize the home page to see your personal account when you log on', says Eileen Gunn of *Fortune* magazine. 'You can set up your own asset-allocation model, screen for the best-performing mutual funds that fit that model, and then buy the funds through Schwab' (Gunn, 7/12/98). Schwab uses prosumer involvement to support mass customization.

Agenting
Agenting is used by Schwab in support of its content integration activities. For example, Schwab has tied up with portal company Excite and Intuit's Quicken.com to provide content about retire-

ment, mortgages, investing, taxes and insurance. To Schwab, being a trusted guide is part of its overall value proposition to customers.

New market forum
Schwab has very effectively disintermediated full service brokers. The company has led the way in empowering a whole generation of investors to assess their own risks, make their own decisions and manage their own portfolios.

Intercustomer relationships
In leveraging freeware to gain network returns on launching eSchwab, the company seems unconsciously to have tapped this Value Lever. Chuck Schwab was 'amazed' at the impact of the Internet on his business, so one can only conclude that Schwab management were unaware of how the network effect could influence the take-up of online broking.

Amazon Inc.

Value Lever	Intensity
Content integration	████████
Freeware	██
Mass customization	██
Real-time activity	██
Prosumer involvement	██████
Agenting	
New market forum	████
Intercustomer relationships	██████

Background
In five short years Amazon.com has grown to become the Internet's biggest seller of books, CDs and videos. Having now added toys, video games, software, home improvement products and auctions,

among other offerings, to its ever expanding range of activities, Earth's Biggest Bookstore is bent on becoming Earth's Biggest Selection, and maybe one day even Earth's Biggest Store. All the same, Amazon's success is rooted in its core business of books, CDs and videos.

Setting up on the World Wide Web in July 1995, Seattle-based Amazon.com was founded by twenty-eight-year-old Jeffrey P. Bezos, former computer system developer. Bezos was determined to use Amazon as a means of demonstrating that the Internet could provide the basis for a viable retail business. With no particular interest in books, Bezos simply selected bookselling as the most likely retail business to succeed over the Internet. Amazon's services quickly proved to be immensely popularly with customers, and by December 1999 Amazon.com was claiming to have more than 17 million customers in nearly 200 different countries. As a result of this success, Jeff Bezos, founder, President and Chief Executive, is now one of the world's best-known businessmen operating in the online environment.

'We want to be the world's most customer-centric company' (*Business Week Online*, 31/5/99), says Bezos and he claims that 'Amazon.com is obsessively focused on providing our customers the best possible online shopping experience, with the best selection, ease of use, and prices' (*PR Newswire*, 10/3/99). These features are not the only ones in the amazon.com shopping experience, with an abundance of general and customer-tailored ancillary services also provided via Amazon's websites. Price has surely been a key factor in the popularity of Amazon's service. Selling over the Internet, the company can offer significant discounts to customers (usually between 20 and 40 per cent on traditional retail outlet prices) as it does not have to cover the cost of running unnecessary physical locations. The cost to customers of a book or CD from Amazon, including postage and packing, is never more than its retail or cover price and is usually significantly less than this, so that postage and packing are, in effect, free.

During 1999 Amazon added a number of new categories of goods, as well as auctions and zShops – an online flea market. By the end of 1999 Amazon claimed to list more than 18 million unique items.

Conscious of the growing competition around him, Bezos is keen to add other categories as fast as possible in pursuit of his vision to build a company where 'customers can come and discover anything they may want to buy online'. In 2000 Bezos plans to double Amazon's offerings yet again, and is now building distribution centres across the USA so that Amazon can continue to meet exacting customer service levels as it pursues its relentless expansion.

In revenue terms, Amazon has also been a runaway success, achieving sales of $1.64 billion in 1999 when in 1996 sales were only $16 million. However, the company has yet to make a profit and a pro-forma loss of $390 million for 1999 against a more modest loss of $74 million for 1998 began to test the nerves of some investors. In January 2000 the market adjusted its valuation downwards by 30 per cent or more to around $25 billion reflecting some of the underlying anxiety. Analysts' opinions vary widely as to Amazon's ultimate realizable potential. One thing is certain: Jeff Bezos will surely surprise a good proportion of them!

Content integration
The Amazon website offers various forms of content to entertain and engage users, enhancing their shopping experience and encouraging purchase. For individual book and CD titles this includes cover art, synopses, annotations, interviews with authors as well as reviews by other users. In addition, the site also offers material such as specially commissioned articles, news stories and events listings.

Freeware
Amazon's meteoric growth owes much to the freely available content on its websites, for which there is no charge. Whether or not this ever-wider enjoyment of content by growing numbers of Internet users actually adds increasing value to all users is debatable. It certainly leads to more customer-generated reviews and participation in chat rooms and interviews with authors.

Mass customization
This is not the most intensively applied lever for Amazon. Account customers do get a personalized web-page greeting. Apart from that

every customer receives more or less the same experience and pays the same price. Customization does occur on selection of a title when users are advised that other Amazon customers who have purchased this book or CD have also purchased the following other titles. Customers will also receive e-mail alerts to new titles that are likely to be of interest.

Real-time activity
With online purchase, physical goods have to be delivered. This cannot be as satisfactory as the immediacy of walking into a music or bookstore and then walking out with your selection. However Amazon works hard to minimize this inevitable shortcoming. Information about order despatch and delivery is communicated by e-mail in an efficient and timely fashion.

Prosumer involvement
The whole Amazon user process is highly participative. By involving customers in an experience that is totally engaging Amazon manages to minimize the detractions of a virtual bookstore. Customers (and prospective customers) are invited to post reviews on books and to participate in chat rooms and virtual meetings with authors.

Agenting
There is no evidence of Amazon applying this Value Lever.

New market forum
Bezos does not view Amazon as simply an online book-seller, but sees his organization as the creator and developer of a new forum for customers to acquire the products and services they need and want. 'We're not a book company. We're not a music company. We're not a video company. We're not an auctions company. We're a customer company', says Bezos.

Amazon also pioneered the concept of syndicated selling on the Internet in 1996, and by early 1999 Amazon more than 200,000 members enrolled in its Associates Programme. Through this 'affiliate networking' programme, individuals or organizations can – for free – seamlessly link their websites to Amazon.com, and receive a 5–15 per cent commission on whatever is spent by visitors they send to Amazon.com.

Intercustomer relationships
Amazon is keen to help its customers feel that they belong to a community of like-minded individuals from the first moment they start to evaluate a book. The presence of customer-authored reviews on site and messages advising what other books buyers of this book have purchased are all part of deliberate process to build a sense of a micro-community around each title. This confers a feeling of involvement in Amazon from the outset that is sustained through other services such as chatrooms and discussion boards related to interests and book titles. Amazon will further enhanced community-related aspect of its services as it expand its auctions and zShops.

Priceline Inc.

Value Lever	Intensity
Content integration	
Freeware	▬▬
Mass customization	
Real-time activity	▬▬
Prosumer involvement	▬▬▬
Agenting	▬▬▬▬▬
New market forum	▬▬▬▬
Intercustomer relationships	

Background
In April 1998 Jay Walker launched Priceline, an Internet-based 'name your own price' service for domestic and international leisure-travel airline tickets. Consumers choose the dates they want to fly, their departure and arrival airports, and the price they are willing to pay

for a ticket and input that information on the priceline.com website. They accept that Priceline will choose the airline and agree to fly at any time between 6:00 a.m. and 10:00 p.m. with the possibility of up to one connection each way. Each ticket request is guaranteed with a credit card. Priceline finds a major airline that is willing to release a seat at the consumer's stated price. Consumers get a reply in one hour for domestic flights, or twenty-four hours for international flights. The customer pays exactly the price they offer, and all ticket requests made are free. Priceline makes its money from the difference between what it charges consumers and what it pays airlines for tickets. In mid-1999 Priceline reported that the average margin was about 5 per cent and could grow to around 12 per cent as sales volumes increase.

By April 1999 there were eighteen airlines participating in the service, with around 36 per cent of reasonable ticket requests (those not more than 30 per cent below the lowest available advance-purchase fares) being fulfilled – a figure rising to more than 70 per cent for popular routes. As a result of its rising popularity with customers, Priceline has become one of the USA's top ten sellers of leisure airline tickets. The innovative nature of the service has also won a significant amount of publicity for the company, so that by early 1999 Priceline ranked as the fifth most recognized Internet brand in America.

In July 1998, Priceline launched a second 'name-your-own price' service for new autos in the New York metropolitan area. Buyers stipulate the exact auto or truck they want and the price they are willing to pay. Priceline then works with all accredited dealers in a customer-specified geographic region to find the auto the customer wants at the named price, and charges a fee to the vendor. Priceline plans to make the auto-purchasing service US-wide. In late 1998 Priceline launched a hotel service to complement its airline ticket service. Leisure travellers could now obtain substantial savings by naming the price they want to pay for quality, brand-name hotel rooms across the USA, and by early 1999 Priceline was selling an average of around 5,000 hotel-room nights a week.

More recently, in February 1999, Priceline teamed up with North Carolina-based Lending Tree Incorporated to offer customers a 'name-your-own-terms' online service for mortgages. Lending Tree is the creator of an online service launched on the Internet in July 1998. It connects a consumer's online loan qualification form to a network of national and regional lending institutions that compete for the consumer's business. The Priceline–Lending Tree strategic alliance is likely to reap benefits for both organizations, and in its first ninety days of operating, the new Priceline service facilitated the approval of $125 million worth of home loans. Priceline's venture into the field of financial services advanced further in May 1999 when Jay Walker brokered a deal with leading Visa card issuer, First USA, for Priceline co-branded credit cards, offering discounts to their users on Priceline services. Walker believes that this deal alone could secure revenues for Priceline of $200 million over the next five years.

Certainly, Walker has big plans for Priceline, and eventually wants to see the company's name-your-own-price service extended to include almost anything people can buy. He plans to sell life and health insurance, and has already added groceries to the range of services in late 1999. As Warburg Dillon Read investment analyst Sara Zeilstra observed, Priceline has developed 'a platform that can be utilized for selling nearly anything over the Internet' (Stone, 29/4/99). Questioned what else Priceline might go into, Walker simply commented that 'This is just the start' (Brady, 22/9/99). However, Priceline has yet to make a profit, making a net loss of $112 million for 1998. Much of the loss can be attributed to Walker's belief – one shared by Jeff Bezos – that success on the Internet necessitates early and lavish spending on marketing. Indeed, Priceline operates an enormous marketing budget; it rose from $24 million in 1998 to $64 million for 1999. Despite its present losses, leading analysts estimate that Priceline will break even in 2001 on revenues of somewhere between $500 million and $1 billion.

Content integration
As an intermediary with a unique customer proposition, Priceline doesn't have to create a content-rich experience for its customers at the interface, so this lever is not applied.

Freeware
Ticket and room requests made of Priceline are free. Experimental usage of Priceline will have helped the remarkable spread of awareness of the service. More value to all users will occur as more suppliers are encouraged to use the Priceline context for meeting their need to fill seats, rooms, etc., as more users put in requests. This in turn will generate more users.

Mass customization
Priceline's initial achievement has not relied upon mass customization. But it is clear that this Value Lever will be important to Priceline in the future. Chairman and CEO Richard Braddock believes that the Internet offers tremendous potential for the deployment of one-to-one marketing strategies:

> It's the ultimate leverage point in what I see as the evolution toward targeted marketing and the ability to treat your customer on virtually a one-by-one basis. Marketing is all about information and knowledge of the customer. We create a basis for a longer-term relationship. Over time we'll be able to offer you [other] things [and] cross-sell [to] you. (Jaffe, 17/5/99)

Real-time activity
Priceline users know whether their requests have been accepted within one hour for domestic flights and twenty-four hours for international flights. To achieve this level of real-time response requires real-time thinking and slick systems linked to all suppliers. When Priceline spreads its wings to non-US markets it will probably have to tighten up on the response times for international flights – European customers will expect a one-hour response on Europe-wide flights at least. Real-time response also underpins other Priceline services.

Prosumer involvement
There is a learning curve up which users will need to progress in order to know with any certainty the threshold at which Priceline will typically find a supplier to meet their request. This learning

experience may involve multiple requests. The Priceline business model implicitly recognizes the importance of active consumer participation in helping to shape a successful outcome from using the Priceline service effectively.

Agenting
As an intermediary Priceline applies the agenting lever to the benefit of its customers. Customers do not personally visit all the suppliers but their requests most certainly do. This is probably one of the best and purest examples of the application of agenting as a Value Lever.

New Market Forum
'In our view, Priceline's business model lends itself to being one of the most successful we've ever seen', reported BancBoston Robertson Stephens analyst, Keith Benjamin, reflecting the global admiration for Jay Walker's applied intuition and boldness in its application. Walker has applied this lever so powerfully that it seems to demand a higher score than five!

Intercustomer relationships
We are unaware of the application of this lever by Priceline, although one could envisage that users of the service might well want to share experiences.

eBay

Value Lever	Intensity
Content integration	————————
Freeware	————————
Mass customization	
Real-time activity	
Prosumer involvement	————
Agenting	—

New market forum	
Intercustomer relationships	

Background

eBay created the concept of person-to-person online trading. It is quite simply 'the world's largest personal online trading community', and the organization's website allows individuals to buy and sell items in an auction format. The range of items offered on the eBay website is very extensive, and covers nearly 3,000 categories, including antiques, collectibles, sports memorabilia, computers, electronics, photographic equipment, toys, coins, stamps, books, magazines, music, china, pottery, glass and jewellery. eBay is now also involved in the traditional auction business through its acquisitions of Butterfield & Butterfield and Kruse International. In its mission statement, eBay states that 'We help people trade practically anything on earth' and the eBay website provides good evidence that this aim is being carried out successfully. Most of the sellers tend to be small businesses or part-time dealers, with many of them having carried out hundreds of successful transactions. The eBay phenomenon has enabled many collectors to turn their hobbies into thriving businesses.

The eBay auction service basically works as follows. Sellers submit the name of an item for sale, accompanied by a short description and often a photograph. Buyers can then submit bids for the item online during the time that the auction lasts (usually several days). When the auction is completed, the successful buyer and the seller are then emailed by eBay, and left to arrange payment and delivery themselves (by doing this eBay is able to minimize its distribution-related costs). For providing its broking services, eBay usually takes around a 6 per cent cut of the selling price from the seller. Despite the obvious potential for scams, the auction model works very well most of the time. This is in larger part because of the rating system that eBay uses to rate its sellers, whereby the details of how buyers have rated previous transactions with a particular seller are clearly displayed. Because of the fact that, having once used eBay, most people go on to use it again, sellers quickly build up a track record which indicates the level of reliability. In order to reduce even further the potential for fraud, eBay has teamed up with Equifax to develop a method of verifying a customer's identity.

The concept around which eBay is based was first conceived as a result of a casual comment made during a dinner-time conversation between Pierre Omidyar – the Chairman and founder of eBay – and his fiancée, who was an avid collector of the colourful sweet dispensers produced by Pez. Pierre's fiancée commented that it would be wonderful it she were able to collect Pez dispensers and interact with other Pez collectors using the Internet. As an early Internet enthusiast, Pierre realized that the Internet could indeed be used to establish a centralized market forum, where people could buy and sell unique items, as well as meet other users with similar interests. Acting on this realization, Pierre subsequently launched eBay in September 1995 as an experiment to assess the demand for an auction-based trading service. The almost overnight success achieved by eBay led Pierre in late 1996 to resign his post in Developer Relations for General Magic so that he could further develop the eBay service. In 1998 eBay's standing as a business was substantially increased by the arrival of Meg Whitman – formerly Senior Vice President of Marketing at the Walter Disney Company's Consumer Products Division, and CEO of the world's largest floral products company, Florists Transworld Delivery (FTD). Meg was appointed to the post of President and CEO of eBay.

By January 2000, eBay had 10 million registered users, making it 'the eighth largest state in the United States' (eBay website). Each day its site was providing a choice of more than 3.5 million auctions with over 400,000 new items being added every twenty-four hours. In the fourth quarter of 1999 eBay hosted 41 million auctions to a value of over $900 million. The site is well-used, and in December 1999 was receiving an average of 1.5 billion page impressions per month. Users were spending an average of 105 minutes per month on the website, making it the world's most popular location in terms of the time spent on the website. Unlike many other well-known Internet businesses, eBay has not only managed to secure massive sales revenues, but has also succeeded in making a profit – from the outset! eBay does not actually handle the goods it sells, and therefore the company does not have the sizeable distribution costs of some other Internet companies, nor does it have to employ many people (currently it employs around 200 employees; Amazon has over 3,000 employees). For the year 1999, eBay secured revenues of $224.7 million, and made a net income of $10.8 million as a result. The market capitalization of the company was around $20 billion at the end of 1999.

The world of the person-to-person auction may have only been born in 1995 but experts forecast that it could be worth a staggering $15 billion by 2001 in the USA alone!

Content integration
In its community-minded way eBay creates a content-rich experience defined by the interests of the user. eBay posts information on everything to do with auctions and online community, but the *pièce de résistance* is the posting of over 400,000 new auctions a day covering nearly 3,000 categories, adding up to over 40 million auctions per quarter.

Freeware
Customer-to customer digital business is the perfect context for this Value Lever. It costs nothing to list an item for auction. The more registered users, the more auctions, the more bids there are, the more liquid becomes the market and the more effective becomes the community. eBay executives have become adept at managing the thirty scrolling message boards to create a sense of almost 'hyper-' activity. The remarkable growth of users throughout 1999 is testimony to the power of network returns.

Mass customization
eBay users shape their own experiences. There is no evidence of any personalization process applied by eBay itself. There is an enormous and growing volume of users with a growing volume and pace of traffic. This may be one of the few sites where mass customization would be of limited value to the overall result.

Real-time activity
This lever is not directly applied. Auctions run for several days. When they close, buyers and sellers complete their own arrangements

Prosumer involvement
There is a great sense of active participation by buyers and sellers. eBay is only an intermediary and both buyers and sellers are responsible for creating and delivering their own value.

Agenting
Agenting is applied in subtle ways. Firstly, eBay provides an online verification of customer service through the Equifax credit-rating agency. The SafeHarbour service also provides a policing service for eBay users and, in effect, an assurance of good performance. There is also an escrow service that holds payments on behalf of buyers pending inspection, thereby assisting buyer–seller relations. In agenting terms this is probably the maximum that eBay can do.

New market forum
This is undoubtedly eBay's finest feature and most intensely applied Lever. eBay pioneered person-to-person trading and virtually gave birth to the concept of the online auction. eBay has created an environment that simply did not exist in the physical world. Imitation, they say, is the sincerest form of flattery. eBay has many imitators, even among other e-champions – Jeff Bezos, John Pluthero and Jay Walker.

Intercustomer relationships
Community is what eBay is about. When Meg Whitman talks of eBay as the eighth largest state in the USA there is more than a hint of reality in her observation. The core values of eBay are about community and are still strongly represented in the guiding spirit of Chairman Pierre Omidyar. For many users, eBay has indeed become a part of their lifestyle with many building up businesses based around its electronic forum. 'We started with commerce, and what grew out of that commerce was community', observes Whitman, 'So

we think of ourselves as sort of a community-commerce model' (*Business Week Online*, 21/5/99).

Freeserve

Value Lever	Intensity
Content integration	▬▬▬▬▬
Freeware	▬▬▬▬▬
Mass customization	
Real-time activity	▬
Prosumer involvement	▬▬
Agenting	▬▬▬▬▬
New market forum	▬▬
Intercustomer relationships	▬▬

Background

In September 1998, Dixons Group, the UK's largest electronics retailer, launched Freeserve, a free Internet service provider (ISP). The new service was developed in conjunction with the telecommunications firm Energis, with the basic aim of providing Dixons with 'the biggest [Internet] portal in the UK'. Amazingly Freeserve achieved this aim within four months of launch in December 1998, when it overtook America OnLine, the previous UK market leader, which at that time had approximately 500,000 registered users. From a standing start, Freeserve had signed up over 900,000 subscriber accounts by the end of 1998.

The free ISP concept is simple. In the UK consumers have to pay for local calls at a metered rate. To connect to the Internet before the arrival of Freeserve they had also to pay a monthly subscription fee. Together the two costs had tended to discourage take-up of Internet access by UK consumers. Freeserve removed one of these costs – the monthly subscription to the ISP – at a stroke. Freeserve partners calculated that the combination of advertising revenues and a share of telephone revenues would make a free ISP service practicable. Freeserve would incur only minimal distribution and administrative costs – there are no fees to collect from customers, so no need for an expensive billing system. Dixons Group has 950 ready-made retail outlets, so there is no need for Freeserve to support expensive advertising campaigns or mail-outs of Freeserve software discs. 'Some estimates put the cost of winning a new subscriber at as much as £40 [$64], but it only costs me £2 to £3 [$3 to $5] to send out a box of ninety disks – that's a potential ninety new customers' (Yates, 30/10/98), said Mark Danby, Freeserve's former General Manager in the heady period when customer growth was truly meteoric, and before imitators had arrived on the scene. Freeserve also achieved significant cost benefits though the use of partner Energis's ISP, Planet Online. 'The whole Freeserve model was very well thought through. Planet was particularly good to tie up with', commented Fletcher Research Director William Reeve, 'They're primarily a business provider so most traffic is between 9 a.m. and 5 p.m. – Freeserve users typically connect from home, outside business hours. They've kept up with demand and Dixons is a good brand. That makes it very difficult for other players to cut corners. (*New Media Age*, 21/1/99).

Freeserve also won a far greater degree of visibility and respect for the Dixons Group as a whole. 'Six years ago Dixons was reporting losses of £22 million [$35 million] and fighting to sustain its brand on the high street. . . . What a difference a Freeserve makes', chirped the April 1999 edition of *Marketing* magazine. 'Dixons, in the past six months has become the darling of the City and a major Internet service provider. Suddenly, its brand and business are looking like good bets for further growth in the next millennium' (Lee, 1/4/99). By January 2000 Freeserve was by far the UK's biggest ISP, reporting more than 1.7 million active subscribers. US investment bank Morgan Stanley Dean Witter predicted considerable growth for Freeserve's customer base. Its April 1999 forecast of almost 5 million users by 2004 is beginning to look like a target that may well be able to achieve. The arrival of unmetered (and effectively free) local calls in the UK in March 2000 for Internet access have hit one of Freeserve's revenue streams, its share of the telephone interconnect charges. After a brief evaluation and a downward adjustment in market valuation, investors remain committed to Freeserve. This seems to reflect the general belief that Pluthero has already demonstrated Freeserve's potential as an integrated business with multiple revenue streams.

Content integration
Typical of a good portal, Freeserve provides its customers with excellent content. It offers at least thirty content channels on topics such as news, business, entertainment, careers, cartoons, shopping and sport. There are also a range of search engines provided by Lycos, UK Plus and iNeed.

Freeware
The Freeserve concept is a classic freeware application where more value accrues to all users – customers and suppliers – with every additional customer or supplier who signs up to Freeserve. New users get a browser that is automatically configured to bring up the Freeserve portal website on which advertisers pay to place advertisements, so numbers count for advertisers. Providers of content and online shopping services will also find every increase in the number of users a further compelling reason to supply the portal.

Mass customization
There is no evidence of the application of this lever yet. Other portals such as Yahoo! do offer personalization driven by initial prosumer involvement in setting up a personalized home page.

Real-time activity
The Internet is about instant intercommunication, so a portal has to provide immediate access to extensive sources of information and other services as a basic component of its offering. Its capacity to create value through this lever will therefore be limited. Freeserve does very well and achieves as high an intensity as a portal is likely to achieve for this lever. Leading portal provider Yahoo! is the benchmark for the application of this lever in this category, setting an example to which John Pluthero is surely aspiring.

Prosumer involvement

Customers do shape their own experiences in using a portal service such as Freeserve in their access or gateway to the Internet. Like real-time activity, this is a basic component of the offering so the opportunity for value leverage is limited. For example, an effective and well-received 'My Freeserve' would merit a higher rating on this lever.

Agenting

Freeserve is an excellent guide and has to be to retain its premier spot as a portal in the UK market. It provides unparalleled access to extensive sources for content, shopping, financial services and interactivity.

New market forum

The concept of a free Internet access service is a brilliant concept that Freeserve appears to have brilliantly executed – so far. It has created a context for its customers that would not have been affordable for many of them. However, an Internet portal is an Internet portal, however good it may be.

Intercustomer relationships

Freeserve offers comprehensive chat facilities and communities for its customers, enabling them to share experiences with like-minded Freeserve users. These are offered rather than being an activity implicit to the offering or business model, so relative intensity of value leverage is low-to-moderate.

Egg

Value Lever	Intensity
Content integration	—
Freeware	——
Mass customization	——

Real-time activity	—			
Prosumer involvement	——			
Agenting				
New market forum	——			
Intercustomer relationships	—			

Background
Egg is a direct banking operation launched in October 1998 by long-established UK insurer Prudential Corporation. Initially, Egg used telephone and post as well as the Internet to interact with customers; it is intending also to use digital television in due course. Egg's initial product range included an instant-access savings account, mortgage and personal loan. Products were designed to be easy to understand and flexible, as well as providing unbeatable interest rates to savers and borrowers. The savings account, for example, offered customers a rate that was higher than the base rate charged by banks for borrowing. 'The launch of Egg reflects our commitment to maintaining Prudential's leading position in a changing UK market', proclaimed Sir Peter Davis, then Group Chief Executive of the Prudential Corporation, 'Egg is a radically new direct financial organization designed specifically for the digital age and backed by the strength of Prudential' *(Daily Telegraph,* 28/8/99).

Egg was developed to compete with the UK's new supermarket banks on the rates it offered, and with Virgin in terms of its overall concept. It was aimed at a set of customers who wish to deal directly with a financial services provider on an execution-only basis and are generally comfortable with the use of newer, computer-based technologies, as Egg Chief Executive Mike Harris affirmed, 'We want to go out and get customers who will use the Internet and use it a lot' (Lumsden, 21/7/99). Egg customers are quite distinct from traditional Prudential customers who value advice and the option of face-to-face contact. Prudential's market research had indicated that as many as 15 million people in the UK would be interested in banking with Egg, ranging from young professionals to retired people. 'The UK needs this sort of new thinking', commented Mercer Management consulting partner Eddy Collier, 'It is great that someone is going to take on the UK banks . . . the market is ready for Egg' (Distribution Management Briefing, 1/11/98).

On launch Egg experienced an unexpected level of demand for its services. By April 1999, after only seven months, Egg had achieved its five-year goal of $8 billion of deposits and half a million customers. The company then switched to Internet-only applications, and by the beginning of 2000 Egg had acquired another 300,000 customers and a total of $12 billion in deposits. The company's aim now is to sign up 2 million Internet customers by 2004. This target now represents a dramatic slow-down in its anticipated rate of acquiring new customers, indicating the belief that the earlier acquisition rate could not be sustained in the longer term.

During 1999 Egg launched more financial products designed specially for the online world. Chief Executive Mike Harris explained the distinct rationale for the Egg credit card:

> With one-in-ten Britons ready to buy online we need to offer something to make online shopping easier, cheaper and safe. We believe the Egg Card will accelerate the growth of Internet shopping considerably. Online shoppers list convenience (47%), price (27%) and speed (11%) as their reasons for using the Web. The Egg Card offers all of these. (Regulatory News Service, 20/9/99)

There is no doubt that Mike Harris and Sir Peter Davis adopted a very deliberate strategy in launching and developing Egg. Jonathan Bloomer, now Group Chief Executive replacing Sir Peter, summed up the thinking: 'Rather than acquiring a company and expensing the goodwill, we are building a new organization and charging the investment to earnings.' Egg will cost approximately $400 million over two years – a lot less than the cost of acquiring a bank – and is expected to turn a profit in 2001. 'It's always been my contention that it's better than buying a bank or building society at three times book value', commented Salomon Smith Barney analyst Trevor May (*Daily Telegraph*, 28/8/99). Analysts' opinions vary widely as to Egg's capital value as a business. At the optimistic end investment bankers Morgan Stanley estimated that Egg could be worth as much as $7 billion, while others are more sanguine and give Egg a value of around $3 billion. The market value will become clear as Prudential completes its intentions to float Egg off later in 2000.

Egg still has much to prove, not least that it can fully break the mould for UK financial services and achieve unprecedented levels of multiple product take-up by its customers. It knows it has to make a move into the broader lifestyle arena in order to extend its appeal to its customers. Plans to provide aggregate buying facilities to Egg customers through Adabra, a shopping business similar to Letsbuyit, represent just one step in the lifestyle direction. It is also planning the launch of a funds supermarket.

Content integration
Egg's success has not involved the specific utilization of this lever. More recently, content channels have been added as the need to build a finance portal to help retain customers has gained some urgency. It is not yet clear how successful this will prove. Intentions to develop a lifestyle emphasis will undoubtedly result in the stronger application of this Value Lever.

Freeware
'Our savings rate is a loss leader but we plan to be offering our customers more products in the future', confessed Egg spokesperson Pema Radha (*Daily Telegraph*, 28/8/99). Unashamedly Prudential has used unprecedented rates of interest to attract customers. The question is whether this 'discount-ware' has tapped the network returns reality or has just been an unparalleled offer that has attracted a lot of people. So, with demonstrable first-mover advantage under the belt whatever the reason, we have attributed this Value Lever as the most powerful one in Egg's profile.

Mass customization
Egg customers do report that the level of personalization has pleased them but that it is limited to the products and does not yet seem to extend to the totality of their relationship with Egg. Mass customizing the relationship will prove a greater challenge.

Real-time activity
Unanticipated demand has led to poor service experiences and serious delays on the launch of more than one product. Customers have also had to deal with a number of website failures. Egg's success has not yet begun to tap the potential of this lever.

Prosumer involvement
Egg customers do report that they have a pleasing sense of control over their credit card and savings accounts that they would not otherwise enjoy. Clearly this only applies to customers using the online capability.

Agenting
This will play a role in Egg's future development. The recently added content channels and lifestyle-related services, such as Adabra, will bring this Value Lever into play. However, it has not yet contributed to Egg's success.

New market forum
Assessing the application of this Value Lever is not straightforward. At the outset and on the face of it, Egg represented a physical world business model transferred almost directly to the virtual world. From this perspective there seemed to be no apparent attempt to address the network dynamic of buyer–seller re-engagement. However, if we look wider the issue is not so clear-cut.

Prudential wanted a bank and a bank needs customers. A bank would have been expensive, perhaps as much as $3 billion. Far better then to leverage your brand and make an unbeatable offer to potential customers, creating a bank by offering them deals that no one else would want to match – savings rates in excess of bank base rates, interest charges lower than deposit rates. So, you rapidly acquire a customer base that costs you perhaps at worst a few hundred millions of dollars. The challenge, though, is that you need to keep these customers and make them purchase much more through you, so you do everything to create a true Internet business. You start to build a portal around the core financial products, encouraging customers to purchase multiple products and services, bolt on lots of additional services and proceed generally in a lifestyle direction. All the time you continue to share value with your customers. So, if we consider this as a deliberate attempt to share value between customers and owners in the creation of a new type of financial service organization based around a portal, we come to a different conclusion on the application of this Value Lever.

For the latter reason we do consider this to be an application of new market forum. Time will tell if this conclusion is right.

Intercustomer relationships
Egg has added the potential for this in the form of chatrooms. It has not yet contributed to its success, so far as we know.

Dell

Value Lever	Intensity
Content integration	——
Freeware	–
Mass customization	——
Real-time activity	————
Prosumer involvement	————
Agenting	
New market forum	
Intercustomer relationships	–

Background
Headquartered in Round Rock, near Austin in Texas, the Dell Computer Corporation, is the world's leading direct computer systems company. In 1999, Dell ranked number 125 among the Fortune 500 companies, and number 363 in the Fortune Global 500. In sales of computer systems, Dell holds the number one position in the USA and is number two in the world (Compaq currently remains slightly ahead in terms of global sales). Dell is a global company, employing

over 24,000 employees in its wholly owned subsidiaries around the world. Dell dates from 1984, when its founder, Chairman and CEO, Michael S. Dell, started selling computers from his dormitory room at the University of Texas. Dell's rapid revenue growth over the last fifteen years has exceeded considerably that of the PC industry as a whole, and has been matched by a equally rapid rise in its stock value, making Dell the best performing stock of all time.

The success of Dell Computer Corporation is largely due to the highly effective exploitation of its direct-sales model. With the aim of eliminating the middleman, Dell subsequently evolved a build-to-order model, in which the company minimized inventory and maximized its ability to serve customers by assembling a computer only when an order had been placed. Michael Dell believes this build-to-order approach is the key to understanding his company's success:

> By following the courage of our convictions and keeping our eyes on what mattered most – our customers, our shareholders, and our people – Dell thrived. . . . Out of these experiences, our strategies for success were born: speed to market; superior customer service; and a fierce commitment to producing consistently high quality, custom-made computer systems that provide the highest performance and the latest relevant technology to our customers. (Dell, 1998)

Dell started selling via the Internet in June 1996. When sales over the Internet climbed to over $1 million a day by the end of 1996, Dell was established as a leader in the field of electronic commerce. Indeed, at that time Amazon was only selling around a sixth of that figure. Dell was also making a profit from its online revenues. The computer company's build-to-order philosophy was ideally suited to the Internet, enabling the company to reduce further already low inventory levels, as well as improve the quality of service provided to customers. 'The Internet will fundamentally change the way that companies do business through its ability to enable people to conduct low-cost, one-to-one customer interactions with rich content', reflected Michael Dell in 1998, 'The Internet would make the direct model even more direct' (Dell, 1998).

Internet customers can access detailed product line descriptions at www.dell.com. They can also use 'configurator' software to design the exact computer system configuration they want and see instantaneously the price implications of their selection. If customers have any queries about their configured computer system, there is a call-back button located on the website, putting them quickly in contact with a Dell call-centre operator. Once customers have developed their desired computer configuration, they can either print out the details for later reference or make an online order. Dell acts speedily on receipt of an online order, manufacturing the required system and delivering it to the customer – usually in less than a week. But the website offers even more. 'Customers can use Dell's web site to track orders and retrieve over fifty three thousand pages of service information, including the same guides that Dell technicians use to diagnose problems', says *Wall Street Journal*'s Scott Thurm.

As well as using the Internet to build closer relationships with its customers, Dell has also sought to use Internet technology to develop strong online communications with the company's partners and suppliers. Many of the latter now have online (extranet) access to Dell's internal databases via secure Internet sites. As a result, suppliers are provided with a direct view into Dell's manufacturing operations and can work collaboratively on product designs, cutting an estimated 30 per cent off development times. A further benefit of Dell's decision to construct a virtual value chain via an Internet protocol-based network is that customers and suppliers can communicate with one another in real time. The benefits are notable. 'If you buy something from us and something is not right, there is a real-time feedback mechanism to the parts supplier. We can remedy things significantly faster', comments Joe Marengi, Dell Computer's Senior Vice President and General Manager for the Americas (McDougall, 13/12/99).

Recently, Dell has diversified the range of products on offer to customers. Perhaps the most significant demonstration of this was the March 1999 launch of the Gigabuys.com website. Dell has designed this as an online superstore for consumers, offering over

30,000 computer-related products, including printers, digital cameras, electronic organisers, scanners, cables, network cards and software. As well as identifying appropriate hardware and software upgrades for specific Dell models, Dell has designed Gigabuys.com to appeal to customers who have purchased other brands of computers. Eventually, Dell plans to expand Gigabuys.com to serve the needs of corporate customers, and offer downloadable software, as that becomes a more mainstream business. Shoppers at Gigabuys.com can use the same virtual shopping cart as at www.dell.com, and can switch between the two sites before making a final purchase. While consumers typically visit the www.dell.com website every few years when they are ready to upgrade, Gigabuys.com provides Dell with the opportunity to sell goods to its customers on a more regular basis.

Content integration
Dell creates a rich experience for the online computer buyer. Detailed product line descriptions are available online, and a 'configurator' helps the customer to cut through the detail to create the desired specification. Customers and engineers alike can access extensive and detailed service information. Dell4me Resources further enrich the experience, if desired.

Freeware
There are the seeds of a weak freeware application. Potential customers can use the 'configurator' to design their ideal Dell product and then print their specification; they do not have to order. This facility may well have contributed to the growth of online sales. As more people select their ideal specification, Dell can use this information as market research to help refine their offerings to suit all future customers. This will include those who have already purchased and may be considering an upgrade.

Mass customization
Once individual customers have ordered the specification to their own design, then they will receive a service that is personalized to their needs. This seems to be limited to the duration of their pur-

chase and the immediate after-sales period. We understand that Dell does advise customers about upgrades and other relevant information. Corporate customers do receive a fully customized service.

Real-time activity
The Dell direct build-to-order business model aims to have the customer's completed order delivered in as few as three days or less where possible. This is effectively the shortest time possible to build a fully personalized computer and get it to the customer. Dell's capacity to operate in every respect in real time is very impressive.

Prosumer involvement
Personalization is the direct outcome of comprehensive prosumer involvement. The customer participates fully in creating the specification, placing the order and then tracking that order through to delivery. This is a fully automated process. Through Dell's Internet protocol-based computer network any online customer can communicate with any online supplier, if necessary.

Agenting
This lever has not been applied in this business model.

New market forum
Dell's outstanding build-to-order direct selling business model was a new business model developed with great prescience in a pre-Internet world. Michael Dell has translated that model perfectly to the network world. However good it is, and however hard we try, we cannot assess it as an application of this Value Lever – even though we feel we would like to!

Intercustomer relationships
Individual users can exchange views with others in the community area of the Dell4me Resources section of the website. This is useful but does not appear to be an implicit application of the Value Lever to underpin the value created by the business model, compared to sharing reviews in Amazon or the sense of community implicit in eBay.

Summary

These seven businesses illustrate remarkably well the application of the Value Lever framework described here. Value Levers also aid our understanding of the nature of their successes, leading to some interesting observations.

The most effective and comprehensive application of customer value leverage is undoubtedly by the Charles Schwab Corporation. Amazon's total obsession with customer centricity shows through in its excellent profile, suggesting that Amazon investors with nerves of steel may well be the ultimate winners. For sheer professionalism in its own sector Dell is unbeatable and we can see clearly why. Whereas both Schwab and Dell have built highly profitable, fully integrated, real-time businesses, only Dell has achieved this with a complex physical good that is built to order. eBay is outstanding for its success in making person-to-person auctions a fact of everyday modern life. Its reach demonstrates the remarkable power of the network economy with 10 million users and over 40 million completed auctions in nearly 4,000 categories in the last quarter of 1999 alone. Priceline is clearly the online consumer's favourite agent and proves again the extraordinary power of applied imagination to the new network economy. Freeserve has illustrated the power of first-mover advantage as its dominant and compelling site continues to leverage network returns and suck in users like a virtual vacuum cleaner. Egg is the business with the most to prove and that is clear from its slightly weaker Digital Value Profile. It has succeeded so far in spite of some service failures, due largely to the strength of its leadership and its boldness. Reports of continuing innovation and attention to earlier shortcomings from the Egg camp suggest that a later reappraisal will probably lead to a much stronger Digital Value Profile.

Now that you understand the Value Lever framework and its power in successful digital business, we will explore in the next chapter how to use it to your own advantage. Specifically, we will:

▶ Take a practical approach to developing digital business

Digital value profiles **227**

- help you to apply Value Levers to your own initiative or new venture
- Reinforce the importance of connections in planning your business

Part Four
Building for success

10
Creating virtual value

▶ How to fit the Value Lever framework to your dream
▶ Turning your dream into a customer proposition
▶ Testing you proposition against a Value Lever checklist
▶ Mapping the connections to plot the revenues
▶ Appreciating the differences in a digital business plan

The connectedness of things

In Chapter 1 we echoed Michael Dell's words – to take advantage of digital business opportunities, all you need is a framework and a dream. We promised you the framework and we've supplied it – Value Levers derived from network realities and emergent customer dynamics. Now is the time to spruce up that digital dream, that business idea, that concept that you have in mind, and test its readiness for launch into the e-world. In this part of *The Buck Starts Here* you can explore how to fit the Value Lever framework to your dream. You can also address some of the organizational issues that may influence whether your dream, once launched, will take wings and achieve the success of your aspirations. And if the challenge is to fit your dream into an established physical-world business, then we'll also consider the task of matching a virtual initiative to a physical organization – the tricky issue of transformation. Once again the experiences of our seven e-champions will inform our thinking. But first, in this chapter, let's evolve the means to fit your dream to the framework.

What is your dream? Whatever it is, it needs to be expressed in terms both of the customers at whom it will be targeted and the set of needs that your dream will address. For your dream to become a proposition that will truly provide value to those customers, you must also evolve the dream from their perspective – what will it mean to them? Take Schwab's proposition, for example. This is about making people into their own brokers and giving them the freedom to make their own investment decisions. In Chuck Schwab's own words, when thinking of his customers, 'It is as simple as turning on your computer, and right there are all the pockets of your financial life on the screen, from your 401(k) and IRA [pension fund and retirement account] to your brokerage and bank accounts. We'll be the consolidator, the integrator' (Gunn, 7/12/98). For John Pluthero and Freeserve the proposition for customers revolves around enabling free access to the Internet through a gateway that can help them to meet all their online needs and wants. Look back at the businesses of the other e-champions, and see

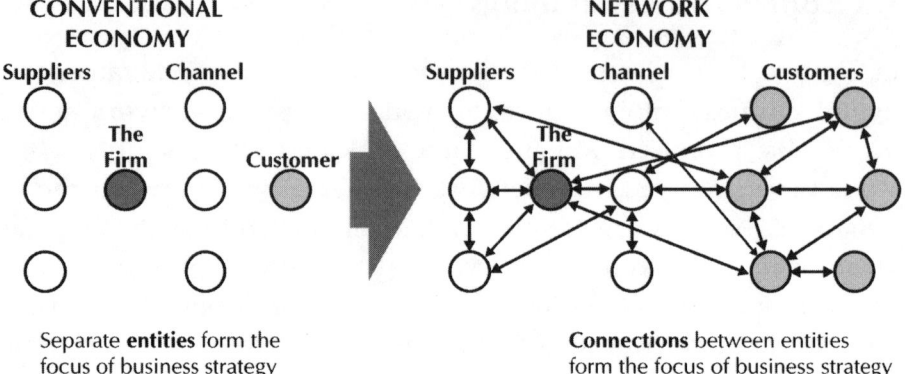

Figure 10.1 Creating value from connection

if you can find more inspiration, if you need to, for turning your dream into a customer proposition.

In extracting that customer proposition from your dream, you may care to remind yourself of the distinctive nature of the network economy, first defined in Chapter 1. What is a network economy? It is an economy that creates significant value from and via digitally based technological, human and organizational connections. It can only flourish when many involved parties have the potential to connect. Connection is key (see Figure 10.1).

The role that connection plays is core to how you now build a plan that will be the basis for putting your proposition into action. You will need to look beyond just the interface between customers and your proposed business to map all the potential connections that may occur in the course of dealing with those customers. This includes, from the customer's perspective, potential connections with:

▶ other customers or prospective customers;
▶ other companies providing part of the total experience through your website;
▶ outsourced suppliers or partners to your organization who might have direct contact with your customer for processing or customer service purposes;

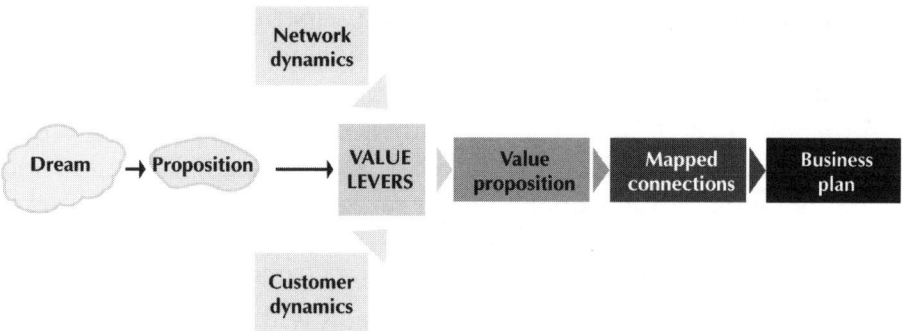

Figure 10.2 Turning dreams into business

▶ other companies, or even competitors conceivably, if there is an intermediary nature inherent in your business model, for example.

Why are connections so important? Because every connection is a relationship and every relationship is a potential financially based exchange. Understand the connections and the relationships they cause, and you have the basis to plot and estimate the revenues that your target customers may generate, as well as the costs they may incur. This mapping of all the connections will add clarity to your thinking, as well as provide key inputs to your business plan (see Figure 10.2).

Before you can proceed to map connections, you need to test the proposition and the extent to which it will create value for your target customers.

A Value Lever checklist

The outcome of going through the Value Lever checklist should be a greater degree of certainty about the soundness of your proposition and its potential to generate value for your customers. In the process of going through the following checklist items you may find that you need to refine your proposition.

▶ **Content integration:** Is a content-rich experience appropriate to your business model and to the customers for whom your proposition is designed? If you think about your proposition in the broadest lifestyle terms, what content does it suggest you might conceivably include, and from what other sectors? Think beyond the obvious and consider the full range of media. Amazon integrates a whole range of content and brings together reviews, editorials and useful information related to the purchase of a book or CD. If you can link content integration with prosumer involvement and mass customization, as Chuck Schwab does, then you can add maximum value through a bubble of personalized content.

▶ **Freeware:** You need to get consumers' attention, encouraging them to change their behaviour – first to try, and then adopt, your offering in preference to others. Can you use freeware to create critical mass and access the effect of network returns? If you think you can, how will you achieve that? Can you provide a component of your offering free? If so, whatever you do must be more than just offering customers a loss leader, its purpose must be to create critical mass. So, can you link the action you take here to the natural propensity for interconsumer collaboration or some aspect of intercustomer relationships? In other words, how can you ensure that your offering leads to those word of mouth and word of mouse referrals? Inspiration should come from how eBay and Freeserve, and other e-champion businesses, achieved just that.

▶ **Mass customization:** This lever may be more important at the outset than you think. The more personalized that you can make customer interactions – and quickly – the richer the experience for the customer will be. Attending to their individual needs will not only enhance their propensity to repurchase but also the likelihood of referral by them to others. Concerns about inherent complexity may dissuade you from addressing mass customization in the early stages of the launch of your business. Many of the e-champions have succeeded without it, but only, we believe, because of the power of their unique business models – e.g. 'name-your-own-price' airline tickets, person-to-person auctions or free Internet access. So, unless you also have a uniquely powerful business model you would do well to consider how to apply this lever in your proposition. If you do decide you have to incorporate this lever, then you will have to consider how to build the learning relationship with the customer and the computer systems this will require.

▶ **Real-time activity:** How important is convenience and instant gratification to your target customers? Will meeting their needs in real-time or near real-time be a source of genuine value to them? What will be the implications of real-time activity for the organization that you put in place? A real-time customer interface means your business will need to think, decide and do in real-time as well. Sustaining a dialogue with customers in real-time presents quite a challenge. One needs only to look at Dell's remarkable 'build-to-order in near real-time' capability here to appreciate the implications for any other business wishing to emulate it. Remember that real-time activity must create value from a customer perspective, so just providing instant access or intercommunication may simply be a necessary or essential component of the offering, and may not provide that added value.

▶ **Prosumer involvement:** A desire for active participation means consumers generally are looking for more control over their experiences, and buyer ascendancy gives them the prospect of achieving just that. So, how will you give your customers the means to create their own value and play an active role in specifying their requirements of the product or service you are offering them? Even better, customers can drive down your operational costs by performing processing activities themselves, while gaining value through a sense of control. This double gain – higher customer value, lower operational cost – features strongly in several e-champions' businesses – Schwab, Amazon, Priceline and Dell.

Slick systems that can provide the capability for 'straight-through' processing are no longer the big ticket items that once they were. The adoption of Internet Protocol as the universal standard linking IT systems inside organizations and the new generation of web application servers mean that you can start small and still think big, scaling up as you go. You will do well to avoid an equivalent of the 'Nike online investment dealing system' where e-mail buy and sell orders received from customers are handed to a runner who rushes them to the dealer and rushes back the confirms – giving customers the illusion of 'straight-through' without the benefits to the business.

▶ **Agenting:** Will your customers see you as facilitating their access to the network economy, or as acting somehow as a guide to them in some way or another? Will you need to use agenting to support the process of content integration, sending customers offsite to complete some aspect of the experience? Agenting may also form an important part of your revenue generation activities with focused 'affiliate network-style' linkages to organizations that can help to provide, and fulfil, related goods and services associated with your core offering. For example, if you were offering an online travel service it might be appropriate to provide linkages, for example, to Amazon for travel books and Lands End for travel clothes. Consider also the branding implications. Remember that the customer dynamic of trust deficit underpins the potential for agenting. What does this tell you about your brand and how you should develop it?

▶ **New market forum:** Are you using your imagination and the potential for buyer–seller re-engagement to put a wholly different business model at the heart of your proposition? Is your business model fundamentally different to any real-world equivalent, or to anything so far launched in the online economy? If it is different, then like Jay Walker or Pierre Omidyar, this Value Lever will underpin the success of your prospective digital business. Are you reorganizing buyers in some new way – such as aggregating buying power; or are you reorganizing sellers – by offering a new type of intermediary service; or are you reorganizing the marketplace – with, say, some variant of the auction model?

Or are you doing none of the above? Reflect on the reality that if your proposition doesn't score highly on this lever, then you will surely need the use of a strong brand to give your business any chance of success. If your proposition doesn't score on this lever at all, then you are probably simply transferring a physical business activity to the virtual world. Unless a strong bricks-and-mortar

based business exists already to support this migration to the virtual world, the odds will be stacked against your success.
- ▶ **Intercustomer relationship:** How are you planning to incorporate in your proposition the natural tendency in network society for consumers to collaborate? Can your idea tap that raw nerve in society that is the absence of affinity? If your customers can actively engage with other users – suppliers and partners, perhaps, as well as other customers, connecting to them through the existence of your business – will that reinforce the value created for them in your overall proposition?

If you can catch the spirit of the Internet and distil it in your proposition and its birth, then you may well harness the increasing tendency of network returns, just as John Pluthero, Mike Harris and Chuck Schwab have managed to do. Like Chuck Schwab, you might find yourself amazed at the impact of the Internet on your business. Only, unlike him, you won't be attributing it to luck! A word of caution, though. Just offering chatrooms and discussion boards is not sufficient to earn anything more than a minimal score for intensity on this Value Lever. Just because you provide these facilities doesn't mean that customers will automatically use them. Ask yourself: how can I make this lever an implicit part of my value proposition?

Take the outputs from the audit of your customer proposition using the Value Lever framework and develop a Digital Value Profile for your own prospective business, using the grid applied to the e-champions' businesses in Chapter 9. Be honest with yourself. What does this tell you? Where are you weak and where are you strong? Use your evaluation to refine your concept into a robust customer-defined value proposition that will truly fly. And if you are not happy with what this process is telling you, try to avoid the old pre-Internet business tendency to conduct lots more research in order to avoid having to make a decision about whether to proceed or not. Intuition and a little research should be enough to fill the gaps in your knowledge and to tell you whether to proceed or not. If your gut feeling is telling you not to proceed – just try another idea! Ideas are ten a penny!

■ Turning connections into dollars

In the network economy, every connection is a potential relationship and every relationship is a possible financially based exchange. Try taking a large blank sheet of paper and putting the typical customer for your dream, your business in the centre of it. Now draw a map of all the connections that might occur. First there will be the link from the customer to a website, that's your business. Then there may be links from the customer to other customers. There may also be links from your website to various organizations, offering a broad range of content and services. There may also be links directly through your website to suppliers or partners with whom you have contracted to process transactions. There may also be direct connections through your website to different people in your own business – providing customer service, accounts queries, for example. Always take the customer perspective in mapping the connections. You may also provide your own core content or product to customers or users of other websites, on an affiliate sales network basis, as Amazon has shown us how to do.

Now calculate the financial implications of all those potential relationships on a link by link, and case by case basis. Your model may tap intercustomer relationships to encourage customers actively to introduce other customers. Is there a commission cost? What is the likely average revenue flow if they do? Using 'click-through' to provide your customers with access to related products and services on other sites (agenting) you will probably receive between 5 and 15 per cent commission on the goods they purchase. Bringing content to your site may be free – there's lots of it on the Internet, but if that content is specific it may incur a cost to you. That content may even generate revenue from customers on your site, particularly in respect of advertising. Don't forget in calculating the financial implications to make sure you put in the revenue of the core offering of your proposition, and the costs of providing it.

Now use the revenue and cost figures you have attached to each link on your customer-connection map to help you to build up the inputs to your business plan. First you will have to ensure you have knowledge of your target market, so that you can make some realis-

Creating virtual value

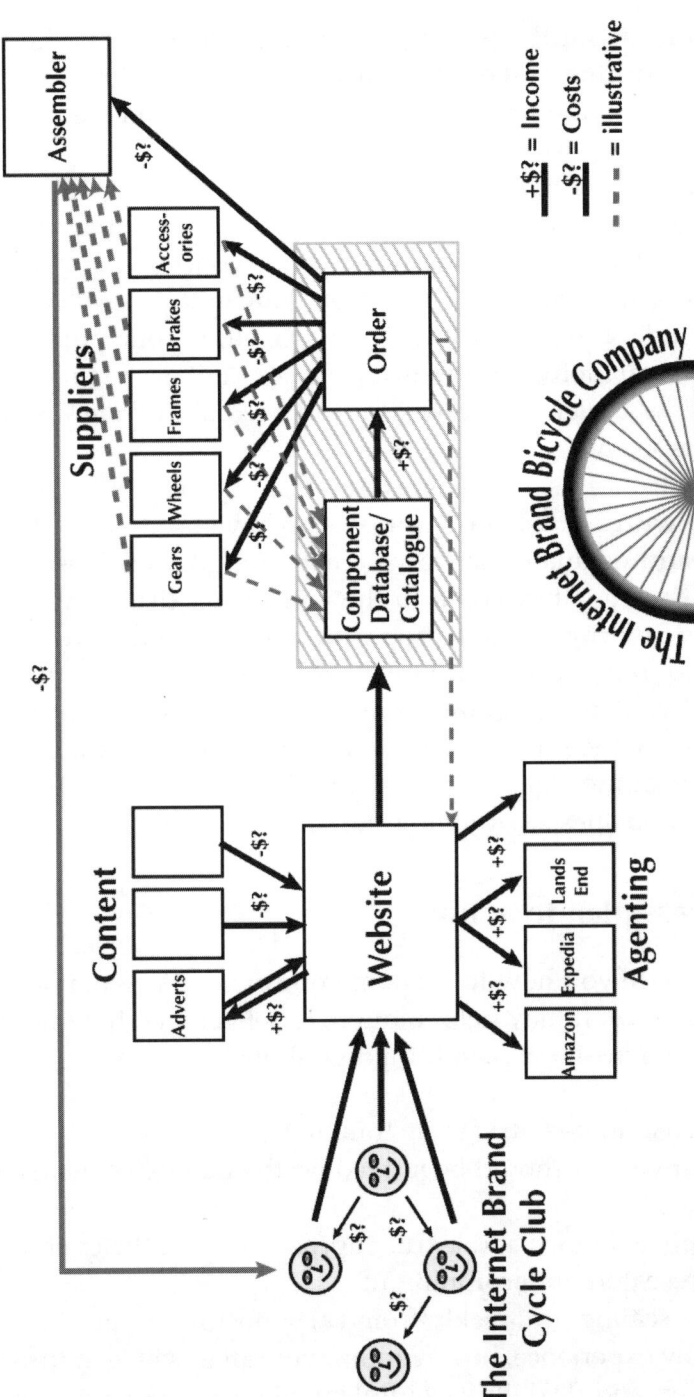

Figure 10.3 Customer-connection map

tic assumptions about the percentage of target customers who may use each link and then take up what is on offer to them. Then use these estimates to build up a comprehensive picture of revenues and costs.

The map in Figure 10.3 is a simplified view that you will need to adapt to your own needs and circumstances. This map for the Internet brand Bicycle Company conveys the concept and provides you with an outline approach to apply. You will probably find it useful to include any physical linkages as well, if your proposition requires physical delivery, for example, or if it is a 'clicks-and-mortar' business, blending physical and virtual channels from a customer perspective.

The results from this mapping exercise can be very revealing. We have worked with a number of groups who have used the technique to assemble and evaluate their own creative digital business ideas. Frequently, it seems, they come to the conclusion that they should treat the core offering in their proposition as 'discountware', if not freeware, and rely upon revenue from other suppliers through agenting and content integration linkages as their source of profit. There must be something in it, because that is the way that Mike Harris is developing Egg. And he's not alone: there seem to other Internet-based businesses applying the same principle.

From business plan to action

Others can advise you how to prepare your business plan, if indeed you need guidance. It may help, though, to reflect on what might be different about a business plan for a digital business. It will:

- ▶ be totally customer-centric in its thinking;
- ▶ be imaginative and should be judged on the quality of the underlying idea;
- ▶ look to apply a 'launch and learn' approach with sufficient but not excessive research underpinning it;
- ▶ provide for scaling up quickly from early positive results;
- ▶ indicate how experience, however unfavourable, will feed through to adaptation and flexibility as implementation progresses;

- evidence how the business will build and consolidate on success rapidly;
- probably ascribe the major proportion of investment to customer-facing developments, including branding and communications.

Using the experimentation, launch-and-learn method will not preclude the attainment of first- or early-mover advantage. Only failure to scale up quickly on positive results will deny its achievement. Prepare to be amazed by your success through, say, a deft application of freeware and intercustomer relationship, rather than be depressed by an early blow-out of your investment on a single throw of the dice that takes you nowhere and threatens to leave you high and dry. With this rigour embodied in your proposed plan you should be able to win the confidence of your investors. Then you'll be ready to push the button . . .

Summary

So, now you have the opportunity to apply the Value Levers. You've got the framework to fit to your dream. The first step is to turn that dream into a clear expression of what it is you are offering your customers – a customer proposition. Remember how important customer-centricity is. Connections are also fundamental. Think in terms of connections and you will start to see your embryonic business in visual terms. As you begin to add shape to your proposition, use the Value Lever checklist to help you flesh out your offering. When you are satisfied with how it's coming together, try mapping all the potential connections starting with the customer. Attach potential revenues and costs to connections, and use this as the basis for preparing your business plan. Accept that customer-facing expenditure will make up a large proportion of your investment capital. In this unpredictable and fast-changing world of the Internet, the source of success in your business may not be wholly clear at the outset. So, be prepared to build your plan on the basis of a scalable experiment – launch and learn then scale up for major success.

In the next chapter we will:

- ▶ Investigate what it will take in organizational terms to make your business grow
- ▶ Identify the key characteristics of the successful online business
- ▶ Find out what commentators and e-champions alike have to say about these organizational features.

11

Creating the network-sensitive organization

▶ Building an organization sensitive to the particular demands of the network economy
▶ Isolating the nine key attributes that a business needs to succeed in the network economy
▶ Establishing why they are so important and what leading commentators and e-champions say about them
▶ Evaluating the implications for digital start up and established company initiative

Characteristics of a successful digital business

In the last chapter we explored how to turn your Internet business dream into a reality. The purpose of this chapter is to evaluate the characteristics of the organization that you will need around you to take your new digital venture to the highest level of your aspirations – an organization that is sensitive to the requirements of the network environment.

'The speed of changes in the global market in an age of accelerating technological innovation means that there are no longer any certainties', reflected Lawrence Bossidy, Chairman and CEO of AlliedSignal Corporation in late 1998,

> New products and competitors emerge almost overnight, and the half-life of market strategies shrinks almost daily. It is the kind of environment in which great companies can be humbled very quickly – but where nimble, creative, and courageous organizations can thrive as never before. (Bossidy, 1998)

Now almost two years on – at least fourteen Internet years, that is – his reflections assume even greater relevance. So, if you are developing a start-up, how do you ensure that your business is nimble, creative and courageous? But, if your business is well established and owes its success to the physical offline economy, how do you avoid being humbled as you address the digital world. 'Humbled' must be exactly how Merrill Lynch and Barnes & Noble felt in the wake of Schwab and Amazon's achievements.

The problem is that successful organizations aren't what they used to be! 'The corporation as we know it, the corporation that was the engine of prosperity throughout the twentieth century, will emerge as something different in the twenty first century', observe respected Wharton School academics Jerry Yoram Wind and Jeremy Main, 'The markets, the technology, and the demands of employees, of customers, and of citizens are driving companies to change boldly and bravely. Today inaction is the riskiest strategy' (Wind and Main, 1999). Their warning applies to all organizations, both new and well established. The only difference is that the well established will find the demands for transformation particularly challenging. But what is common to all organizations embarking on a digital journey are the characteristics that they will need if they are to succeed in the network economy.

Extensive research and experience of working with client companies on innovation and entrepreneurship issues has proved invaluable in understanding the pressures that the network economy imposes upon organizations. This has led to the identification of nine attributes that are core to any successful business in the network economy:

- Ideas intensive
- Action oriented
- Partner biased
- People centred
- IT integrated
- Customer centric
- Risk conversant
- Channel fluent
- Lean focus

In the major part of this chapter we will consider each of these attributes and explore what makes them critical to digital business success, contrasting the issues for the young start-up with those for the older established business.

Ideas intensive

In a world of almost light-speed change, the need for businesses to be imaginative in everything they do takes on an unprecedented urgency. Success in today's competitive landscape is more likely to be achieved by an 'ideas-intensive' organization than one that is preoccupied with the status quo. 'The new battle lines are between the insurgents and incumbents', argues Professor Gary Hamel, 'The way to win is not through scale but creativity, imagination and experimentation' (Maitland, 28/9/99).

The incumbents ought to have a head start when it comes down to ideas. But, sadly, that just isn't the case. All too often they focus on cutting cost from existing business operations and 'doing things right', rather than exploring new opportunities for sources of income and 'doing the right things'. Most companies that have built their success in the old pre-Internet world of the physical economy just haven't valued creativity and innovation among their employees. Now they are finding it difficult to motivate them to be creative and apply their imagination to future business. Mike Harris thinks he has an answer:

> The key to creativity in any business is generating as many different and novel solutions as you can. If you're not being creative you tend to go down one track – you think, 'I know how to deal with this because I've done it before'. Most businesses are like that. But if you are looking at things creatively you think, 'how many possible approaches are there and how novel can I be?' (Cozens, 6/11/98)

The task is still to generate all those novel solutions, though.

For the digital start-up, too, the continuing generation of ideas is equally demanding. Most entrepreneurs develop a vision and then put in place a team to help them proceed doggedly in the vision's general direction. Frequently that progress is achieved with a tenacity that can blind the team to better options, different ways of doing things or fresh opportunities. In the network economy, the capacity to generate a constant source of fresh thinking really counts, so fast are markets changing. Opportunities will spring up and disappear with alacrity. The dogged tenacity of the entrepreneur may prove as much a liability as it is laudable in this climate.

'Out there in some garage, an entrepreneur is forging a bullet with your company's name on it', declares Gary Hamel, 'Once that bullet leaves the barrel, you won't be able to dodge it. You've got one option: you have to shoot first. You have to out-innovate the innovators, out-entrepreneur the entrepreneurs' (Hamel, 9/99). As Hamel so graphically describes, whether you are an incumbent or an insurgent, 'ideas intensity' is now an essential attribute of every business.

■ Action oriented

Being action oriented is about speed. It's about doing something rather than waiting for yet another piece of confirmatory research. It's about doing something even though it may not prove wholly successful – in fact it's about accepting it may even fail! 'Faster, in almost every case, is better', wrote General Electric CEO, Jack Welch, as long ago as 1994: 'From decision-making to deal-making, to communications to product introduction, speed, more often than not, ends up being the competitive differentiator' (General Electric, 1994). If it was true then, it is even truer now, and for every company. David Pottruck at Schwab has no doubt that action orientation is a major factor in Schwab's success. 'Our advantage is in our ability to innovate faster – to make the discontinuous leap' (Lappen, 29/4/96).

'The decade of the 90s has witnessed significant and discontinuous change in the competitive environment', explains respected management guru, Professor C. K. Prahalad, 'As all traditional companies are confronted with disruptive changes, the capacity to learn and act fast is increasingly a major source of competitive advantage' (Prahalad, 4/10/99). The watchword now is 'launch and learn, don't learn and launch'. 'Analysis paralysis' as an excuse for inaction has become the fast track to the corporate graveyard. 'If your instinct is to wait, ponder, and perfect, then you're dead', observes Ruthann Quindlen, partner in California-based Institutional Venture Partners (IVP), 'Now that product cycles are being compressed from eighteen months to six months or even three months, you have to be willing to try something and see if it works – and, if it doesn't work, to change it fast' (LaBarre, 6/99). Quindlen should know – IVP are successful investors in many Internet start-ups.

Action orientation is where the start-up has an advantage over the incumbent. That propensity for action needs to be enshrined and a sense of energy sustained as the business develops. If you hope to tap and sustain first-mover advantage. then you will have to be fleet of foot – and remain so.

Partner biased

There are a number of very good reasons why every business, big or small, old or new, needs to develop a bias towards finding partners rather than trying to do most things themselves. These include: sharing costs, reducing risk, tapping fresh thinking, acquiring knowledge, moving faster, bringing new products to your markets, shedding non-core work, accessing new or different skills. 'Creating the future is a task that involves more than the traditional stand-alone company', affirms C K Prahalad, 'Resources available to the company are dramatically enhanced through alliances and networks' (Prahalad, 4/10/98). In the fast-moving world of the network economy you need to keep your options open.

Creating a web of partners is a clever ploy that the information technology sector originated when it seemed that only high-tech companies needed to worry about speed and time as competitive factors. Companies in the high-tech sector actively participate in relatively loose and highly flexible networks of businesses that enable them to share costs, resources, risk, capital, capacity, and even R&D investments. Often such networks are overlapping in nature, and incorporate the phenomenon of 'co-opetition', with organizations often collaborating with potential and actual competitors in order to compete more effectively in the marketplace as a whole.

We can now draw on that high-tech experience as a guide to our own needs as we launch our digital business. Think about how you will apply the Value Levers and ask yourself whether you can be effective without a partnering philosophy at the core of your business. Content integration means accessing diverse content from other sectors – Schwab and Amazon each ally with diverse content providers. Value through agenting depends upon more than just suppliers – for a major portal such as Freeserve, partnering may even extend to taking small equity stakes. Real-time activity requires a level of flexibility and adaptability that can only properly be achieved with a web of partners who can respond rapidly – order a computer from Dell and the order goes to Fedex who consolidate orders and then organize component suppliers, in real time. 'Increasingly the strategic focus of successful companies is not the company or even the industry but the value-creating system itself, within which different economic actors – suppliers, business partners, allies, customers – work together to co-produce value', observed management gurus Richard Normann and Rafael Ramirez prophetically in 1993, 'Their strategic task is the reconfiguration of roles and relationships amongst this constellation of actors in order to mobilize the creation of value in new forms' (Normann and Ramirez, 7/93).

For the start-up digital business, partnering should be fundamental and almost natural. It will conserve investment, should reduce risk and enable 'upscaling' very quickly. For the 'e-' development inside the established business partnering may require a more purposeful consideration. First, it may well mean stopping doing some things that have always been done inside the business. This will have ramifications. Organizations tend to develop a very stable view of the world where everything may change but the status quo. Partner bias may require reformulating that worldview.

People centred

'Probably the biggest single component . . . is bringing together a talented and diverse group of people' (Hazleton, 7/98). This is Jeff Bezos's view about making ideas work at Amazon. Finding those people and bringing them together into a motivated high-performance team will be quintessential to your success. Ask Dave Pottruck at Schwab, if you are in any doubt, and you will get the following answer. 'The next great product does not give us the competitive edge. It's recruitment of terrific people that creates the ability to innovate' (McReynolds 12/7/98).

For all the light-speed activity that is creeping into successful digital business, getting the people bit right is critical. 'Despite all of our focus on speed, we consciously slow down for one thing: hiring people', comments Alan Naumann of software company Calico Technologies, 'That's tough to do when you're growing as fast as we are, but it's the one aspect of business today in which the cost of mistakes is greater than the advantage of acting in real time' (LaBarre, 6/99). The issue of 'slowing down' spreads much wider than just the hiring process; it extends to the way we see the people who work with us, and to the way we behave towards them as co-workers, if we want to get the best out of them. 'But there is a deal you have to do to get people to bring their creativity to work. You have to treat them like human beings', acknowledges Egg's Mike Harris (Hall, 11/10/98), reflecting the truth that employment for many in Western society remains a demeaning experience, devoid of motivation.

'Developing the Destiny Factor' is an interesting exercise that established businesses can use to get in touch with themselves and their future (Senge, 1994). Managers roll the clock back to remember the earliest entrepreneurial days of their business and rediscover what it must have been like at the early cutting edge. The exercise seems almost invariably to reveal, in the distant recesses of the past, a small and dedicated team beavering away, with a vision and a sense of purpose. Even in today's network economy where smart ideas, winning technology and new business models are the game, 'team' is still what counts. 'Teamwork is the only way we can accomplish anything', emphasizes Chuck Schwab, 'We are not built like a traditional brokerage house. We are not about outselling everyone else but about growing the company, which will create jobs and allow people to grow their careers.'

But perhaps we should allow the last word on this to Michael Dell, an e-champion who has built his success on a constant and successful search to accumulate high-grade talent. 'Making sure you have the right people to support the growth of the business and complement the strengths that are already within the company is probably the most important lesson' (Dell, 1998).

IT integrated

As the established business organization transforms from a full-service hierarchy towards Normann and Ramirez's prophetic value-creating system or 'value constellation', it becomes almost amorphous in its nature. Information replaces structure and becomes the glue that holds the organization together. Bill Gates talks of a Digital Nervous System (DNS) which 'is the corporate, digital equivalent of the human nervous system, providing a well-integrated flow of information to the right part of the organization at the right time' (Gates, 1999). So, if information plays this absolutely fundamental role, then information technology and the business itself have become completely inseparable.

This doesn't mean that you need to be a technologist to have any chance of building a successful digital business organization; far from it. You do need to understand the critical role that Internet-based technology plays in making all this possible. Transmission Control Protocol/Internet Protocol, better known as TCP/IP, or just IP for short, is the building block of all Internet and related technologies. IP-based software now provides an open standard and universal basis that enables businesses to connect with everyone who might be in their 'value constellation' – from supplier, through employee, to intermediary and right on the customer.

For the start-up, IP-based software puts new businesses on an even footing with established ones, and may even give them an advantage! IP-based software, such as powerful web application servers from aggressive young companies like SilverStream, makes 'industrial strength' applications affordable even to start-ups because the solutions they provide are completely scalable. You just pay for what you want when you want it, and add to it as your business grows. You may not even buy the software, preferring to rent your growing needs from the new breed of application service provider. You can also configure this new progeny of software quickly and relatively easily to your business needs. For the established company those same solutions are equally available, but all too often established thinking is wedded to the big-ticket proprietary systems that have underpinned their real-world success. These are less flexible, and generally lead to solutions that are less than wholly satisfactory and take longer to configure.

IP-based infrastructure is the key to Gates's Digital Nervous System and to the application of key Value Levers. It is elemental to achieving real-time activity-based value for customers. Effective prosumer involvement will be well nigh impossible without it. Mass customization is similarly dependent. Once again, Michael Dell seems to qualify for the last words on this:

For Dell, online commerce was only the beginning. Because we viewed the Internet as a central part of our IT strategy, we started to view the ownership of information differently, too. Rather than closely guarding our information databases, which took us years to develop, we used Internet browsers to essentially give that same information to our customers and suppliers – bringing them literally inside our business. This became the key to what I call a virtually integrated organization – an organization linked not by physical assets, but by information. (Dell, 1998)

Customer centric

The need to put the customer at the centre of your thinking is, as this book has established, completely integral to digital business success. As we have seen, it has driven the success of all of our e-champions. Others have similarly used the conviction of 'customers above all else' in a pre-network economy context and gained. 'The purpose of being in business is not to make money; the purpose of being in business is to be of unique, important and meaningful help and value to the customer', says marketing consultant and publisher, James Wendell Forbes, 'Then it will follow, "as night the day", that you cannot help but make money' (*Trade Marketing*, 9/97). Adherence to the principle has surely stood Wendell Forbes in good stead.

In this new 'value constellation', where IP-based systems have enabled us to include the customer as an integral part of the system, it naturally follows that the customer becomes a part of your organization. As Ron Ashkenas and colleagues put it, 'The boundaryless organization begins and ends with customers. . . . Its entire focus is to anticipate and serve changing customer needs. Moreover, it works to see itself from the customer's point of view' (Ashkenas *et al.*, 1999). Once you see the customer as part of the organization, this will free up your thinking and all sorts of things will become possible. Customers can work with you to co-design products and services for the benefit of all customers, as well as helping you to personalize to their own specific needs and wants. Customers of network solutions provider Cisco Systems reduce their installation costs by co-creating features on the routers they purchase. The sale of these co-created products contributed as much as two-fifths to the $3.8 billion revenues that Cisco generated in 1998. European car manufacturer Fiat wanted to test new design concepts for its Punto model. It invited potential customers to visit the Fiat website and express their preferences for a large array of the prospective Punto's features. More than 3,000 people participated, and Fiat was thereby able to capture valuable insights into the preferences of a targeted consumer group and test different design concepts at low cost. For their part, customers got a car that was better matched to what they actually wanted.

Almost without exception our e-champions are partnering with customers to co-create value for the benefit of the whole customer base. 'A critical difference in running an Internet company is our closeness to our customers', explains Meg Whitman, Pierre Omidyar's CEO, 'This is especially true for eBay, because we enable individuals to do business with one another in a way that's completely new and powerful . . . We get products into the community as quickly as possible; then we listen to reactions to those products and make changes accordingly. Some of our best ideas . . . have come from our community of users' (LaBarre, 6/99).

■ Risk conversant

In the roller-coaster business environment of the network world, risk is endemic. Businesses need to take a more positive attitude and develop an effective risk-sharing and risk-taking culture to adapt and thrive in this uncertain landscape.

While companies focus on shareholder value as their prime directive, it is natural that they will tend to be more risk averse, seeking to achieve a return that restricts their business risk and smoothes their earnings. Yet shareholders too are becoming aware of the world around them, and recognizing that without risk there cannot be reward. Internet investors are acutely aware of this and are taking significant risk to achieve significant returns. Without this sea change in attitude among investors the development of the network economy might never have been funded. We owe the existence of Amazon, Priceline, eBay, Freeserve and many other Internet-based businesses to this calculated acceptance of risk by so many investors. We owe them a debt of gratitude!

The attitude to business risk is the one arena where there still needs to be a change of tack inside many established companies. Their prevalent outlook is the principal factor holding them back from taking those important steps towards developing effective digital business and success in the network economy. Failure remains a hanging offence for far too many management teams. Fear of failure creates indecision and inaction. If companies are to be action oriented and apply their ideas in a launch-and-learn manner, they must expect that a goodly proportion of their ideas will fail. Rather than dwelling on the failures, they need to see them as essential to provide the experience they need to refine their experiments and get them right next time around. This negative attitude to failure is much more evident in Europe than it is in the USA. It is also a major reason for Europe continuing to lag behind the USA in network economy development.

For the start-up business, being risk conversant is equally an issue. Launch and learn and scalable experimentation apply as for any other digital business initiative, whatever its provenance. That doogged tenacity of entrepreneurs that can blind them to better options and more creative approaches can also make them risk averse, seeking to conserve their limited, and probably dwindling, capital resources. Boldness characterizes the really successful Internet successes.

Channel fluent

Channel fluency is about making it easy for customers to do business with you. It is also about recognizing that they will decide how and when to deal with you, so this means evaluating what access channels your business needs in order to be successful, and not relying just upon PC-based Internet access because that's all you've got. By 2003 there will be more than a billion mobile phones with digital capability in use around the world, and interactive digital TV is also spreading rapidly. Today's customers are becoming increasingly capable at using a growing range of network access devices, including telephone, Internet, hand-held digital appliances, multimedia kiosks and interactive television. They are also still happily employing that trusted means of access from the original primitive network economy – face-to-face contact.

Channel fluency is also about how you manage and share the knowledge of interaction with your customers. 'In order to be successful in electronic commerce, everyone who touches the customer needs to be able to see the total picture – a 360 degree view – of that customer's relationships with your firm', says Internet author and consultant, Patricia Seybold, 'While it's important for customers to have one-stop shopping and to feel that everyone they interact with knows who they are and what they need, it's equally important for your employees and key business partners to have access to the complete customer picture' (Seybold, 1998).

For a digital start-up the potential for physical contact with the customer base may quite possibly be important, in addition to the virtual channel that you will inevitably establish as the initial and primary access for your business. 'Clicks-and-mortar' is the phrase Dave Pottruck coined for this. 'Sooner or later, you need more than an outpost in cyberspace. When you have a problem affecting customers, that's when you know the true meaning of the word "mortar", and that is people', advises Pottruck, 'Online commerce has got to be about technology plus people. It's a false dichotomy to think you're either doing business online or you're doing it the old fashioned way. We're all embedded in the real world' (*PR Newswire*, 19/07/99). Pottruck's point is important; it is not a question of virtual or physical channels. It may well be both, depending upon the needs of your customers. Remember that you can achieve a physical interface with your customers by partnering businesses that already have those 'on-the-ground' capabilities. If you are worried that you may be in a weak position to negotiate as a start-up, remember that, as more retailing moves online, those real world-rooted businesses will have to look a lot harder for the means to achieve a turn on their physical outlets. Just choose your partners wisely!

For established businesses launching into the digital world, physical channels will probably be available to you as an option. These may be very useful, but they may be a liability. Dixons' retail outlets provided Freeserve with an extremely low-cost route to market, so Freeserve gained. On the other hand, the presence of a physical option may mean you feel obliged to use them when you are trying to compete on equal terms with the lower-cost, nimbler virtual organizations. That, however, may be more a matter of developing lean focus.

Lean focus

A key characteristic of the network environment is its capacity to reduce the need to tie up capital in physical assets, such as offices, retail outlets and branches, and in unnecessary organizational trappings and processes that tend to accumulate around the real-world physical business over time. This means that most digital business start-ups can apply the maximum proportion of their available capital to customer-based development, compared to real-world based competitors.

Lean focus is a useful way of contrasting the differing mental attitude between the virtual start-up and the digital initiative of the established real-world business. The issue is distinctly one of value enhancement over cost reduction. Once again the established business should have an automatic advantage over the start-up but it isn't always quite so clear-cut. Mindset gets in the way and attachment to physical assets and redundant processes can provide a real drag on progress. 'In getting companies to start thinking about the ways of rewriting the industry rules', say management consultants Fiona Czerniawska and Gavin Potter, 'we have found that the challenge is to make people ask, not "How can we convert this physical process into information?" but "What – if any – physical processes do we truly need?"' (Czerniawska and Potter, 1998). These authors advocate a technique termed 'zero-based physical budgeting' whose purpose is to get real-world managers to think about how they will create virtual value for customers starting without any physical assets and processes, adding in only those that are really necessary.

Among our e-champions the lean focus principle is well understood. Schwab operates an expanding branch network of over 300 branch offices and four national service centres, maximizing the value that can be created by the integration of physical and virtual assets. David Pottruck strongly believes Schwab will gain a significant competitive edge by being able to serve its customers wherever they happen to be, whether that means in a store, on the phone, or online. Dell's direct build-to-order model has an implicit lean focus foundation that Michael Dell is keen to maintain. This low physical asset count has undoubtedly made a major contribution to Dell's meteoric growth. As for Amazon, Jeff Bezos has recognized the need to add physical assets if he is to maintain service standards and high levels of customer satisfaction as he embraces that bigger vision for Amazon. He is adding distribution centres across the USA, and reportedly some flagship bookstores. Physical asset acquisition by Amazon will probably not help the nervous disposition of his more timid investors. Pluthero's Freeserve, on the other hand, can stay almost fully virtual since Freeserve taps the parent company's physical outlets in building its customer base. Nearly a thousand stores and a customer base of many millions have had a lot to do with Freeserve's rapid early success. Egg, too, will be able to count on its parent's physical assets when required. As for Priceline and eBay, both can remain confidently virtual, reflecting the inherent power of their virtual business models. Draw once more on the experience of the e-champions to inform your approach to lean focus.

Summary

Success in launching a digital business depends upon more than an excellent business plan based around a neat idea that will create outstanding value for customers. It requires attention to detail in how you go about it. Remember that entrepreneurs cannot succeed on their own, they need an effective team and organization around them. Look at the success of each and everyone of our e-champions and you will see that they all owe their success as much to the people around them as they do to their own abilities and perseverance. Look also at the nine attributes defined here, and note that a digital business is not a quiet life. It is a world of constant experimentation, in surroundings that are continually moving and never

Attribute	Action
Ideas intensive	"Encourage imagination and creativity"
Action oriented	"Adopt a 'launch & learn' approach"
Partner biased	"Develop partnerships with win–win collaborators"
People centred	"Evolve an adaptable and capable human resource"
IT integrated	"Build a flexible IT infrastructure"
Customer centric	"Develop a total customer focus"
Risk conversant	"Create a risk taking/sharing culture"
Channel fluent	"Construct the right interface"
Lean focus	"Remove excess physical assets"

Figure 11.1 Attributes and actions for the network-sensitive organization

certain but always exciting. 'There's no rest for the weary', chortles an irrepressible Jeff Bezos (Figure 11.1).

In the next chapter we will:

▶ Define the imperative for established companies of transforming to a business suited to the distinct demands of the network economy
▶ Learn that the challenge of transformation isn't new
▶ Find out what that challenge entails now and how others have fared

12

Transformational options

▶ Why embracing the network economy is essential for the sustained wellbeing of established businesses
▶ Appreciating the revitalizing efforts of companies over the past two decades
▶ Understanding the stages of transition from conventional, real-world to digitally literate, virtually enabled business
▶ Exploring the transformation options, their implications and e-champion experience of them

Change is not optional

In the previous chapter we evaluated the characteristics of the network-sensitive organization. These attributes represent standards for the successful digital business to aspire to, as it smartly leaves its starting blocks. In this chapter we will explore the twist – those nine attributes will define the nature of *all* future organizations, not just the Internet start-ups, and not just those established businesses that have embraced the virtual world and launched specific digital initiatives. This fact may come as a rude shock to some companies but the reality is that the virtual world will define the future business landscape and competitive environment. Why does the virtual always win over the physical? Because it is usually faster, cheaper, better and easier. This doesn't mean the virtual will always replace the physical. There will be many cases where it won't, but add some virtual element to an existing physical business model to provide some value-based refinement, and the integrated proposition will almost certainly set a new competitive standard for the existing physical offline business environment. So whether they like it or not, established companies have got to face up to digital business and become network-sensitive organizations if they are to thrive. In this penultimate chapter of the book we will explore the case for transformation of all businesses and the options available to them.

The emergence of the network economy is bringing about a sea change in the competitive dynamics of today's business environment. As the network economy gathers strength, companies will find that the risks associated with adopting a 'business as usual' approach will become far greater than the risks associated with embarking on a course of significant organizational change. Given the rapid pace at which the network economy is taking shape, it's a strong possibility that many of today's businesses will find themselves faced with the option of either keeping the organization as it is and definitely failing, or of changing the organization and possibly failing. This is the realistic, if unsavoury, prospect (see Figure 12.1).

Should you be in any doubt as to the speed with which the change will take place and network economics take over, then the experi-

Figure 12.1 Value networks

ence of the US domestic airline market should provide a cautionary tale of what can happen and how quickly.

In the mid-1970s the US Government deregulated domestic air transport. All of a sudden, new airlines could enter what had been a tightly controlled, competitive world. In their previously regulated existence airline corporations accepted high costs, focused on their engineering qualities and were preoccupied with first-class passengers. Load factors on aircraft were, on average, relatively low. As one observer put it, all that mattered was wiping the plane down with an oily rag and getting it back in the air – passengers were just walk-on cargo, unless they were first class. With deregulation came a new breed of competitors. Corporations like People's Express and Braniff arrived on the scene, bent on a low-cost, no-frills, customer-focused airline experience. They quickly caught everyone's attention, including the incumbent airlines. Their success led to all the established players converting their own business dynamics to compete on the same terms as these aggressive new competitors. But for the incumbents it meant a painful transformation in order to adjust. Within a couple of years or more the new entrants found, too late, their low-cost business model was unsustainable. People's Express and Braniff went to the wall, but their legacy of low-cost, customer-focused competition lived on. There was no way to put the lid back on Pandora's box. And so, like dominoes, the incumbents fell one by one – Eastern, Delta, Pan Am – also unable to sustain the new basis of competition where revenues could not match costs. The moral of the story is simple. Once the competitive dynamics of a sector change due to some external factor, they are unlikely ever to revert – even if the harbingers of that new competition themselves fall by the wayside as a consequence.

We can apply this lesson to what is going on around us now, but there are some differences. First, the external factor – in this case the Internet – is technologically driven unlike the sudden intervention of the US government, although it is similarly irreversible. Second, the principal new entrants responsible for new competitive dynamics have yet to go to the wall, and may not. Third, and perhaps the most important, this external change affects every corner of commerce and business, not just one sector. In fact, many sectors have yet to feel how cold the wind of change can be.

But change is not easy

Experience shows that change is not something that comes easy to most established companies, particularly if they are mature organizations used to operating in stable markets. This is an age-old problem, as advice to aspiring rulers from medieval political theorist, Niccolo Machiavelli, reveals:

> There is nothing more difficult to plan, more doubtful of success, nor more dangerous to manage than the creation of a new system. For the initiator has the enmity of all who would profit by the preservation of the old institutions, and merely lukewarm defenders in those who should gain by the new ones.

But the problems aren't all political. Organizations are developed for permanence and gain stability through inward focus. Usually this is achieved through reinforcing the status quo. In times of turbulence this inherent behaviour presents some difficulty. As long ago as the late 1970s more forward-looking corporations became sensitive to the accelerating pace of change around them and to their own slowness to adapt to its demands. Senior managers adopted and applied a variety of techniques in an attempt to make their organizations more responsive to changing external circumstances. Success was limited. 'Over the past decade, I have watched more than one hundred companies try to remake themselves into significantly better competitors', reported leading authority on business change, Professor John Kotter, in 1995:

> These efforts have gone under many banners: total quality management, reengineering, right sizing, restructuring, cultural change, and turnaround. But, in almost every case, the basic goal has been the same: to make fundamental changes in how business is conducted in order to help cope with a new, more challenging marketplace. A few of these corporate change efforts have been very successful. A few have been utter failures. Most fall somewhere in between, with a distinct tilt toward the lower end of the scale. (Kotter, 3/95)

In addition to the initiatives specifically noted by Kotter there were also various attempts at introducing innovation and entrepreneurship – corporate venturing, intrapreneurship programmes and skunkworks were just some of them. These produced even fewer reports of success or lasting benefit.

In the 1980s there was a sense that attention to corporate renewal, in other words firms revitalizing themselves, represented good corporate citizenship. It was important, but seemed almost optional because expectations of success were uncertain and were kept deliberately low. Besides, things were changing but not that radically. So, the activity was treated as non-essential in most cases, and efforts were allowed to wither away as soon as senior managers thought the going was becoming a little rough. Invariably this happened not long after the start, when new ventures continued to demand capital. Managers were generally uncomfortable with the risk and the uncertainty. The final outcome was inevitable. So, largely discredited as a management technique, corporate renewal languished through the 1990s.

Awareness of the network economy and of its implications for established companies is now growing fast, and with it the realization that change is no longer optional. In every sector there is a groundswell of belief that transformation is now absolutely essential, there is no alternative. This is reflected in virtually every survey of senior managers in businesses, both global and domestic. There is only one difficulty. Just because change is now compulsory doesn't make it any easier. In fact it becomes more difficult, principally because the timescale within which that transformational change has to take place has been foreshortened. The same challenges apply as they did in the 1980s.

Transition to digital business

It seems there are typically three stages of transition to the fully digitally capable business, as Figure 12.2 illustrates. So, where do you start? Most organizations take their first faltering steps into e-business by way of *ad hoc* experiment, instigated perhaps by some Internet buff in IT. Like a child learning to walk, this experimentation, if successful, leads to a more confident attitude and preparedness to be wholly committed to the task – falling over happens less often and doesn't hurt too much anyway if you are wearing a diaper/nappy. For the business as a whole this second more confident stage of transition typically integrates digital capability into the current way of doing things. Only a limited part of what is done in the integration step will be truly 'network sensitive', providing a full-scale appreciation of what may yet be required.

Having reached the second stage, there's still a long way to go to transform the organization to a business that is digitally capable and fully adapted to the competitive demands of the network economy. The achievement of this third stage requires a giant leap. It's like the child learning to run or to jump; it doesn't have to think about how to walk any more. The new game now is how to use that new mobility mischievously to get into all sorts of interesting things. It's

	Experimentation	Integration	Transformation
Digital strategy	None	Supports current business strategy	Integral to business strategy
Business strategy	No digital input	Limited digital implementation	Digital-thinking driven
Scope	Within function	Cross functional	Enterprise-wide full value network: interconnected suppliers and consumers
Return	Uncertain	Cost reduction and process enhancement	Revenue enhancement and consumer satisfaction
Levers	Infrastructure and software applications	Business processes	People, knowledge, connections and relationships
Role of information	Secondary to technology	Supports process efficiency/ effectiveness	Information asymmetries used to create business opportunities

Adapted from Kettinger & Hackbarth, 15/3/99

Figure 12.2 From experimentation to transformation

about thinking differently and doing differently, adapting the business to the network economy and to all it entails – not trying to adapt the network economy to the business. It's about assuming all the attributes of the network-sensitive organization.

Ask any single team of managers where they think their company is on the three-stage transition and almost certainly you will get the full range of opinions. At the one extreme there will be the realists who know that a 'brochure-ware' website is dabbling and experimentation at best. At the other extreme there will be the blissfully ignorant who believe any web presence is tantamount to transformation. So, let's take a closer look at what each stage involves.

In that early stage of *experimentation* there is usually a lack of leadership on digital issues. Different departments will possess disparate online applications. Purchasing may have developed an EDI (electronic data interchange) system to link up with its largest suppliers. Marketing might have created a public website to improve its public relations, while Research and Development may have established an intranet to facilitate the sharing of product specifications and designs. These applications operate to the benefit of functional interests and senior managers are unlikely to have any expectation of the returns these may produce.

The second stage of *integration* results from a much wider appreciation of the inescapable advance of the network world. Recognizing what is possible and what is required to compete, managers see that they have much to do to ready their businesses to achieve digital capability. The real task is to build vision beyond integration, and use imagination to envisage what might just be possible. Yet, their focus characteristically remains on the existing way of doing things and how those might be made more efficient, with little emphasis on how to use the new competitive environment for revenue-generating activities. Typical among these are the airlines that have suddenly become aware, once again, of a new generation of low-cost airlines using the network economy to gain an advantage. In the UK, the success of EasyJet, with a high proportion of bookings fulfilled over the Internet, has goaded British Airways into action. Among the e-champions, Dell, Schwab and Amazon have had a similar effect upon their competitors.

The third stage – *transformation* – demands a major leap forward. It is the point where digital thinking drives business strategy, where businesses embrace automatically the characteristics of the network-sensitive organization as fundamental to future well being and success. Managers see the broader picture with every supplier, partner and customer as part of an interconnected network. They energize and motivate colleagues to share knowledge and apply imagination to discern new ways to provide services to customers. They are sensitized to how information flows around their networked organization, aware of how those network flows create both opportunities and threats. As e-champion Michael Dell reminds us:

The Internet must become your business. The use of the Internet throughout the business will be what ultimately distinguishes successful firms in all industries. In the future, there will be no distinction between 'dot-com' and traditional businesses, just winners and losers. (*Business Wire*, 25/8/99)

Transform, disaggregate or perish

So, there is no option. Every business has to become fully network sensitive, and the sooner the better. The first two stages are relatively easy. It is the third stage – *transformation* – that is most exacting and maybe beyond the capacity of many organizations to achieve readily. Rather than attempt to transform the organization, 'disaggregation' – where the business creates its own digital start-up while the parent organization can undertake a more gradual transformation process, or is wound-up – may be the only achievable route to the future. Disaggregation as a strategy doesn't obviate the need for the parent to transform itself, unless of course winding up the old pre-network economy business is the ultimate goal; it just removes some of the urgency. Figure 12.3 displays the four principal options and routes to transformation. Three of the options involve disaggregation.

The generally poor experience of corporate renewal, intrapreneurship and reinvention programmes of the 1980s and 1990s highlights the scale of difficulty in achieving effective transformation. The three-stage transition process can seem deceptively easy. It is anything but. Four of our e-champions have undertaken some form of transformation and are sensitive to this fact. Three are using, or have used, disaggregation strategies to support their own transformations. One, Dell Corporation, has used the most challenging and direct route, option 1.

Since Michael Dell founded his business in 1984, arguably its transition to a fully digitally enabled business has been less troublesome than for other longer instituted companies. If you look closer, though, you will see that Dell's transformation to a business that uses the Internet effectively throughout its operations has required leadership, vision, a distinct management style and a propensity for action. The intention is clear in Michael's visionary thinking: 'The

Transformational options

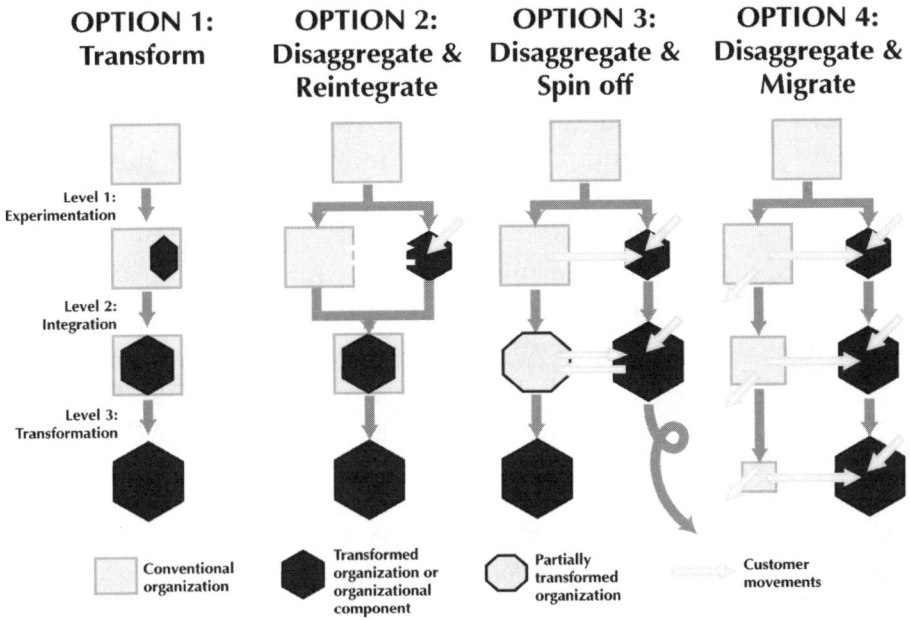

Figure 12.3 Transformation options

Internet will fundamentally change the way that companies do business through its ability to enable people to conduct low-cost, one-to-one customer interactions with rich content' (Dell, 1998). There are clues, too, in his style of management and in the flat organization structure that he has put in place. Michael has little time for formal chains of command when they get in the way of getting the job done, and he likes to make it known that his company is 'allergic to hierarchy'. His approach to recruitment also indicates why a direct transformation has proved a sensible option. He believes that success in business requires one 'to add talent and organize a business correctly'. Michael believes that the ideal employee is someone who has an open and questioning mind, a healthy balance of experience and intellect, and an eagerness to make innovations despite the risk involved of making mistakes. How many leaders of incumbent businesses would be prepared to recruit on that basis? The answer is very few. But that is what is required for a successful business suited to the demands of the network economy.

Chuck Schwab took a different route. He chose option 2 with equally outstanding success. Charles Schwab Corporation, too, is a relative youngster and a maverick among financial businesses. Chuck Schwab founded his business in 1971 as a discount broker offering a cheap, convenient and 'no-frills' share-dealing' service. So, like Michael Dell, one might expect Chuck to have taken the direct route of option 1 when he developed eSchwab, evolving it at the core of the main business. He quite deliberately did not. The decision to set up eSchwab as a separate electronic commerce unit was done in part to enable Charles Schwab Corporation to learn how to compete with deep-discount brokerages, such as E*Trade and Ameritrade. These recent arrivals on the scene were also working hard to offer an Internet-based service. 'We had to figure out how to compete with these small brokerages', explains Chuck's lieutenant, Dave Pottruck, 'So we needed a group that felt like they did: nimble, unshackled from the larger bureaucracy.'

There was a second reason why Schwab chose option 2. It was a matter of the risk to which it might expose the core business, as Dan Leemon, Schwab's Head of Strategy notes: 'We created e.Schwab because we wanted to learn. But we did not want to risk the whole company' (Gunn, 7/12/98). The success of eSchwab speaks for itself. Putting eSchwab at the heart of the core business consummated Schwab's transformation, and demonstrated the importance of leadership in achieving transformation. Chuck Schwab was prepared to take a major hit in terms of his firm's revenues by giving every client access to the standard $29.95 stock trade fee, because he believed it was the right thing to do, demonstrating inspired intuition and decisive leadership.

Both Freeserve and Egg are examples of disaggregation using option 3. Both businesses have spun off from their parents. One has floated and achieved its Internet status, the other is in the process of doing so. Freeserve is a different type of business to Dixons, so a separate existence is more natural. It had to be that way, as John Pluthero explains: 'We called it Freeserve rather than Dixons.net for good reason. It wasn't a retailer's online brand strategy; it was never designed to be a promotional device for Dixons. It was designed to be an Internet business' (Hall, 11/7/99). Vision, conviction and persuasion were essential to achieving the right outcome. John Pluthero persuaded Dixons' senior management that the best way forward for Freeserve would be spin off the new organization and float it on the stock market. 'If this is as big as we think it could be, then we are going to have to play on a level playing field with other Internet businesses', argued Pluthero to Dixons CEO, John Clare, 'which means we will need to float and generate our own currency and resources because that is the way this market is going' (Waples, 13/6/99). It is conceivable that Dixons Group might one day put Freeserve back at the heart of the group's business, but probably not until a majority of UK consumers are actively using the Internet through one access device or another.

Egg is a financial business operating in a similar field to its parent, Prudential Group. It has a separate existence to free it from the stifling culture of the parent business. Flotation will complete that separation, and this independence will be vital if Mike Harris is to prove that Egg deserves its pre-eminent position and full Internet status. Egg's Digital Value Profile in Chapter 10 suggests there is still much to do. It is also imaginable that Egg might one day find itself a role assisting the transformation of its parent. As with Freeserve, that role is likely to be some years off. A separate profitable existence needs to be established by each of them respectively before they are in a strong enough position to use their own success to drive their parent companies' operations and transformation.

Examples of option 4 as a disaggregation route are likely only to occur when established businesses experience real difficulty in transforming their existing pre-Internet businesses to a form that is fit for the network economy. Finally acknowledging the inevitable, senior managers in these businesses are likely to put their investment wholly into their Internet vehicle, hoping to migrate their customer base over time to this new and separate entity. They will then expect to run down the core business as a form of 'cash cow', extracting the maximum value from its customers as it shrinks.

There is a twist to the disaggregation model. The reality is that the vast majority of businesses have yet to decide on how to transform.

Many will decide on option 3, hoping to enjoy the halo effect on their own stock value of an Internet subsidiary's enhanced market valuation. The outcome, though, may be very different. Unable to achieve any impact upon their old pre-Internet core business, managers may find themselves with an unplanned option 4 on their hands. Worse still, it may turn out to be an option 5. In this case the new Internet-based business is unsuccessful and withers, as well as the old core business!

Summary

So, there's no soft option. Every business has to become an Internet business and that means assuming the characteristics of a network sensitive organization. Changes to current competitive environments are likely to be sudden and irreversible as smarter businesses find the way to merge virtual and physical to gain a real advantage, so every business needs to prepare, and do it now. However, changing the status quo won't be easy if the experiences of forward-thinking and acting companies throughout the 1980s and 1990s are anything to go by. Becoming network sensitive is bound up in a full transformation of the business and there are steps towards achieving that. The danger is that many managers will not be able to build vision beyond the integration of the network economy into current business thinking. They need to look beyond that and adapt both business thinking and the business to the network economy. Vision beyond integration is vital. There are different routes to transformation, and dis-aggregation may well be most suited to your business. But beware the shrinking core and option 5, unless you plan it to be that way!

In the last chapter, let's put the spotlight on you. Find out:

▶ That you probably share many of the characteristics that have enabled our e-champions' successes
▶ That the key learning points from these last twelve chapters provide a map for your own prospective digital success
▶ That action is probably all that separates you from them

Reflections

The bucks start here

13
A personal agenda

▶ Recognizing that our e-champions are just a bunch of regular guys
▶ Isolating the shared characteristics that have underpinned their personal endeavours
▶ Relating those characteristics to your own capabilities
▶ Reviewing the key learning points of the past twelve chapters.

Curtain call for the e-champions

Over the course of thirteen chapters our e-champions have played an important and active role, guiding us with their successes to plan and develop our own. Their achievements have all the elegance of a gliding swan – serene and powerful above the water, lots of frantic movement below as they and their teams grapple daily with a rapidly changing landscape. 'The Internet changes so fast,' agrees Jeff Bezos, 'The set of competitors changes every day' (Hof, 27/9/99). So, let's pause for a moment, and catch our breath, reminding ourselves just who these seven guys are when you strip away their Internet success and their fortunes.

First, there's the dyslexic graduate who found that an effective compensatory learning style helped him to see the business world in a different way to others, and realize that investors wanted more than they were being offered. Curiosity about the Internet drove one very successful young financial executive to give up his lucrative job to prove to himself that he would never have any regrets. The following day he borrowed his father's old Chevrolet pick-up and got his wife to drive him, their dog and a few belongings from Fort Worth to Seattle, while he sat in the passenger seat drafting his business plan. There's the self-described ideas man and addicted serial entrepreneur whose Walter Mitty-like admiration for Thomas Edison led him to emulate his hero and create a laboratory for developing Internet business concepts and models. Then, for one smart and inquisitive planning executive, the potential of the Internet proved much more exciting than accountancy. He was determined to provide his employer with a meaningful Internet strategy, one way or another, and did. And then there's the dark horse, the soft-spoken and unassuming software developer whose admiring friends think his success and consequent fortune can only be accidental. A love of developing businesses, creating things and inspiring others may seem an unlikely combination to find in a finance sector senior executive but it's one that has led to success twice for another of our champions. Finally, there's the one-time little boy who had a passion for computers and money and who grew up pursuing his dream with remarkable results.

So who are they then? They're just a bunch of regular guys. But what is different about them? What makes them distinctive? To find out we looked carefully to establish what they have in common, and there are indeed some characteristics that most, if not all, of them share. Our e-champions tend to be:

▶ **Energetic self-starters** – they are all self-motivated and action-oriented individuals. They don't just dream, they do – accepting some risk as inherent in pursuing the main chance. When John Pluthero successfully persuaded Dixons' senior management of the merits of his free ISP concept he knew he had to act quickly. Only eight weeks after he and colleagues had worked out the innovative business model, Freeserve was up and running.
▶ **Motivating leaders** – they are confident about where they are going and can inspire others to follow, even through occasional setbacks. Most people warm quickly to Mike Harris, and a former colleague speaks appreciatively of their time together. 'Board meetings with Mike were creative, expansionist, supportive and he relied on people's good nature to get things done . . . Mike is a charismatic leader, but he is not hard-nosed' (Hall, 11/10/98).
▶ **Creative thinkers** – they all have that ability to think 'outside of the box', and can appreciate, generate, and apply fresh ideas. They each have their own way of being creative – harnessing the creativity of others, as well as their own. In his search for the DNA of business, Jay Walker reportedly 'picks apart a process and looks at the pieces in a different way' (Brady, 22/09/99). As Jay himself confesses modestly, 'I think the invention part may be the thing I am good at' (INC, 1/11/98).
▶ **Customer advocates** – they see things from the customers' perspective and act accordingly. Chuck Schwab received lasting praise from investors for having removed the shroud from investing. Ever the customers' friend, Jeff Bezos walks the talk: 'Our business is helping people make purchase decisions' (Bezos, 16/09/99).
▶ **Technology innovators** – they are sensitive to the business benefits offered by information technology, even though they may not be specialists themselves. Chuck Schwab is typical. He has always

sought to use technology as a means of adding value to the service provided to his customers, believing that leadership in his sector would be defined by technology innovation.
- **Team players** – as individuals they may have developed their initial dreams and turned them into business models and customer propositions, but as team players they mobilized the capabilities of a group of individuals to help them achieve shared goals. With community at the core of eBay's business model, Pierre Omidyar has successfully imbued that sense of community into the eBay team. He built a socially aware organization where employees even run a charitable organization issuing grants to community-oriented projects.

So, how do you measure up against these six characteristics? Against how many of these could you place a tick and say with confidence that you could match the basic requirement? It's not that complicated. All of the attributes can be learned or acquired, so if you have a shortcoming, a missing tick, just ask yourself how will you compensate for it, or remedy the deficiency.

Time for departure

Confident now that you can match up to the e-champions in developing your own digital business, you should be ready to get out there and build your own great digital company. Remember the lessons you have learned from the e-champions and use the checklist below to prepare for action.

- **Appreciate the network economy:** Recall how connections are king – one-to-one, one-to-many, many-to-many and many-to-one. Connections are relationships. Every connection, face-to-face and virtual, is also a potential financially based exchange.
- **Develop a sixth sense:** Become sensitive to the role that information technology is playing in shaping society and commerce. Technology will influence every aspect of your business and how you compete. Don't worry, you don't need to be a technologist to become an e-champion – a healthy interest in IT will be sufficient.

- **Feel the social context:** Reflect on the nexus of social trends and how they conspire to create new standards for the behaviour of consumers. Remember that the rise of customer power changes the nature of business.
- **Put customer value first, always:** Remind yourself that the market realigns from supplier to buyer. Create value-based relationships with customers that are fit for the network economy. Unless you put customer value ahead of all else, even shareholders, you are unlikely to be successful. Profits will flow but be patient.
- **Turn your dream into a proposition:** Spruce up your digital business idea and make it ready for launch into the e-world. Express your idea in terms of the customers at whom it will be targeted and the needs that it will address. Spell out what it will do for them from their perspective.
- **Apply the Value Lever framework:** Be certain about the soundness of your proposition and its potential to generate value for your customers. Use the Value Lever framework as a checklist to refine your proposition
- **Build your business plan:** Map your connections, starting with the customer. Attach potential revenues and costs, and use this as the basis for preparing your business plan. Build your plan on the basis of scalable experiments – launch and learn, then scale up for major success.
- **Assemble your team:** Remember that business success on any scale requires a first-class team. In the fast-changing Internet world this is doubly the case. Make sure the organization that you build is network sensitive.
- **Become the intrapreneur, if applicable:** If expecting to succeed as an internal entrepreneur inside a company, beware the forces that are aligned against you. Transformation to a network-sensitive state of being is imperative for all companies. So, don't let the status quo inside the organization derail your digital business initiative. Grasp the nettle and help to facilitate the right transformation option for your company.

■ Rush!

In the nineteenth century reports of gold strikes galvanized the hopeful, the ambitious and the greedy across the world. Tens of thousands of ordinary people used every last cent to purchase a one-way ticket to the gold-fields: California, South Africa, Australia, the Yukon – it didn't matter where. The reaction was always the same. News of gold electrified society, acting like a clarion call to everyone and anyone prepared to risk all to seek their fortune. Many went, but few found gold in any quantity. Usually most arrived at the gold fields by the time the gold had either been dug out, or all the suitable land had been claimed. Frequently those who did make money did it more simply, providing supplies and succour to the hapless prospectors – at a price!

Internet entrepreneurs strike virtual gold on a daily basis, it seems, turning embryonic businesses into stock market titans. The Internet boom has for the budding Internet businessperson all the hallmarks of a virtual gold rush. There are some big differences, though. As prospector you can stake your own claim wherever you like – there's plenty of virtual territory still available. There's plenty of gold in the ground, too, but you alone will determine whether you can recover it. And best of all, you don't need to up sticks and set off to the ends of the earth. That fortune is there in that virtual claim right under your nose.

Just do it.

References

Introduction

Bezos, Jeffrey P. (16/9/99) 'Q&A with Jeff Bezos – Amazon: Nurturing a New Species of Business', *E.Biz – BusinessWeek Online*.
Brady, Diane (22/9/99) 'Jay S. Walker: The Priceline Mogul Races for New Markets', *E.Biz – BusinessWeek Online*.
Cozens, Claire (6/11/98) 'The Boardroom Players – Mike Harris', *Campaign*, p. 32.
Darby, Ian (25/3/99) 'Banks Face Up to their Online Challengers', *Marketing*, p. 17.
Dell, Michael (1998) *Direct from Dell: Strategies that Revolutionized an Industry*. Harper Collins: London.
Gunn, Eileen (7/12/98) 'The E-Corporation: Schwab Puts It All Online', *Fortune*.
Hall, Amanda (11/10/98) 'I am the Egg Man', *Daily Telegraph*, p. 7.
Halper, Mark (1/10/99) 'The High Flyers: Richard Braddock and Jay Walker', *Business 2.0*.
Harris, Mike (16/1/99) 'Mike Harris Visits', *Guardian*, p. 4.
Hazleton, Lesley (7/98) 'Jeff Bezos', *Success*, Vol. 45, No. 7.
Hunter, Jennifer (21/6/99) 'Amazon's Kingpin', *Maclean's (Canada)*, p. 30.
Lappen, Alyssa A (29/4/96) *Institutional Investor (US Edition)*, p. 63.
Lynn, Matthew (26/4/99) 'PC Whiz-kid Piles Up the Billions', *Sunday Times*.
Machan, Dyan (17/5/99) 'An Edison for a New Age', *Forbes Magazine*.
Pinchot, Gifford, III (1985) *Intrapreneuring: Why You Don't Have to Leave the Corporation to Become an Entrepreneur*. Harper and Row: New York.
Preston, Morag (31/3/99) 'When Book Sales Speak Volumes', *The Times*..
Stone, Amey (29/4/99) 'Why Priceline.com Could Be the Net's Next Superstar', *Business Week Online*.
Sunday Times (26/9/99) 'Top 20 in Finance – Power List 1999'.
Waples, John (13/6/99) 'The Making of Freeserve', *Sunday Times*.

Chapter 1

Castells, Manuel (1996) *The Information Age: Economy, Society and Culture – Volume 1: The Rise of the Network Society*. Blackwells: Cambridge.
European Commission (1998) *Content and Commerce Driven Strategies in Global Networks – CONDRINET*. Commission of the European Communities: Luxembourg).
Kelly, Kevin (1998) *New Rules for the New Economy: 10 Ways the Network Economy is Changing Everything*. Fourth Estate: London.
Toffler, Alvin (1970) *Future Shock*. Random Books: New York.
Toffler, Alvin (1981) *The Third Wave*. Pan Books: London.

Chapter 2

Barnatt, Christopher (1997) *Challenging Reality: In Search of the Future Organization*. Wiley: Chichester.

Hutchings, Andrew (2/10/97) 'All the World Loves a Techno Megatrend', *Money Marketing*, p. 32.

Negroponte, Nicholas (1995) *Being Digital*. Hodder and Stoughton: London.

Tapscott, Don (1995) *The Digital Economy: Promise and Peril in the Age of Networked Intelligence*. McGraw-Hill: New York.

Taylor, Paul (7/4/99) 'How the Internet will Reshape Worldwide Business Activity', *Financial Times – Information Technology*, pp. 1–2.

Chapter 3

Arthur, W. Brian (7/96) 'Increasing Returns and the New World of Business', *Harvard Business Review*.

Barnatt, Christopher (1999) *Valueware: Technology, Humanity and Organization*. Adamantine Press: London and New York.

Barnatt, Christopher (1997) *Challenging Reality: In Search of the Future Organization*. Wiley: Chichester.

Butler, Patrick, Ted W. Hall, Alistair M. Hanna, Lenny Mendonca, Byron Auguste, James Manyika and Anupam Sahay (1997) 'A Revolution in Interaction', *The McKinsey Quarterly*, No. 1, pp. 4–23.

Cairncross, Frances (1997) *The Death of Distance: How the Communications Revolution Will Change Our Lives*. Harvard Business School Press: Boston, MA.

Choi, Soon-Yong, Dale O. Stahl and Andrew B. Whinston (1997) *The Economics of Electronic Commerce: The Essential Economics of Doing Business in the Electronic Marketplace*. Macmillan Technical: Indianapolis, IN.

Deighton, John (11/96) 'The Future of Interactive Marketing', *Harvard Business Review*, pp. 151–166.

Downes, Larry and Chunka Mui (1998) *Unleashing the Killer App: Digital Strategies for Market Dominance*. Harvard Business School Press: Boston, MA.

Gage, John (4/96) 'The Network is the Company', *Fast Company*.

Gates, Bill with N. Myhrvold and P. Rinearson (1995) *The Road Ahead*. Penguin Books: New York.

Hagel III, John & Armstrong A.G. (1997) *Net Gain: Expanding Markets through Virtual Communities*. Harvard Business School Press: Boston, MA.

Hamel, Gary with Jeff Sampler (7/12/98) 'The E-Corporation More Than Just Web-based: It's Building a New Industrial Order' *Fortune*.

Hamel, Gary and C. K. Prahalad (1994) *Competing for the Future*. Harvard Business School Press: Boston, MA.

Kelly, Kevin (1998) *New Rules for the New Economy: 10 Ways the Network Economy is Changing Everything*. Fourth Estate: London.

McIntyre, Paul (5/5/98) 'Online Puts Old Habits Out of Line', *Australian Financial Review*.

Negroponte, Nicholas (1995) *Being Digital*. Hodder and Stoughton: London.

Papows, Jeff (1998) *Enterprise.com: Market Leadership in the Information Age*. Nicholas Brealey: London.

Porter, Michael E. (1980) *Competitive Strategy: Techniques for Analyzing Industries and Competitors* (The Free Press: New York).

Pritchett, Price (1994) *New Work Habits for a Radically Changing World*. Pritchett & Associates: Dallas, TX.

Rheingold, Howard (1994) *The Virtual Community*. Secker and Warburg: London.

Skelly, Jessica (7/10/98) 'Charles Schwab Leverages Net', *Retail Banker*, p. 2.
Tapscott, Don (1995) *The Digital Economy: Promise and Peril in the Age of Networked Intelligence*. McGraw-Hill: New York.
Tellzen, Roland (24/11/98) 'Technology Nullifies Time', *Australian*.

Chapter 4

Chappell, Caroline (6/99) 'Keeping the Customer Satisfied', *IT Consultant*, pp. 29–34.
Cyber Dialogue (22/6/99) *Online Branding: The Internet's Impact on Branding* (Cyber Dialogue).
Dempsey, Margaret (3/2/99) 'Why So Many Organisations are Embracing the CRM Trend', *Financial Times – Information Technology*, p. 7.
Doyle, Peter and Teresa Knight (1998) *The Role of Marketing: Research Report*. KPMG: London.
Drucker, Peter F. (5/10/98) 'Peter Drucker: Interview', *Forbes Magazine*.
Frost & Sullivan (8/99) *The European Market for Customer Relation Management* (Frost & Sullivan).
Dyson, Esther (6/98) 'Consumers in Control', *Outlook Magazine*.
Economist (9/10/99) 'Cutting the Cord'.
Heil, Gary (1996) *One Size Fits One*. Wiley: New York.
Levitt, Theodore (7/60) 'Marketing Myopia', *Harvard Business Review* (reissued 9/75).
Millennium Group (11/99) *Competing in the Network Economy – Customer Power* Millennium Group: Winchester.
NFO Interactive (5/99).
Venes, Robert (8/7/99) 'Are Customers Really King?', *New Media Age*.

Chapter 5

Balls, Andrew (28/7/97) 'Study Shows 'Unprecedented' Rise in Inequality', *Financial Times*, p. 8.
Barnatt, Christopher (1995) *Cyber Business: Mindsets for a Wired Age*. Wiley: Chichester.
Beck, Ulrich (1992) *Risk Society: Towards a New Modernity*, trans. M. Ritter. Sage: London.
Business Wire (1/4/98) 'Expanding Consumer 'Time Deficit' Creates Demand Consumer Services'.
Cooper, Cary (8/99) 'Hard Decade at the Office', *Director*, p. 34.
Fukuyama, Francis (1999) *The Great Disruption: Human Nature and the Reconstruction of the Social Order*. Free Press: New York.
Future Foundation (1998) *The 24-hour Society*. Future Foundation: London.
Gates, Jeff (5/99) 'Statistics on Poverty and Inequality', *Global Policy Forum*.
Gavigan, James P., Mathias Ottitsch and Celia Greaves (4/99) *Demographic and Social Trends Panel Report – Series 2*, Document EUR 18729 EN. European Commission/Institute for Prospective Technological Studies: Seville, Spain.
Hall, Celia (14/1/99) ' How Children have Changed in 50 Years', *Daily Telegraph*, p. 7.
Handy, Charles (1994) *The Empty Raincoat: Making Sense of the Future*. Hutchinson: London.
Harris Poll (6/99) 'Time at Work and at Play'.
The Henley Centre (1999) *Planning for Social Change 1999*. Henley Centre: London.
The Henley Centre (1998) *Planning for Social Change 1998*. Henley Centre: London.
The Henley Centre (1997) *Planning for Social Change 1997*. Henley Centre: London.
ICL (9/98) *The Lifestyle Revolution*. ICL: Slough.
Institute for Fiscal Studies (1997) *Inequality in the UK*. IFS: London.

Johnston, Philip (15/6/98) 'Divorce to Affect One Child in Four as the Family is Rejected', *Daily Telegraph*, p. 5.
Jones, Helen (8/1/99) 'Tunnel Vision', *Design Week*.
Mantle, Jan and David Bowers (14/10/99) *European Pensions Reforms*. Merrill Lynch: London.
Mazaar, Michael J. (1998) 'The Five Paradoxes: Business Competition in the Knowledge Era'. Centre for Strategic and International Studies: Washington, DC.
Mazarr, Michael J. (1997) 'Global Trends 2005: The Challenge of the New Millennium'. Centre for Strategic and International Studies: Washington, DC.
McQuivey, James L. (8/99) 'The Net-Powered Generation'. Forrester Research: Cambridge, MA.
Morgan, Patricia (7/99) *Farewell to the Family? Public Policy and Family Breakdown in Britain and the USA*, 2nd edn. Institute for Economic Affairs: London.
OECD (1994) *Employment Outlook*. OECD: Paris.
Office for National Statistics (1999) *Social Trends 29*. The Stationery Office: London.
Patton, Lucy (14/5/99) 'Parent's Absence at Work makes Young Grow Fonder of Sex, Drugs and Drink'.
Pillot de Chenecey, Sean (21/5/99) 'Targeting Teenagers', *Brand Strategy*.
Popcorn, Faith with Lys Marigold (1996) *Clicking: 16 Trends to Future Fit Your Life, Your Work, and Your Business*. Harper Collins: London.
Popcorn, Faith (1992) *The Popcorn Report: Revolutionary Trend Predictions for Marketing in the 1990s*. Arrow: London.
Poster, Mark (1992) *The Mode of Information: Post Structuralism and Social Context*. Polity Press: Cambridge.
PR Newswire (3/5/99) 'Two Sides of the Coin'.
RSA (1998) *Redefining Work*. Royal Society for the Encouragement of Arts, Manufactures and Commerce: London.
The Salvation Army/The Henley Centre (1999) *The Paradox of Prosperity*. The Salvation Army: London.
Scase, Richard (5/97) 'The Changing Consumer', *Strategy*, pp. 10–11.
Schultz, Charles L. (10/98) 'Downsized and Out: Job Security and the American Worker', *Brooking Review*.
Swiss Re Life & Health (1998) *The Insurance Report 1998*. Swiss Re Life & Health: London.
Tapia, Andrés (12/9/94) 'Reaching the First Post-Christian Generation', *Christianity Today*, pp. 18–23.
UNDP (1999) *United Nations Human Development Report*. UNDP: Geneva.
US Census Bureau (1/10/98).
Waugh, Patricia (ed.) (1992) *Postmodernism: A Reader*. Edward Arnold: London.

Chapter 6

Bowen, David (17/9/99) ' I Spy with My Little Eye', *Financial Times*.
Burgess, Rob (10/99) 'Let's All Get Together and Go Shopping', *Revolution*, p. 31.
Cable Europe (12/05/99) 'BSkyB Targets Cable with Free Box Offer'.
Castells, Manuel (1996) *The Information Age: Economy, Society and Culture* – Volume 1: *The Rise of the Network Society*. Blackwells: Cambridge.
Cova, Bernard (1996) 'The Postmodern Explained to Managers: Implications for Marketing', *Business Horizons*, Vol. 39, No. 6.
Davis, Stan and Christopher Meyer (1998) *Blur: The Speed of Change in the Connected Economy*. Capstone: Oxford.
Dell, Michael (1998) *Direct from Dell: Strategies that Revolutionized an Industry*. Harper Collins: London.

Fournier, Susan, Susan Dobscha and David Glen Mick (1/98) 'Preventing the Premature Death of Relationship Marketing', *Harvard Business Review*, pp. 42–51.
Green, Heather (31/8/99) 'Can Kozmo be the 7-Eleven of the Internet?', *Business Week e.biz*.
Gunn, Eileen P. (7/12/98) 'The E-Corporation: Schwab Puts It All Online', *Fortune*.
The Henley Centre (1998) *Planning for Social Change 1998*. Henley Centre: London.
The Henley Centre (1997) *Planning for Social Change 1997*. Henley Centre: London.
Jaffe, Thomas (17/5/99) 'Bouncing Around', *Forbes Magazine*.
Lieber, Ronald B. (23/6/97) 'Selling the Sizzle', *Fortune*, p. 80.
M2 Presswire (28/10/99) 'Charlottestreet.Com Set to become the UK's Number One Online Community for Women'.
MacKenzie, Dorothy (15/4/97) 'Consumers and Brand: How Will Future Relationship Develop', *Brand Strategy*.
Marketing (21/10/99) 'SkyDigital Signs Up 1.8 Million in Surprise Results', p. 12.
Online Marketing Tips (1/2/99) 'A Medium or a Tool'.
Pine, B. Joseph and James H. Gilmore (7/98) 'Welcome to the Experience Economy', *Harvard Business Review*, pp. 97–105.
Sheiner, Leo (21/10/98) 'Do You Offer a Rich Experience', *ClickZ Network*.

Chapter 7

BAH/EIU (1999) *Competing in the Digital Age: How the Internet will Transform Business*. Booz Allen & Hamilton/Economist Intelligence Unit.
Downes, Larry and Chunka Mui (1998) *Unleashing the Killer App: Digital Strategies for Market Dominance*. Harvard Business School Press: Boston, MA.
Ghosh, Shikhar (3/98) 'Making Business Sense of the Internet', *Harvard Business Review*, pp. 126–135, 180.
IBM/EIU (1998) *e-business . . . is Europe Ready?* IBM/Economist Intelligence Unit.
InterForum (1998) *Electronic Commerce – The Challenge for UK Business*. InterForum: Englefield Green, Surrey.

Chapter 8

Barnatt, Christopher (1999) *Valueware: Technology, Humanity and Organization*. Adamantine Press: London and New York.
Business Week Online (21/5/99) 'Q & A with Meg Whitman'.
Downes, Larry and Chunka Mui (1998) *Unleashing the Killer App: Digital Strategies for Market Dominance*. Harvard Business School Press: Boston, MA.
European Commission (1998) *Content and Commerce Driven Strategies in Global Networks – CONDRINET*. Commission of the European Communities: Luxembourg.
Evans, Philip and Thomas S. Wurster (11/99), 'Getting Real about Virtual Finance', *Harvard Business Review*, pp. 85–94.
Gates, Bill with Collins Hemingway (1999) *Business at the Speed of Thought: Using a Digital Nervous System*. Penguin Books: New York.
Hagel, John III & Armstrong A.G. (1997) *Net Gain: Expanding Markets through Virtual Communities*. Harvard Business School Press: Boston, MA.
Hamel, Gary with Jeff Sampler (7/12/98) 'The E-Corporation More Than Just Web-based: It's Building a New Industrial Order' *Fortune*.
Kelly, Kevin (1998) *New Rules for the New Economy: 10 Ways the Network Economy is Changing Everything*. Fourth Estate: London.
Marcus, Eric (4/3/99) *The eBusiness Imperative*. The Concours Group: Cambridge, MA.

Martin, Chuck (1997) *The Digital Estate: Strategies for Competing, Surviving, and Thriving in an Internetworked World*. McGraw-Hill: New York.
Mougayar, Walid (1999) *Opening New Digital Markets: Battle Plans and Digital Strategies for Internet Commerce*, 2nd edn. McGraw-Hill, New York.
Peppers, Don and Martha Rogers (1997) *Enterprise One-to-One: Tools for Building Unbreakable Customer Relationships in the Interactive Age*. Piatkus: London.
Pine, B. Joseph, Don Peppers, and Martha Rogers (3/95) 'Do You Want to Keep Your Customers Forever?', *Harvard Business Review*, pp. 103–114.
Pine, B. Joseph (1992) *Mass Customization: The New Frontier in Business Competition*. Harvard Business Press: Boston, MA.
Schwartz, Evan I. (1997) *Webonomics: Nine Essential Principles for Growing Your Business on the World Wide Web*. Penguin Books: London.
Shapiro, Carl and Varian, Hal R. (1999) *Information Rules: A Strategic Guide to the Network Economy*. Harvard Business School Press: Boston, MA.
Tapscott, Don (1995) *The Digital Economy: Promise and Peril in the Age of Networked Intelligence*. McGraw-Hill: New York.
Toffler, Alvin (1981) *The Third Wave*. Pan Books: London.
Wilson, David L. (29/6/98) 'New Internet Frenzy is Over Portals', *San Jose Mercury News*.

Chapter 9

Brady, Diane (22/9/99) 'Jay S. Walker: The Priceline Mogul Races for New Markets', *E.Biz – BusinessWeek Online*.
Business Week Online (31/5/99) 'Q & A with Jeff Bezos'.
Business Week Online (21/5/99) 'Q & A with Meg Whitman'.
Daily Telegraph (28/8/99).
Dell, Michael (1998) *Direct from Dell: Strategies that Revolutionized an Industry*. Harper Collins: London.
Distribution Management Briefing (1/11/97) 'Citibank to Build a Virtual Community on the Internet'.
Flynn, Laurie J. (Summer 1998) 'Eating Your Young', *Context Magazine*.
Gunn, Eileen P. (7/12/98) 'The E-Corporation: Schwab Puts It All Online', *Fortune*.
Lee, Julian (1/4/99), 'How Dixons Reinvented Itself ', *Marketing*.
New Media Age (21/1/99) 'Freeserve Fever Running High', p. 15.
PR Newswire (10/3/99) 'Dell and Amazon.com Announce Online Agreement'.
Regulatory News Service (20/9/99).
Skelly, Jessica (7/10/98) 'Charles Schwab Leverages Net', *Retail Banker*, p. 2.
Stone, Amey (29/4/99) 'Why Priceline.com Could Be the Net's Next Superstar', *Business Week Online*.
Yates, Karen (30/10/98) 'Behind the Hype: Dixons Freeserve', *Campaign*, p. 35.

Chapter 10

Gunn, Eileen P. (7/12/98) 'The E-Corporation: Schwab Puts It All Online', *Fortune*.

Chapter 11

Ashkenas, Ron, Dave Ulrich, Tidd Jick and Steve Kerr (1998) *The Boundaryless Organization: Breaking the Chains of Organizational Structure*. Jossey-Bass: San Francisco, CA.
Bossidy, Lawrence (1998) 'Foreword', in Ron Ashkenas, David Ulrich, Todd Jick, Steve Kerr, *The Boundaryless Organization: Breaking the Chains of Organizational Structure*. Jossey-Bass: San Francisco, CA.

Cozens, Claire (6/11/98) 'The Boardroom Players – Mike Harris', *Campaign*, p. 32.
Czerniawska, Fiona and Gavin Potter (1998) *Business in a Virtual World*. Macmillan Business Press: London.
Dell, Michael (1998) *Direct from Dell: Strategies that Revolutionized an Industry*. Harper Collins: London.
Gates, Bill with Collins Hemingway (1999) *Business at the Speed of Thought: Using a Digital Nervous System*. Penguin Books: New York.
General Electric (1994) *GE Annual Report 1994*.
Hall, Amanda (11/10/98) 'I am the Egg Man', *Daily Telegraph*, p. 7.
Hamel, Gary (9/99) 'Bringing Silicon Valley Inside', Harvard Business Review, pp. 71–84.
Hazleton, Lesley (7/98) 'Jeff Bezos', *Success*, Volume 45, Number 7.
LaBarre, Polly (6/99) 'Leaders.com', *Fast Company*, Issue 25, p. 95.
Lappen, Alyssa A (29/4/96) *Institutional Investor (US Edition)*, p. 63.
Maitland, Alison (28/9/99) 'How to Create the Creativity of a Silicon Valley', *Financial Times*, p. 17.
McReynolds, Rebecca (12/7/98) 'Doing It the Schwab Way', *US Banker*.
Normann, Richard and Rafael Ramirez (7/93) 'From Value Chain to Value Constellation: Designing Interactive Strategy', *Harvard Business Review*, pp. 65–77.
Prahalad, C. K. (4/10/99) 'Changes in the Competitive Battlefield', *Financial Times – Mastering Strategy, Part Two*, pp. 2–4.
PR Newswire (19/07/99) 'Winning in Online Commerce means Mastering "Clicks and Mortar," Says Schwab Co-Ceo'.
Senge, Peter M. (1994) *The Fifth Discipline Fieldbook: Strategies and Tools for Building a Learning Organization*. Nicholas Brealey: London.
Seybold, Patricia with Ronni T. Marshak (1998) *Customers.com: How to Create a Profitable Business Strategy for the Internet*. Random House: London.
Trade Marketing (9/97).
Wind, Jerry Yoram & Jeremy Main (1999) *Driving Change: How the Best Companies are Preparing for the 21st Century*. Kogan Page: London.

Chapter 12

Business Wire (25/8/99) 'Michael Dell Says Online Sales Represent a Fraction of Internet's Massive Business Potential'.
Dell, Michael (1998) *Direct from Dell: Strategies that Revolutionized an Industry*. Harper Collins: London.
Gunn, Eileen P. (7/12/98) 'The E-Corporation: Schwab Puts It All Online', *Fortune*.
Hall, Amanda (11/7/99) 'Freeserve's 'Paranoid' Dynamo', *Sunday Telegraph*, p. 7.
Kotter, John P. (3/95) 'Leading Change: Why Transformation Efforts Fail', *Harvard Business Review*, pp. 59–67.
Waples, John (13/6/99) 'The Making of Freeserve', *Sunday Times*.

Chapter 13

Bezos, Jeffrey P. (16/9/99) 'Q&A with Jeff Bezos – Amazon: Nurturing a New Species of Business', *E.Biz – BusinessWeek Online*.
Brady, Diane (22/9/99) 'Jay S. Walker: The Priceline Mogul Races for New Markets', *E.Biz – BusinessWeek Online*.
Hall, Amanda (11/10/98) 'I am the Egg Man', *Daily Telegraph*, p. 7.
Hof, Robert D. (27/9/99) 'Jeffrey P. Bezos', *E.Biz – BusinessWeek Online*.
INC (1/11/1998) 'Face-To-Face – Walker Digital's Jay Walker'.

Index

Adabra 137
agenting: characteristics 177; and connection 238; and content integration 195; described 177–8; e-champion businesses 199–200, 203, 208, 212, 216, 220, 225; importance of 179–80; role of 178–9
agrarian society 27, 28
Alladvantage 168
Amazon Associate Program 132, 203–4
Amazon Inc. 13, 16, 46, 57, 72, 75, 121, 122, 127, 129, 132, 135, 142, 172, 182, 186–7, 211, 252; agenting 203; background 200–2; content integration 202; digital value profile 200–8; freeware 202; inter-customer relationships 204; mass customization 202–3; new market forum 203–4; prosumer involvement 203; real-time activity 203; value levers 200
Amazon zShops 201, 204
America Online (AOL) 13, 165, 213
American Banking Association 49
Ameritrade 18
Apple Computer 141
Armstrong, Arthur 59, 74, 75, 184–5
Arthur, Brian 61
Ashkenas, Ron 255

BancBoston 14, 208
Barclaysquare 182
Barnatt, Christopher 47, 58–9, 86, 113, 159
Barnes & Noble 121–2, 247
Barrett, Craig 44
Beck, Ulrich 112
beliefs erosion: consequences of diminished trust 110–12; key facets 108; rise of 109–10; and rise of risk society 112; and sense of moral decline 110
Benjamin, Keith 14, 208
Bezos, Jeffrey P. 4, 5, 8, 9, 10, 12, 13, 15–16,
51, 60, 72, 121, 127, 129, 132, 142, 201–2, 252
Bloomer, Jonathan 218
Booz Allen Hamilton 149
Bossidy, Lawrence 247
Boston Consulting Group (BCG) 164
BottomDollar 137
Braddock, Richard 14, 127
brands 69–71; emotional marketing of 120–1; and trust/authority 134–5
Braniff 266–7
BSkyB 124
BT 138
business performance: drivers 45, 51; friction-free transactionality 48–50; global interactivity 46–7; hypermedia environment 47–8; physical asset independence 50–1
business plans 242–3, 284
Butterfield & Butterfield 209
buyer ascendancy: defined 66; described 66–7; impact of 68
buyer–seller re-engagement: defined 71; described 71–2; impact of 72–3

Cairncross, Frances 50
Calico Technologies 252
Cap Gemini 163
Castells, Manuel 27, 88, 116
Chambers, John 69
change/transformation disaggregate or perish 272–6; experimentation 270–1; integration 271; key points 276; not an option 265–7; as not easy 267–70; options 273; stages 270–2; and transition to digital business 270–2
Charles Schwab Corporation 17–18, 32, 55, 132, 154, 172, 176; agenting 199–200; background 196–8; content integration

198; digital value profile 196–200; freeware 198–9; intercustomer relationships 200; mass customization 199; new market forum 200; prosumer involvement 199; real-time activity 199; value levers 196
CharlotteStreet 141–2
Choi, Yong 47
Cisco Systems 69, 255–6
Citicorp 14
Clare, John 11, 13, 275
Coase, Ronald 49
Coca Cola 60
Collier, Eddy 218
3Com Corporation 42
Compaq 153, 221
CompareNet 137
competitive forces 55–6; buyer ascendancy 66–8; buyer–seller re-engagement 71–3; convergence 56–9; immediacy 646; information/estimation 62–4; interconsumer collaboration 73–5; key points 75–6; network returns 59–61; provider equalization 69–71
Concours Group 160
connection: and agenting 238; and content integration 236; creating value from 233–43; and freeware 236; from business plan to action 242–3; importance of 235–6; and intercustomer relationships 239; and mass customization 236–7; and new market forum 238–9; and prosumer involvement 237–8; and real-time activity 237; role of 234–5; turning into dollars 240–2
consumers *see* customers
content integration: and agenting 195; and connection 236; and cost 163–4; e-champion businesses 198, 202, 206, 211, 215, 219, 224; importance of 165–6; key points 163; reach-richness trade-off 164–5
convergence: challenge of 58–9; defined 56; described 56–7; impact of 57–8
cookies 62
Cooper, Cary 99
Cotsakos, Christos 132
Cova, Bernard 131
Crunch 129
customer dynamics: access freedom 136–9; active participation 130–3; affinity gap 139–43; attention scarcity 123–6; experience richness 119–23; individualism 126–8; key points 143; now mentality 128–30; trust deficit 133–6

customer relationship management (CRM) 83–4
customers: access to twenty-four hours a day seven days a week consumption 93–5; attracting attention of 166–7; average spending per UK consumer per year 87; changing behaviours of 85–7; and collective power of individuals 87–8; empowerment of 182; experience-oriented 115–16; gaining attention of 152–3; interest in 10–12; key points 88–9; learning relationships with 62–4; and marketing 82–4; obsession with 81; and online purchasing 85–7; power of 66–8; rise of vigilante 107–8; time pressures/management 95–6; transfer of power to 84–5; and value 159–60
Cyber Dialogue 84

Daily Mail 141
Danby, Mark 11, 16, 214
Davenport, Charlotte 142
Davis, Sir Peter 14, 150, 217
DealPilot 137
Deighton, John 63
Dell4me Resources 224, 225
Dell Computers Corporation 17, 65, 129, 133, 153, 172, 175, 176, 272; agenting 225; background 221–4; content integration 224; digital value profile 221–5; freeware 224; intercustomer relationships 225; mass customization 224–5; new market forum 225; prosumer involvement 225; real-time activity 225; value levers 221
Dell, Michael S. 7, 9, 10, 12, 17, 19, 51, 60, 63, 81, 129, 132, 172, 182, 222–3, 253, 254–5, 273–4
Demon 138
Demos 140
Dettore, James 69
digital business: action checklist 283–5; action oriented 250; apply value lever framework 284; appreciate network economy 283; assemble team 284; attributes/actions 261; become intrapreneur 284; build business plan 284; channel fluent 257–9; characteristics of 247–8; customer centric 255–6; develop sixth sense 283–4; ideas intensive 248–9; IT integrated 253–5; key points 260–1; lean focus 259–60; partner biased 251–2; people centred 252–3; put customer value first 284; risk conversant 256–7; rush!

Index **295**

284–5; transition to 270–2; turn dream into proposition 284
Digital Nervous System (DNS) 253–4
digital strategy: getting first-mover advantage 152–3; new mindsets needed 149–50; and quest for digital business tools 153–6; understanding conventional/digital difference 151–2
digital value profiles 195–6; Amazon 200–8; Charles Schwab Corporation 196–200; Dell 221–5; eBay 208–13; Egg 216–21; Freeserve 213–16; key points 226
Dixons Group 8, 11, 13, 16, 17, 125, 213–14, 275
Dobscha, Susan 127
Downes, Larry 72, 151, 169, 176
Doyle, Peter 82
Drucker, Peter 66, 82, 88
Dyson, Esther 84

E*Trade 18, 132, 155, 176
e-champions: as creative thinkers 282; as customer advocates 10–12, 282; described 281–3; as energetic self-starters 282; introduction to 4–8; as motivating leaders 282; as regular guys 8; success of 18–19; as team players 15–18, 283; as technology innovators 282–3; vision of 10, 12–15
eBay 11, 12, 16, 55, 73, 122, 142, 150, 183; agenting 212; background 209–11; content integration 211; digital value profile 208–13; freeware 211; intercustomer relationships 212–13; mass customization 211; new market forum 212; prosumer involvement 212; real-time activity 212; value levers 208–9
eBay Café 186
eBay Foundation 11–12
Economist Intelligence Unit (EIU) 149
Egg 10, 14, 16, 44, 65, 125, 135, 150, 155, 167, 275; agenting 220; background 217–19; content integration 219; digital value profile 216–21; freeware 219; intercustomer relationships 221; mass customization 219; new market forum 220–1; prosumer involvement 220; real-time activity 220; value levers 216–17
Emmott, Stephen 42
employment: changing structure of 98; as flexible 96–9; paternalism in 134
Emusic 129
Energis 11, 214
eSchwab 17, 18, 60, 138, 153, 154, 187

European Commission, Social Trends Panel Report 97, 104–5, 163
European Union (EU) 97, 102
Evans, Philip 164
eWorld 141
Exppedia 165

Federal Express (FedEx) 65, 251
Fiat 256
Filo, David 179
financial services 57
Financial Times 137
First Direct 8, 10
flexible working 95; bellwether nation 97–9; challenges posed by 99–100; key facets 96; rise of 96–7
Florists Transworld Delivery (FTD) 210
Fortune magazine 122
Fournier, Susan 127
Freeserve 11, 13, 17, 32, 43–4, 57, 123, 125, 138, 155, 165, 182, 274–5; agenting 216; background 213–15; content integration 215; digital value profile 213–16; freeware 215; intercustomer relationships 216; mass customization 215; prosumer involvement 216; real-time activity 215; value levers 213
freeware: characteristics 166; and connection 236; e-champion businesses 198–9, 202, 207, 211, 215, 219, 224; and intercustomer relationships 195; law of increasing returns 166, 167–8; mindshare 166–7
friction-free capitalism 48–50
Fukuyama, Francis 112
Future Foundation 94

Gage, John 67
Garden Escape Incorporated 176–7
Gates, Bill 48, 103, 253
General Electric (GE) 153
Geocities 140
Ghosh, Shikhar 150
Gigabuys.com 182, 223–4
Gilder, George 44–5
Gilder's Law 44–5
Gilmore, James 121
Global Market 122
Grant, Robin 85
Grenz, Stanley 116
Gunn, Eileen 127

Hagel, John 59, 74, 75, 184–5
Hamel, Gary 68, 173–4, 248, 249

Handy, Charles 99
Harley-Davidson 121
Harris, Mike 7–8, 9, 10, 12, 13–14, 16, 55, 81, 125, 135, 150, 155, 183, 217, 218, 249, 253
Harris polls 100
Heil, Gary 83
Henley Centre 95, 96, 98, 104, 109, 111–12, 130, 140
Hewson, Nick 84
Hoff, Ted 41
Howell, Rupert 10
hypermedia: audio/video-streaming 48; bandwidth constraints 48; described 47–8; three-dimensional images 48

IBM 149, 182
immediacy: challenge of 65–6; defined 64; described 64–5; impact of 66
individualism: customer dynamic 87–8, 126–8; and inequality 104–5
industrial society 27
inequality: growth of 103–5; and world of individuals 104–5
infomediaries 72
information over estimation: defined 62; learning relationships 62–4; remote tracking 62
information society 26, 27
Institute of Fiscal Studies (IFS) 104
Institutional Venture Partners (IVP) 250
Intel Corporation 41, 44
interactive multimedia sector 57
interconsumer collaboration: defined 73; described 73–4; development of 74; impact of 75; as reinforcement of buyer ascendancy 74–5
intercustomer relationships: characteristics 183; and connection 239; described 183–4; e-champion businesses 200, 204, 208, 212–13, 216, 221, 225; facilitation of 185–6; and freeware 195; opportunities of 187; in practice 186–7; significance of 184–5
Internet 11, 12, 17, 43, 47, 49, 87; adult/children use of 114–15; brand awareness on 70; as centralized market forum 122–3; influence of 134; and now mentality 129–30; one-to-one marketing on 127–8; online communities 141–3; portal websites 165, 179; as questionable environment 177–8; reassessment of business on 72; shopping comparison sites on 137–8; travel sites 165
Internet service provider (ISP) 213–14

Joyner, Joan 18

Kelly, Kevin 30, 166
Koogle, Tim 179
Kotter, John 268
Kozmo 129–30
Kruse International 209

Lastminute.com 174
law of increasing returns 43, 61, 166, 167–8
Leemon, Dan 18, 274
Lending Tree Inc. 205–6
Lepore, Dawn 17
LetsBuyIt 137, 182
Lotus Development Corporation 66

McGinn, Richard 173
Machiavelli, Niccolo 267
MacKenzie, Dorothy 134
McKinsey & Co. 46, 114
McLuhan, Marshall 29
McNealy, Scott 65
Main, Jeremy 247
Marcus, Eric 160, 173
Marengi, Joe 223
marketing: aggregate vs one-to-one 170–1; and the customer 82–4; emotional 120–1; one-to-one strategies 127–8
Martin, Chuck 184
Martini Principle 50
mass customization: application of 170–2; characteristics 169; and connection 236–7; customer information 169; e-champion businesses 199, 202–3, 207, 211, 215, 219, 224–5; individual treatment 169; production/marketing functions 170; and prosumer involvement 193–4; use of digital technology 169
May, Trevor 218
Mazaar, Michael 107, 112
Meeker, Mary 14
Mercata 137
Merrill Lynch 107, 247
metamedia consumption: broadening of communications media 113; and coming of 'netpowered generation' 114–15; experience-oriented consumer 115–16; key facets 112; technology meets society 112–14
Metcalfe, Robert 42
Metcalfe's Law 42–3, 59
Mick, David Glen 127
Moore, Gordon 40–1
Moore's Law 40–1

Morgan Stanley Dean Witter 14, 124, 214, 219
motor insurance 60–1
Mougayar, Walid 181
Mountainzone 180
MP3 129, 177
Mui, Chunka 72, 151, 169, 176
Mulgan, Geoff 140
My Freeserve 216
My Stuff 177

Naumann, Alan 252
NCR 42
Negroponte, Nicholas 40, 42
Netscape Online 165
network economy: challenge of 25–6; competitive forces 46; and creation of value 33–4; and customers 119; defined 31; development of 28–9; differences in 31–2; dynamics 45; historical background 26–8, 29–30; importance of connections in 31–2; key points 34–5; macro-level dynamics 39–51; macro-realities 45–51; micro-level dynamics 55–76; and navigability/effective search engines 67; as revolutionary 30–1
network returns: defined 59; impact of 61; inflection point 59–60; possibilities of 60–1
network society 139–43
new market forum: characteristics 180; and connection 238–9; creation/reorganization of 182–3; described 180–2; e-champion businesses 200, 203–4, 208, 212, 216, 220–1, 225; and real-time activity 194
News Corporation 124
NFO Interactive 87
Nicoski, Rob 95
Normann, Richard 252

Omidyar, Pierre 6, 8, 9, 11, 73, 81, 122, 142, 150, 183, 210
Open Market 150
Opinion Research Corporation International 69

Palmer, John 182
Papows, Jeff 66
PAWWS Financial Network 167
Peapod 171
People's Express 266–7
Pepper, Don 170
Pez 210

Pillot de Chenecey, Sean 109
Pine, Joseph 121
Pipex 138
Planet Online 11, 214
Pluthero, John 6–7, 8, 11, 12, 16–17, 45, 123, 125, 138–9, 150, 155, 275
Popcorn, Faith 108
Porter, Michael 160
Pottruck, David 17, 18, 68, 155, 252, 258, 260
Prahalad, C.K. 250, 251
Priceline Inc. 14, 55, 60, 67, 73, 124–5, 127, 135, 137–8, 174, 179, 183; agenting 208; background 204–6; content integration 206; digital value profile 204–8; freeware 207; intercustomer relationships 208; mass customization 207; new market forum 208; prosumer involvement 207–8; real-time activity 207; value levers 204
prosumer involvement: characteristics 175; and connection 237–8; described 175–6; e-champion businesses 199, 203, 207–8, 212, 216, 220, 225; and mass customization 193–4; reality of 176–7
provider equalization: and brand awareness 69–71; defined 69
Prudential Group 8, 14, 44, 125, 150, 217

Quindlen, Ruthann 250

Radha, Pema 219
Radikal Communications 128
Ramirez, Rafael 252
real-time activity: characteristics 172; and connection 237; e-champion businesses 199, 203, 207, 212, 215, 220, 225; effective 173–4; and new market forum 194; speed/immediacy 174–5
RealAudio 48
Reeve, William 214
Revolution magazine 137
Rheingold, Howard 74
risk society 112, 156–7
Rogers, Martha 170

Salomon Smith Barney 218
Santa Fe Institute 61
Scase, Richard 99, 105
Schultz, Charles L. 96
Schwab, Charles R. 6, 8, 9, 10, 12, 17, 18, 32, 60, 68, 81, 122, 127, 138, 155, 172, 175, 183, 253, 274
Scwartz, Evan 176
self-determination: key facets 105; and pressures on welfare state 106–7; rise of

105–6; and rise of vigilante consumer 107–8
Seybold, Patricia 258
Sheiner, Leo 122
Shell Oil 110
ShopGuide 137
Silicon Valley motto 66
Simplyfood 180
Skoll, Jeff 11
Sky Digital 124
social fragmentation: changing households in USA/Europe 101–2; key facets 100; rise of 100–2
social trends 93; erosion of beliefs 108–12; flexible working 96–100; fragmentation 100–2; growth in inequality 103–5; key points 116; metamedia consumption 112–16; self-determination 105–8; 24/7 society 93–6
24/7 society 136; introduction of 93–5; key facets 93; time management 95–6; time pressures 95
Stephens, Robert 208
strategy *see* digital strategy
Sun Microsystems 65, 67
Swiss Re 107

TalkCity 141
Tapscott, Don 40, 57, 64, 173
technology: acceptance/adoption of 112–15; and customer dynamics 3; in digital age 3–4; impact of 3; profit from 1–2; revolution in 34–5; understanding 2–3
technology drivers 9, 39, 51; digitization 39–40; interconnectivity 42–4; processing power 40–2; transmission speed 44–5
Teerlink, Richard 121
TheGlobe 141
ThomasCook 165
Thurm, Scott 223
Time Warner 165
Toffler, Alvin 27, 175–6
Toyota 131–2

transactions 48–50
transformation *see* change/transformation
Transmission Control Protocol/International Protocol (TCP/IP) 254
Tripod 141

UN Human Development Report 103
UPS 49

value: competition and customers 160–2; creating from connection 233–43; customer perception of 159–60
value levers 162; agenting 177–80; combining for advantage 193; content integration 163–6; framework 25–6, 188; freeware 166–8; intercustomer relationships 183–7; key points 187, 189; and making the net work for you 193–5; mass customization 169–75; new market forum 180–3; prosumer involvement 175–7; realtime activity 172–5
virtual communities 74

Walker Digital 15, 16
Walker, Jay 5–6, 8, 9, 14–15, 49, 60, 73, 127, 135, 174, 206
Welch, Jack 153, 250
welfare state 103–4; pressures on 106–7
WELL (Whole world WLectronic Link) 74
Welsner, Mike 84
Whitman, Meg 142, 186, 212–13, 256
Wilkinson, Peter 11, 13, 16
Wilton, Peter 63
Wind, Jerry Yoram 247
Wired magazine 30
World Wide Web 48, 49, 64, 68, 133
WorldAvenue 182
Worldcom 138
Wurster, Thomas 164

Yahoo! 165, 179, 215
Yang, Jerry 179